THE CINEMA OF AUSTRALIA AND NEW ZEALAND

First published in Great Britain in 2007 by
Wallflower Press
6a Middleton Place, Langham Street
London W1W 7TE

ISBN 978-1-904764-96-0 (paperback)
ISBN 978-1-904764-97-7 (hardback)

Printed by Replika Press Pvt Ltd. India

THE CINEMA OF
AUSTRALIA AND
NEW ZEALAND

EDITED BY

GEOFF MAYER & KEITH BEATTIE

 **WALLFLOWER PRESS** LONDON & NEW YORK

24 FRAMES is a major new series focusing on national and regional cinemas from around the world. Rather than offering a 'best of' selection, the feature films and documentaries selected in each volume serve to highlight the specific elements of that territory's cinema, elucidating the historical and industrial context of production, the key genres and modes of representation, and foregrounding the work of the most important directors and their exemplary films. In taking an explicitly text-centred approach, the titles in this list offer 24 diverse entry-points into each national and regional cinema, and thus contribute to the appreciation of the rich traditions of global cinema.

Series Editors: Yoram Allon & Ian Haydn Smith

CONTENTS

INTERNATIONAL EDITORIAL BOARD

NOTES ON CONTRIBUTORS

KEITH BEATTIE has taught at universities in both Australia and New Zealand and is currently senior lecturer within the Faculty of Arts, Deakin University, Melbourne. He is the author of *The Scar that Binds* (1998 and 2000) and *Documentary Screens* (2004) and numerous essays on cultural theory, cultural history and documentary studies. Between 1996 and 1999 he edited the *Australasian Journal of American Studies*.

PHILIP BELL is Head of the school of Media, Film and Theatre at the University of New South Wales, Sydney. He has published widely on Australian-American cultural relationships and on the Australian press, cinema and television.

INA BERTRAND has researched, published and taught on Australian film and television for many years, and is currently a Principal Fellow in the Cinema Programme at the University of Melbourne.

ROLANDO CAPUTO lectures in the Cinema Studies Program, La Trobe University, Melbourne, and is co-editor of the online film journal *Senses of Cinema*. His work has appeared in such critical anthologies as *The Cambridge Companion to the Italian Novel* (2003) and *Australian Film, 1978–1994* (1995). He has contributed the audio commentary to the Region 4 DVD release of Luchino Visconti's *The Leopard* (AV Channel/Potential Films).

FELICITY COLLINS teaches in the Cinema Studies Program at La Trobe University, Melbourne. She is the author of *The Films of Gillian Armstrong* (1999) and co-author, with Therese Davis, of *Australian Cinema after Mabo* (2004).

IAN CONRICH is Senior Lecturer in Film Studies at Roehampton University, an editor of *Journal of British Cinema and Television*, and chair of the New Zealand Studies Association. Guest editor of a special issue of *Post Script* on Australian and New Zealand cinema, he is also co-editor or editor of eight books, including *New Zealand – A Pastoral Paradise?* (2000), *Contemporary New Zealand Cinema* (2006) and *New Zealand Filmmakers* (2006).

BARBARA CREED is Professor of Cinema Studies at the University of Melbourne. She is the author of numerous articles and books, including *The Monstrous-Feminine: Film, Feminism, Psycho-analysis* (1993), *Pandora's Box: Essays in Film Theory* (2004) and *Phallic Panic: Film, Horror and the Primal Uncanny* (2005).

ADRIAN DANKS is Head of Cinema Studies in the School of Applied Communication, Royal Melbourne Institute of Technology. He is President and co-curator of the Melbourne Cinémathèque, co-curator of the Australian Cinémathèque and editor of *Cteq: Annotations on Film*, which is published in *Senses of Cinema*. His writing has appeared in a range of books and journals. He is currently co-editing a book on overseas-financed films made in Australia.

ANNA DZENIS is a lecturer in the Cinema Studies Program at La Trobe University, Melbourne. She is book review editor for the online journal of visual media and history *Screening the Past*. She is also currently writing a book on the cinema of Michael Mann.

WENDY HASLEM teaches in the Cinema Studies Program at the University of Melbourne. Currently she is researching the impact of Hollywood on post-war cinema in Japan. She is co-editor of *Super/Heroes: From Hercules to Superman* (2007).

ROGER HORROCKS has been Head of the Centre for Film, Television and Media Studies at the University of Auckland. He has served as Deputy Chairperson of New Zealand's Broadcasting Commission (NZ on Air) and on other funding agencies, and has contributed widely to film culture in New Zealand. He was Len Lye's assistant late in Lye's life and is a member of the Len Lye Foundation. Among other works he is the author of *Len Lye: A Biography* (2001).

PETER HUGHES is coordinator of the Media Studies Program at La Trobe University, Melbourne. His research is mainly in the fields of documentary and new media. He is co-author, with Ina Bertrand, of *Media Research Methods* (2005) and editor of *Screening the Past*, an online journal of media and history.

HESTER JOYCE is a lecturer in the Cinema Studies Program at La Trobe University, Melbourne, specialising in script analysis and development. She is a professional scriptwriter and consultant and has credits as a theatre director and as an actor in theatre, film and television.

ROSE LUCAS teaches in the School of Literary, Visual and Performance Studies, Monash University, Melbourne, and has published widely in the areas of cinema, gender studies, and literature and psychoanalysis.

BRIAN McDONNELL is a New Zealander of Irish and Maori descent, with a PhD in Film Studies from the University of Auckland. He is currently Programme Coordinator of Media Studies at Massey University's Albany campus in Auckland. He has published widely on New Zealand film and television and on Hollywood cinema. His books include the textbook *Fresh Approaches to Film* (1998).

GEOFF MAYER is Reader and Associate Professor at La Trobe University, Melbourne, and he has taught in Australian and New Zealand universities. He is currently Head of the School of Communication, Arts and Critical Enquiry at La Trobe. He is co-author of *The New Australian Cinema* (1992), co-editor of *The Oxford Companion to Australian Film* (1999) as well as author of *Film as Text* (1991), *A Guide to British Cinema* (2003) and *Roy Ward Baker* (2004). His most recent book, a comprehensive study of film noir, will be published by Greenwood in 2007.

GABRIELLE MURRAY is a lecturer in the Cinema Studies Program at La Trobe University, Melbourne. She is the author of *This Wounded Cinema, This Wounded Life: Violence and Utopia in the Films of Sam Peckinpah* (2004) as well as articles in various journals such as *Metro* and *Senses of Cinema*.

RICHARD PASCAL has taught at several universities in the United States, New Zealand and Australia. He is currently a Senior Lecturer in the School of Humanities at the Australian National University. Publications in recent years include articles on Shirley Jackson, Walt Whitman, Oliver La Farge and Kim Scott.

INGO PETZKE was born in Germany and from 1983 to 2001 was Professor for Film and Video at Fachhochschule (University of Applied Sciences), Würzburg, Germany. Since 2001 he has been Associate Professor for screen-based media at Bond University, Queensland. In 2004 he published *Phillip Noyce: Backroads to Hollywood*.

WILLIAM D. ROUTT taught for many years within the Cinema Studies Program of La Trobe University, Melbourne. Nowadays he does more or less what he likes.

LAURENCE SIMMONS is Associate Professor in the Department of Film, Television and Media Studies at the University of Auckland. His recent publications include *Baudrillard West of the Dateline* (with Victoria Grace and Heather Worth) (2003), *The Image Always Has the Last Word: On Contemporary New Zealand Painting and Photography* (2002) and *Freud's Italian Journey* (forthcoming).

ROCHELLE SIMMONS wrote her doctoral thesis on John Berger at the University of Toronto. She now teaches English at Otago University, where she has also taught New Zealand film. She has published articles on Michael Ondaatje, New Zealand cinema, Canadian cinema and digital multimedia. Her current research involves relations between the verbal and the visual across a range of media.

DEANE WILLIAMS is Senior Lecturer in the School of English, Communications and Performance Studies, Monash University, Melbourne. He has published widely on Australian documentary film and is the author of *Mapping the Imaginary: Ross Gibson's Camera Natura* (1996). He is currently writing a biography of John Heyer and is a member of the international Advisory Board for the *Encyclopedia of Documentary Film* (forthcoming).

To Lesley Mayer, and to the memory of Reg Beattie

PREFACE

The essays collected here affirm the actuality, necessity and the seeming impossibility of cinema in Australia and New Zealand. 'Impossible' in the sense that notions of a 'distinctively' culturally specific national cinema are predicated on a disavowal of the globalising political economy of world cinema. The notion of 'national cinema' also requires the disavowal of the transnational, discursive character of genre, narrative and aesthetics that constitute moving image forms and works. Yet the term 'national cinema' retains utility in that, in relation to Australia and New Zealand, it bespeaks the shadow of colonialism, with its intimations of identity, often worrisome, and sometimes empowering.

Admitting the particularity of national cinemas brings with it the need to construct and to trace innovation, tradition, insight and expression as they have emerged in the cinemas of Australia and New Zealand. At this time a decade-long reign of a national government in Australia dedicated to waging a series of 'culture war' assaults on hard-won ideals of democratic liberties and rights has for the moment successfully reformulated 'national identity' in terms that give privilege to atomised individualism against collective and community interests. Neo-liberal ideologies have carefully divided an 'us' from a 'them' with borderlines wrought by xenophobia, fear and war. A similar set of conditions prevailed in New Zealand during the 1980s. The opportunity represented by the essays collected here to trace some histories of other kinds of provisional national identities can only be welcomed.

The promotion of cinema in Australia and New Zealand has benefited from significant government support since the late 1960s, though in recent decades the cinemas of both nations have, of necessity, been implicated in circuits of global finance and linked in the chains of distribution and exhibition stemming from the USA. Culturally, the projection of Australian and New Zealand national identities have at times repressed differences in favour of a tendency to proclaim various myths of origin and unifying, homogenous identities. In recent times more complex representations have emerged giving expression to more variegated experiences of sexuality, ethnicity, gender and cultural difference. However, small domestic markets in Australia and New Zealand present filmmakers here with a dilemma common to the creative industries elsewhere, that is, how might the particularity of our perspectives and experience best be formulated in ways that work for international markets? Many of the films discussed in this collection provide historical instances of imagined national identities as artefacts 'negotiated' with international expectations and reception.

Actors, writers, directors, cinematographers, art directors and editors from Australia and New Zealand also straddle the Pacific in other ways. They are welcomed in Los Angeles because they bring an extraordinary versatility and freshness to the industry, born out of the creative agility of these small countries. This is at once a symptom of 'underdevelopment' – a form of cultural brain-drain – while at the same time contributing certain specific and recognisable sensibilities and expressions to world cinema.

Despite the problematic contours of notions of national cinemas today there remains a necessity to affirm its possibility as it carries with it the potential to register the lived complexity of everyday life in Australia and New Zealand as we formulate the variety of ways we might live together in the world today.

The circulation of world cinema, and an Australian and New Zealand contribution to this, constitutes a moment of hope, insofar as the very diversity of Australian and New Zealand film cultures at the present time – from the 'art house' features that are our 'mainstream', through activist documentary, to the extraordinarily imaginative, playful, dark animation and short fiction films of both countries – contest the tendency to lock off possibilities that exist for articulating other kinds of perspectives, voices and imaginings.

This collection of essays offers an international readership generous and informed slices of Australian and New Zealand film scholarship and an Australian and New Zealand reader an all too scarce opportunity for invaluable critical engagement with the traditions of our film cultures. The book will have done an even better job if it leads its readers back to the films themselves.

John Hughes
Melbourne
January 2007

INTRODUCTION

Australians embraced film from the beginning. In the five months following the arrival of Edison's Kinetoscope' 35mm film-viewers in Sydney, in November 1884, 25,000 Australians flocked to witness the new technology. In 1898 Henry Lawson's 'The Australian Cinematograph' was published and the story's imaginative use of colour and movement encouraged film historian Ina Bertrand to describe it as 'Australia's first screenplay'. Lawson's story appeared two years after Australia's first film, *Passengers Alighting from the Paddle Steamer 'Brighton' at Manly*, which was filmed by Frenchman Marius Sestier in October 1896. However, it was Sestier's next venture the following month at the Flemington Racecourse, in Melbourne, that captured the public imagination, when he filmed a number of races, including the *1896 Melbourne Cup*.

Early film production came from an unlikely source, the Limelight Department of the Salvation Army. Beginning in 1891, the Limelight Department, under the supervision of its chief technician Joseph Perry, developed slides to accompany religious presentations. In 1897 Perry began using motion pictures and he established Australia's first film studio behind the Salvation Army's Bourke Street headquarters in Melbourne where Commandant Herbert Booth scripted and directed 'feature length' presentations of one-minute films and slides. The most well-known presentation, first screened on 13 September 1900, was *Soldiers of the Cross*, a lecture on the Christian martyrs which consisted of 15 one-minute films and 220 slides. The popularity of these films encouraged the Salvation Army to undertake secular projects and in 1901 it produced a 35-minute film, *The Inauguration of the Australian Commonwealth*, on behalf of the New South Wales Government.

The Story of the Kelly Gang, Australia's first fully integrated, secular, fictional narrative film appeared in 1906. Stage productions dramatising the exploits of Australia's most famous bushranger, Ned Kelly, were common even before his hanging in 1880, and theatrical entrepreneurs J. and N. Tait, who held the stage rights to the exploits of the Kelly Gang, encouraged Melbourne chemists Milliard Johnson and W. A. Gibson to make a film on Kelly's life up to the point where he was captured by the police at the Glenrowan Hotel. With a budget of £1,000, filming took place over a series of weekends in the bush around Melbourne. Although the running time at the first screening on 26 December 1906 was reported to be 40 minutes, advertisements for the film claimed its length to be approximately 4,000 feet, or 67 minutes. This subsequently provoked speculation that it was the world's first feature film. The film enjoyed great success in Australia and Britain, where it was advertised as the longest film ever made. It also encouraged the development of the 'bushranging genre', Australia's most popular film genre until it was banned by the New South Wales Police Department in 1912.

Although strong patriotic feelings during World War One encouraged the production of propaganda films such as *The Hero of the Dardanelles* (1915), *Within Our Gates, or Deeds That Won Gallipoli* (1915) and *The Martyrdom of Nurse Cavell* (1916), the American domination of Australian screens escalated during the war. Before 1914, less than half of the films screened in Australia were American. By 1923 the figure had grown to 94 per cent. Local film production was sporadic until the establishment of Cinesound in 1932, under the supervision of Ken G. Hall. Beginning with *On Our Selection,* Hall produced, directed and (often) wrote, 17 films between 1932 and 1940 – Cinesound's total output except for one film. Every Cinesound production was profitable although *Strike Me Lucky* (1934), starring Australia's most popular stage and radio comedian Roy Rene, only recovered its costs some time after its initial release.

Hall, who visited Hollywood in 1925 to observe film production techniques, modelled Cinesound on the Hollywood studio system. He tried to minimise failure with a formula that emphasised the 'Australianness' of Cinesound Productions through dialogue and settings within a narrative structure that appealed to audiences familiar with Hollywood films. The most successful Cinesound productions were the series of 'Dad and Dave' films starring Bert Bailey as Grandad Rudd and Fred McDonald as his slow-witted son Dave. Loosely based on the characters created by Steele Rudd, Hall directed *On Our Selection, Grandad Rudd* (1935), *Dad and Dave Come to Town* (1938) and *Dad Rudd M.P.* (1940), Cinesound's last production.

A Royal Commission was established in 1927 to investigate the influence of Hollywood films and although there were concerns over the state of the Australian film industry, the Commission was equally concerned by the decline of the number of British films screened in Australia. In 1913, British films represented 26.3 per cent of the total number of imported films and by 1923 this figure had fallen to 3.4 per cent. Although the Commission recommended protection for the British industry with an exhibition quota, it did nothing to change American domination of the Australian industry. In the 1930s the Fox film company purchased a controlling share in Hoyts cinemas while MGM and Paramount secured their own first-run theatres. In 1945 the British Rank Organisation acquired a controlling interest in Union Theatres.

In 1934, an inquiry established by the New South Wales Government recommended a five-year distribution and exhibition quota for Australian films. The resultant NSW Cinematograph Films (Australian Quota) Act required that five per cent of all films handled by distributors and four per cent of films screened by exhibitors in the first year should be Australian. This Act also led to the establishment of a new film studio, National Studios at Pagewood in New South Wales, which was modelled on the Gaumont-British National Studios in London. However, its first film, *The Flying Doctor* (1936), with American actor Charles Farrell, failed at the box office, resulting in the company making only one more film.

The release of Charles Chauvel's *Forty Thousand Horsemen* (1940), which premiered six months after Cinesound's final film, *Dad Rudd M.P.*, marked the end of an era. For the next thirty years the Australian film industry diminished to a point where, in the 1960s, it barely existed. Only nine Australian feature films, produced independently, were released during World War Two. The high point, however, was not a feature film but *Kokoda Front Line!* (1942), a special edition of the weekly newsreel *Cinesound Review*, which won an Academy Award for the best documentary in 1942.

The 1950s was a decade of lost opportunities, a period dominated by overseas companies. While the feature film industry languished in the 1950s and 1960s, this was a relatively rich period for documentary and non-fiction film. The visit to Australia in 1940 by John Grierson helped the establishment of the National Film Board in 1945, which was modelled on the Grierson-inspired Canadian Film Board. This evolved into the Commonwealth Film Unit and in 1973 it became Film Australia. By the late 1960s there was a pool of talent eager to make feature films. All that was needed was an adequate infrastructure that could assist with financing, distribution and exhibition. This took shape when Prime Minister Holt established the Australian Council of the Arts, with a Film and Television Committee, in 1967. In May 1969 this committee recommended the establishment of a national film and television school, which opened in 1973, a film development corporation and an experimental film fund. All three recommendations were accepted by the government and with the passage of the Australian Film and Television Corporation Bill in 1970 Australian film was finally recognised in a parliamentary act.

Among the first films to benefit from government assistance were two 'Ocker' comedies: *Stork* (1971) and *The Adventures of Barry McKenzie* (1972). The success of this latter film in both Australia and Britain encouraged local investment and it was followed by a succession of sex comedies, such as Tim Burstall's *Alvin Purple* (1973), in the early 1970s. These films were much less confrontational in their criticisms of Australian attitudes than *The Adventures of Barry McKenzie* or *Stork*. *Alvin Purple*, for example, was based on the simple premise of a naïve young man (Graeme Blundell) who cannot understand why every woman he meets wants to have sex with him. It became Australia's most successful film in the 1970s and was followed by a sequel, *Alvin Rides Again* (1974), and a television series.

In 1972 the Premier of South Australia, Don Dunstan, established the South Australian Film Corporation and three years later this organisation produced two films that changed the nature of the Australian film industry: Ken Hannam's *Sunday Too Far Away* (1975) and Peter Weir's *Picnic at Hanging Rock* (1975). The Corporation was also involved in many other notable productions during this period including *Storm Boy* (1976), '*Breaker' Morant* (1980) and Weir's *The Last Wave* (1977) and *Gallipoli* (1981). Its success not only inspired the other states to establish similar organisations, it provided an ideal environment for directors such as Peter Weir to develop a style of filmmaking that was noticeably different from the prevailing Hollywood style. The best film to emerge from this period was *Sunday Too Far Away*. In addition to winning awards in Australia, it was selected for the Director's Fortnight at the Cannes Film Festival. Similar praise greeted *Picnic at Hanging Rock* which was more in keeping with the style of European art cinema, and the film was heralded as evidence of the artistic maturity of the Australian film industry.

The success of both films was influential and they were followed by a series of low-key period films in the next four years, including Henri Safran's *Storm Boy*, Peter Weir's *The Last Wave*, Donald Crombie's *Caddie* (1976) and *The Irishman* (1978), Ken Hannam's *Break of Day* (1976), John Power's *The Picture Show Man* (1977), Bruce Beresford's *The Getting of Wisdom* (1977), Kevin Dobson's *The Mango Tree* (1977) and Carl Schultz's *Blue Fin* (1978). The languid pacing and downbeat tone of these films encouraged producer, author and radio commentator Phillip Adams to catalogue them as 'elegiac images of failure'.

Bruce Beresford's *Money Movers* (1979) and George Miller's *Mad Max* (1979) were both tough crime genre films and they represented a significant change. *Mad Max*, which was made on a very tight budget, was popular with audiences in Australia, America and elsewhere as the film – which was rooted in the most elemental of all melodramatic storylines, the revenge story – had a sense of energy and dramatic power that was unusual in the Australian cinema at that time. It was lean, violent, humorous, with little interest in the nuances of characterisation. While some critics condemned it, its success resulted in two sequels, *Mad Max 2: The Road Warrior* (1981) and *Mad Max Beyond Thunderdome* (1985). The success of this trilogy, in conjunction with changes in the nature of government support for the industry, provoked a rapid increase in the production of crime films and other forms of melodrama. In 1981 the Income Tax Assessment

Act offered a tax deduction of 150 per cent of eligible film investment, and exemption from tax on the first 50 per cent of net earnings from that investment, providing that the projects could verify their Australian credentials and could be financed, completed and released in the year of the deduction (this was changed to two years in 1983). This encouraged a boom in production although, unfortunately, there were many sub-standard films as some producers, motivated solely by the tax rebate, churned out films that went straight to video or even remained unreleased. As a consequence, the tax benefits were constantly reduced throughout the 1980s as the debate over the nature, and level, of government support inten-sified until a major review of film funding was conducted in 1997. The resultant Gonski Report, however, received only a luke-warm reception by the Federal Government and a mixture of tax concessions and incentives for private investment emerged as a compromise between a government reluctant to continue large-scale financial support and an industry still reliant on external funding.

Australia, with its population of little more than 20 million, will always struggle to maintain a feature film industry that can compete in the same marketplace with the Hollywood blockbusters. In the 1970s, there was a concerted effort by directors such as Tim Burstall, Ken Hannam, Bruce Beresford, Peter Weir, Gillian Armstrong, Paul Cox, Fred Schepisi and Philip Noyce to distinguish their films from usual Hollywood fare. This trend has been maintained by subsequent filmmakers such as Jane Campion, Baz Luhrmann, John Ruane, Scott Hicks, Jonathan Teplitzky, Clara Law and Cate Shortland. These directors have been able to fashion a distinctive place somewhere between the 'poetic realism' of the European art film and the narrative demands of the classical Hollywood cinema. It is a difficult terrain as commercial failure is always precipitously close.

A similar situation has confronted, and in many ways continues to confront, the film industry in New Zealand, a fact that can be gleaned from one of the more resilient attempts to summarise New Zealand cinema, the documentary *Cinema of Unease* (1995). Produced as part of the British Film Institute's *Century of Cinema* series, *Cinema of Unease* was written by documentary filmmaker and historian Judy Rymer in association with New Zealand actor Sam Neill, the film's on-screen presenter. Unlike the US and UK episodes within the *Century of Cinema* series (which offer wide-ranging surveys of the histories of their respective cinemas) Neill constructs his appraisal around a specific thesis. Centrally, Neill argues, New Zealand films are characterised by dark and brooding qualities that reflect the existence of these features within the nation itself. One difficulty with such a thesis – apart from its essentialisation of what are arguable, if not dubious, national characteristics – is that Neill, or any student of New

Zealand cinema, is forced to draw conclusions from a small sample. The total number of feature films produced throughout the history of New Zealand cinema is approximately 150.

Working with this limited archive, Neill identifies the road as a central theme in the films of the late 1970s and early 1980s, and indeed *Good Bye Pork Pie* (1980) and *Smash Palace* (1981) adopted and adapted the road movie genre leading to popular success among New Zealand audiences. According to Neill, road films gave way to the production of films which were more complex and sophisticated in terms of narrative structures and production values, among them *Vigil* (1984) and *The Navigator* (1988) by Vincent Ward, and Jane Campion's 'breakthrough' drama, *The Piano* (1993). Such films, he argues, are works of a mature cinema which, he insists, continues to return to dark, troubled and menacing narratives.

As with any thesis the cogency of this interpretation resides in its applicability. A broader survey of New Zealand cinema exhibits other works and themes not easily reducible to road films or those of the 'dark and brooding' thesis. Notably, *Cinema of Unease* ignores the deep tradition in New Zealand cinema of films directed by and about Maori, and with them the opportunity for analysis of New Zealand's colonial and postcolonial history of confrontation and negotiation between Maori and Pakeha. In this way, for example, Neill refers to the presence of Maori in *The Piano*, though omits reference to the tradition of films based on Maori characters, among them what is arguably New Zealand's first feature-length film, *Hinemoa* (1914, now lost). Feature films directed by Maori include, among others, *Mauri* (1988) by Merita Mita, *Te Rua* (1991) by Barry Barclay and *Once Were Warriors* (1994) by Lee Tamahori.

Documentary, a major category within New Zealand cinema, is also omitted from *Cinema of Unease*. John Grierson's brief visit to New Zealand in 1940 served as the impetus for the establishment the following year of the government's National Film Unit, which oversaw production of newsreels and government promotional films. More recently independent documentary production in New Zealand has focused on political and social issues, as exemplified in *Patu!* (1983), Merita Mita's powerful direct cinema account of the protests against the 1980 tour of New Zealand by South Africa's rugby football team, and Barry Barclay's *The Neglected Miracle* (1985), which examines issues surrounding the use and abuse of plant genetic resources and their importance to indigenous cultures worldwide. In a different way, *War Stories* (1995) by Gaylene Preston combines archival footage and on-screen interviews to recreate the experiences of New Zealand women in World War Two, and *Punitive Damage* (1999) by Annie Goldson uses a journalistic mode to investigate the death in East Timor of a young New Zealand human rights campaigner.

Beyond Maori film, documentaries and experimental film (another category ignored in *Cinema of Unease*), the production of mainstream fiction film has expanded since the 1970s. A key film for Neill's survey is Roger Donaldson's political thriller *Sleeping Dogs* (1977), which he credits with inaugurating the so-called revival of New Zealand cinema. The notion of a revival or renaissance of New Zealand cinema gathers force in light of the parlous state of film production in New Zealand immediately prior to the 1970s, as exemplified in the fact that between 1940 and 1970 only three fiction features were produced in New Zealand (*Broken Barrier* (1952), co-directed by Roger Mirams and John O'Shea, and *Runaway* (1964) and *Don't Let it Get to You* (1966), both directed by O'Shea). In contrast to the lean years prior to 1970, 63 feature films (and 15 international co-productions) were made in New Zealand between 1977 and 1982. Many of these films were produced with the assistance of the New Zealand Film Commission (NZFC), the establishment of which in October 1978 provided the funding which served as the platform for the revival.

The Commission was mandated by the government 'to encourage and also to participate and assist in the making, promotion, distribution and exhibition of films'. This basic task was linked to issues of national identity and cultural nationalism in that the Commission was charged with providing assistance to films that were 'distinctively New Zealand'. In this way national identity was to be packaged as a filmic commodity that would help to ensure the existence of a New Zealand film industry. Questions of what constitutes a 'distinctively New Zealand' film were outlined in the Film Commission Act (1978). The Act links national distinctiveness to 'significant New Zealand content' defined through reference to subject matter, the nationality and place of residence of chief members of a film's production team, and the national origin of financial sources and production facilities and equipment. The foundation of an ethnocentric, culturally exclusionist (and with it, economically circumscribed) film industry inherent in such a definition provoked debate within the local film industry. On one side, commentators argued that New Zealand cinema should be structured along lines of international co-productions and offshore capital to produce films aimed at the world market. Opposing viewpoints supported the notion of national identity and its inscription in a state-subsidised cinema.

Interestingly, both sides of the debate, while rallying issues of 'New Zealandness', implicate levels of funding available for filmmaking in New Zealand. At the time of its establishment, the NZFC operated on a modest budget derived from a direct government subsidy and a grant from the national Lottery Board. A significant impetus to film production under the auspices of the Film Commission occurred for a brief period around 1982, when production finance increased as a result of a taxation scheme that enabled investors to deduct their investments in New Zealand films. This situation was eclipsed in 1984 by the election of a Labour government under Prime Minister David Lange and Finance Minister Roger Douglas. The practices of the new government embodied the paradox of what were, essentially, New Right polices implemented by a Labour government. The policies converged in the form of rapid economic deregulation and privatisation of all sectors of the economy, a situation that continued in a dramatic and disastrous way for a decade. Within the midst of rampant supply-side economic policies the new government, surprisingly, and again paradoxically, increased the total annual budget of the NZFC from NZ$7.3 in 1986 to NZ$14.5 in 1991.

Despite the funding increases received by the Commission in these years, the situation facing New Zealand filmmakers in the 1990s was anything but rosy. Whereas in 1995 Sam Neill in *Cinema of Unease* saw a burgeoning film industry, reflecting a healthy New Zealand economy (an opinion that would satisfy the 'Chamber of Commerce', as a reviewer of the series in the US journal *Film Comment* put it) other commentators at the time saw a fragile industry attempting to survive in a precarious economic environment. The filmmaker Gaylene Preston, for example, noted that it was more difficult in the late 1990s to make and distribute a film than it had been in the late 1970s. Difficulties facing filmmakers in the prevailing climate of economic rationalism were further highlighted by the fact that stipulations in the NZFC's funding guidelines, among them the requirement that filmmakers supply their own agent, had become prohibitive.

The chronic conditions prevailing in the 1990s were reflected in the fact that a number of New Zealand filmmakers chose, or were forced, to work outside of New Zealand. In particular the trans-Pacific route from Auckland to Los Angeles became a well-worn one for many directors (Lee Tamahori, Geoff Murphy, Roger Donaldson, among others) lured to Hollywood by the opportunity to direct big-budget films. During the 1990s this migration produced mixed responses in the perennially parochial New Zealand press, which tended to either hail the directors as local heroes who had achieved international success, or figures who, in effect, subverted attempts to maintain a local film industry.

Such assessments are revised in the experience of director Peter Jackson, which presents a 'third way' between the call of Los Angeles and the production of small-budget local films supported by NZFC funds. Beginning with *The Frighteners* (1996) Jackson was able to opt out of the reigning alternatives open to New Zealand directors by persuading Hollywood to finance his productions in New Zealand. The outstanding financial and critical success of Jackson's *Lord of the Rings* trilogy (2001–2003), financed by Ted Turner's New Line studio, has, it would seem, silenced the demands of cultural nationalists for New Zealand content and an indigenous identity on screen. Also overlooked in the success of the trilogy is the experience of countries which have served as branches or outposts of Hollywood, notably Italy in the 1960s and Spain in the 1970s and Canada over a longer period. In most of these cases evidence points to the fact that serving as a host to US productions does not ensure the health and longevity of a local film industry. The emergence of a comprador cinema, one which exists through the intervention of US financial investment, is a reality often overlooked in the success of big-budget filmmaking 'New Zealand' style. In terms of the number of people it employs, its range of expertise and the production funds it wields, Peter Jackson's Weta Studios in Wellington (once the government National Film Unit) *is* New Zealand cinema, a situation likely to continue at least in the short term due to Jackson's and Weta Studios' remaking of *King Kong* (2005) with US financial backing.

With the *Lord of the Rings* trilogy 'New Zealand cinema' has definitely entered a new phase of international finance and large-scale productions. Such tendencies, and the globalising trends they signal, are redefining the conditions that produced the films of the revival, those films that Sam Neill in *Cinema of Unease* interprets as unique New Zealand cinematic artefacts. In his answer to the question he poses in his analysis of New Zealand cinema – 'who are we?' – Neill refuses to acknowledge the high degree of international production finance which has created a product that is, arguably, non indigenous in content, form or production funding. Reference to the context within which films are currently produced in New Zealand answers Neill's question of identity: 'we' are subjects of intensifying global influences grounded within a local cultural environment.

Finally, a comment on the organisation and content of this volume. It does not seek to offer an encyclopaedic coverage of films produced in Australia and New Zealand. The aim of the book is, on the one hand, more modest than such an endeavour (it comprises a selection of films from the history of Australian and New Zealand cinema) and is, on the other hand, much more focused than a general overview (we have sought to include films which, in various ways, demonstrate significant formal, technical and cultural dimensions of Australian and New Zealand cinemas). The selection includes 'foundational' works and significant lesser-known films from the histories of both cinemas which point to the diversity of filmmaking in Australasia.

Geoff Mayer & Keith Beattie

THE STORY OF THE KELLY GANG

01

CHARLES TAIT, AUSTRALIA, 1906

In the Australian community, the historical process has produced two incompatible versions of the story of the outlaws known as the Kelly Gang, encapsulated in the two phrases 'game as Ned Kelly' and 'blame it on the Kellys'. If you consider that Ned Kelly and his gang were driven to crime by a corrupt administration and a brutal police force, that their rebellious actions demonstrated determination not to be ground down by the system, that they were personally brave and admirable, and that the blame for any adverse results (including the death of police officers) rests with those who drove them to it, you are likely to use the former phrase. The second phrase comes from the theme song of the 1972 film *Ned Kelly*, starring Mick Jagger, and it sums up the attitude of the Kelly detractors at the time – those who feared and hated the gang were willing to believe that they were capable of violence and were probably responsible for many more crimes than those officially attributed to them. This attitude continues among those who believe the gang were simply criminals who deserved their fate.

Ned Kelly was the eldest son of former convict John Red Kelly and his wife Ellen (née Quinn). When his father died, Ned – at the age of twelve – became head of the household, responsible for his mother and the other seven children in the family. In his teens, he was imprisoned several times for minor crimes, then for three years he was steadily employed, though he may also have been cattle duffing with his stepfather, George King, whom Ellen had married in 1874. In 1878, Constable Fitzpatrick visited the Kelly household in an attempt to serve a warrant on Ned's brother, Dan, for horse-stealing. Fitzpatrick returned to the police station with a bullet wound in his wrist, which he claimed had been inflicted by Ned himself. Ellen Kelly was arrested on a charge of attacking the constable, and a £100 reward was posted for the capture of Ned. Ellen was jailed for three years, and Ned went on the run with Dan and two friends, Steve Hart and Joe Byrne. The police pursued them relentlessly, but ineffectually, as the gang were both familiar with the terrain and protected by the local people. Ned's sister Kate became an expert at throwing pursuing police off the scent as she rode into the ranges with supplies or messages.

The die was finally cast when four police officers were sent in to the Wombat Ranges to capture the gang, and in a gunfight three of the police were killed, with only Constable Macintyre escaping to take the news into town. The gang's exploits after that became more sensational and reckless, while the police crack-down (under the new Felons' Apprehension Act) caused severe hardship among their friends and supporters, and the reward for information leading to their capture rose to £8,000. One of their associates, Aaron Sherritt, took this bait and acted as a double agent. On discovering his dual role, the gang killed him. Support in the general community, however, never wavered, making the authorities fearful of a general uprising.

The climax of the series of events occurred in the small northern Victorian town of Glenrowan in June 1880. The gang destroyed a section of the railway line into town, then seized the hotel and kept the patrons hostage while they waited for the crash of the train carrying police reinforcements. But the schoolmaster, Curnow, whom Ned had allowed to go home to his ailing wife, walked back along the line with a lantern, preventing the train crash. The police surrounded the hotel, and after a bloody gun battle, during which Dan, Steve and Joe were killed, captured Ned and took him to Melbourne for trial. He was convicted and hanged on 11 November 1880, aged 26 years.

The site of the hanging, in the old Melbourne Gaol, continues to be a tourist attraction, and representations of the story in many different forms remain popular. Indeed, there has been something of a Kelly revival in recent years, with at least two novels (*True History of the Kelly Gang* by Peter Carey and *Our Sunshine* by Robert Drewe), several large exhibitions, two feature films and a number of television programmes devoted to the Kellys. But the version of the story which concerns us here was a film, produced in 1906 – Australia's (and arguably the world's) first feature-length dramatised film.

The second history that needs to be explored here is the history of film in Australia – both in terms of production and exhibition. We might follow Chris Long's view that this begins with kinetescope images, registered sequentially on a strip of celluloid, projected as a loop through a peep-show, with the audience limited to one viewer at a time. My personal preference for a founding moment of Australian cinema is the screening on 28 August 1895 by Carl Hertz at the Melbourne Opera House, as this was the first public screening of projected moving pictures. It was when hundreds, even thousands, of people could view a film simultaneously that the production of films became economically viable and the future of the cinema assured. At this time, films recorded actuality in real time (factual films) and had started to enact primitive stories in front of a camera (fiction). The public seemed to enjoy both. Before the turn of the century, recording technology dictated the length of a film: a one hundred-feet reel of film stock recorded approximately one minute of projected film, which was the standard length for all films.

At the end of the nineteenth century, Melbourne was Australia's second-largest city, and by 1906 it had a population of around 530,000. Purpose-built, hard-top cinemas were still in the future, but the city was well-supplied with theatrical venues. Her Majesty's Theatre, the Theatre Royal and the Princess Theatre offered live performances: musical shows from orchestral concerts to Gilbert and Sullivan, and stage drama from Shakespeare to weekly repertory. The Opera House was the home of Harry Rickard's vaudeville company. None of these venues showed film during 1906. Four other variety theatres, however, offered film occasionally during the year: the Cyclorama, the Bijou, the Temperance Hall and the New Gaiety Theatre. There were also multi-purpose venues, where films were occasionally advertised: the Melbourne Town Hall, the Melbourne Cricket Ground, the Exhibition Buildings, the Aquarium, the Austral Hall, the Masonic Hall and several tent shows, some of which were semi-permanent. In the suburbs of Melbourne and Victorian country areas, film was most likely to be found in the Town Hall or Mechanics' Institute, or in one of the outdoor pleasure gardens that were popular during the summer.

In all these venues, the films being offered were both a mix of local and imported productions, fact and fiction. It was still common for films to be presented as a segment within a vaudeville programme or other live theatrical performance. In such cases a number of short films of different styles might be presented on the sandwich principle of interleaving drama and/or actuality with comedy. But by then it was not unusual for a full programme to be devoted just to film – either again on the sandwich principle, or with the programme built around a subject of current interest (for instance, the Boer War in 1899, or the funeral of Queen Victoria in 1900). Longer films were unusual, but not unheard-of. Fight films were popular with one segment of the audience. These recorded the full contest, such as the Corbett/Fitzsimmons prize fight, 11,000 feet recorded in 1897. The Oberammagau Passion Play had been recorded on film in 1898, and – listed variously as being between 2,100 and 3,000 feet – was one of the longest dramatic subjects yet presented in the medium. By 1906, the technology had improved, so that a standard reel held 1,000 feet of film, which was presumed to run at sixty feet per minute, but might take between 15 and twenty minutes to present, depending on the speed of the hand-cranked projector. So, Melbourne audiences were by this time accustomed to a full programme of films, with some films considerably longer than one reel.

Audiences were also accustomed to seeing locally produced films. The first known local productions were taken during the Melbourne Cup carnival of 1896, and soon films were produced in several of the major cities, recording historical events such as the Inauguration of the Commonwealth in 1900, or sporting events such as football matches. The Biograph Company of the Salvation Army was one of the first production companies to regularly produce fiction. Out of its Melbourne studio came dramatisations of the evangelical work of the Army as well as Bible stories, most notably the 13 short films concerning the Christian martyrs, incorporated into the multi-media presentation *Soldiers of the Cross* in 1900.

By 1906 the groundwork had been laid for an expanding film industry. The real events in which the Kelly gang had been engaged were a quarter of a century old; far enough away to have acquired historical distance, but near enough to still hold public interest. Film had an established place in the entertainment scene and public taste was beginning to incline towards fiction over fact. With Melbourne as one of the main centres of Australia's thriving film production industry, the scene was set for the production of Australia's first feature-length dramatised film.

A synopsis printed in the programme booklet available at early screenings of *The Story of the Kelly Gang* outlines the film's narrative, which began with Constable Fitzpatrick's unwelcome advances to Kate Kelly and finished with the capture of Ned at Glenrowan. The plot established the police as the villains, and left the hero alive (even though the audience knew the real outcome). Other facts about the film, such as who made it, who played in it, its length, where it was made and how it was presented, remain in doubt. The film survives only in fragments, and the ancillary evidence that remains is circumstantial and contradictory.

There are contemporary advertisements and reviews, notorious for exaggerating, or for at least repeating uncritically what was supplied to them by the exhibitor of the film (not the distributor, who only began to appear in the industry after 1909). There is also confusion in these sources about the functions listed. For instance, 'under the direction of' usually means presented in the cinema by, that is, it is a reference to the exhibitor rather than to what we would nowadays think of as the director of a film. Later articles, even from those who claim to have been involved at the time, are fallible and it is difficult to evaluate competing claims.

It appears that the film was made by a team, consisting of three theatrical entrepreneurs (brothers Charles, John and Frank Tait) and two industrial chemists who had moved into the business of hiring out cinematograph projectors and films (William Gibson and Millard Johnson). All seem to have had a financial stake in the film, although Charles Tait put up most of the money. I have argued elsewhere that the distribution of roles within any production team at that time did not usually correspond to the way tasks are distributed nowadays, so it is hard to allocate labels, even when there is more evidence about a production. It seems that Charles Tait was the driving force. A mixture of what we would now think of as producer and director, he also claimed to have written the film. The cinematographer may have been William Gibson, or perhaps Charles Byers Coates (who was employed as camera operator by Johnson and Gibson on several of their films), or they may have shared the task. Actors were hired by the day, and the extended Tait family also took part. The production took place over six months, with the cast and crew travelling out from Melbourne each Wednesday and Saturday afternoon (traditional half holidays for actors) to the Chartersville Estate, in what is now suburban Heidelberg, but was at that time a rural area. Johnson and Gibson developed and edited the footage.

The result was the longest dramatised film yet produced in Australia, advertised as a featured, or 'star', entertainment, presented on the second half of a double bill, with the first half comprising vocal and instrumental musical numbers. In its first season, the film was variously advertised as 4,000–6,000 feet long, or taking over an hour in presentation, though all that remains, even after a virtually complete scene was recently discovered in Britain, is about 17 minutes in total. One suggestion is that the compression of the story within the surviving fragments indicates that the film was never as long as it was claimed at the time, and that the advertised screening time was actually how long it took to present six short reels with breaks for reel changes, filled in with live performance of songs and instrumental music. If so, it follows the fragmented story outline published in the programme booklet, which was divided into six scenes. The remaining film appears to correspond with this narrative structure. However, this position ignores the references to the physical length of the film. Screening on a hand-cranked projector at an average of 16 minutes per 1,000-feet reel, 4,000–6,000 feet of film would take 64 to 96 minutes to screen. It also seems unlikely that in 1906 exhibition venues still operated with a single projector, as they had done in 1895. Surely, after ten successful years of film exhibition, the larger venues would have had two projectors and so no need to stop to change a film spool. One early manual for managers and operators speaks of the projector as though there were only one in the booth, but occasionally assumes that there are two.

In addition, the film itself grew longer as material was added. In those days it was the exception rather than the rule for a film to remain as it was on first release. We know from advertisements that footage was added early in 1907 – the scene of the robbery of the Jerilderie bank. There is also evidence of this process of change in the fact that the surviving film has intertitles. These must have been added later, as the original film ran without any explanatory titles, instead relying on the audience's prior knowledge of the events being depicted, combined with the narration performed by an actor (or, in some larger venues, more than one) behind the screen. In those early years, before the advent of film distribution companies, exhibitors purchased films outright and ran them until they were unwatchable, making running repairs as they saw fit, which might reduce the film by repeatedly eliminating worn segments, or lengthen the film by the addition of scenes from other films. Perhaps what we have in these surviving fragments is such a reduced reel, with the action cut to the bone, barely allowing the viewer to follow the story. We know that plays about the Kelly gang had no trouble providing a full evening's entertainment.

It is clear from the surviving fragments that the film was surprisingly sophisticated for its time. It is difficult to engage in close analysis of short segments without reliable evidence of the whole from which they have been extracted, but the most immediate impression is of skilful use of locations and of action presented naturalistically and economically. There is no stage gesturing or posturing (as there certainly is in a fragment of another Kelly gang film, of similar vintage but probably not of similar length, found in Perth), making the film closer in spirit to the early work of Edwin S. Porter in the US or Cecil Hepworth in Britain than to the Italian primitives.

The emphasis in this film is on the action, rather than on the spectacle: it is melodrama rather than epic. However, viewers (at the time, as well as later) were also impressed with the grandeur of the scenery, and one of the admirable qualities of the cinematography is the capacity to place figures in the landscape in a manner that advances the narrative while also establishing a visual style. The two policemen left alone in the bush camp are seen to the left of the frame, in front of their tent, sighting a rifle at unseen birds in the top right. The viewer's attention is drawn to these birds, allowing the gang to creep up unobtrusively, and therefore convincingly, into the base of the frame, and so to surprise the police. Another example is the capture of Ned, where the camera is placed low, among the troopers taking cover behind a log. Ned advances, weaving across the image as he staggers, but also growing larger as he approaches the camera – as well as approaching the shot that will bring him to his knees and to eventual capture.

There is impressive use of a mixture of long shots and closer shots, though in most cases not enough of the film has survived to provide evidence of how these were cut together. One case is particularly remarkable – the final confrontation between the gang and the police at the Glenrowan Hotel. We see the hotel in long shot, identified by a sign on a post, with the police firing towards the building from just in front of the camera. A policeman carries a bundle of sticks up towards the hotel. Soon after smoke begins to rise as the building catches fire. Some people escape through the smoke, including one in the robes of a priest. He reaches the police and argues with them, apparently to no avail, so he returns into the burning building. This action is presented in long shot, with the backs of the police close to the camera and tiny figures moving about in the middle to far distance. Then an intertitle tells us that Steve and Dan shoot each other. A following cut moves to the interior of the building, to the bar of the hotel, where Steve Hart and Dan are facing each other across the image, and we see the two puffs of smoke that represent the shots, and the two men fall. Then another intertitle, 'Gallant rescue by Father Gibney of the wounded platelayer', and we see the priest from the earlier scene enter the bar, help a wounded man to his feet, and support him as they both stagger out the door. We then cut to the reverse-shot, outside the door: it opens, and Father Gibney helps the wounded man out, brings him round onto his shoulders and carries him, apparently unconscious, out of frame to the left of the camera.

What makes this sequence impressive is the sophisticated (for that time) mix of close shots and long shots, and of proscenium shots (Steve and Dan facing each other) with movement across the frame in every direction, including directly towards the camera (Father Gibney carrying the wounded man). The performances are natural, though the scene of the two men shooting each other is presented in a balanced and formal composition. The whole sequence is tinted red to represent both fire and danger/excitement. There are cuts between narrative elements (the police and Father Gibney outside, Steve and Dan inside, then Father Gibney and the wounded man inside), and that single reverse-shot (despite not being particularly well-matched) carries the action from the inside to the outside of the hotel. We have, of course, no way of knowing how accurately this version of the sequence reflects what audiences saw in 1906. The current version may have had pictorial elements added or removed; it has certainly had intertitles added, but it is not clear when this was done.

The new footage is less adventurous. It consists of several medium to long shots, all from very similar vantage points in front of the Younghusband station homestead. Here the gang hold up the family and its visitors, rob them and one rides off with the loot. Action occurs across the frame, in a sequence that closely matches the description in the programme booklet.

Another short fragment of Kelly footage survives and for many years it was thought that this was the 1906 film, re-cut and re-issued in 1910. However, it is most likely that this was a completely different Kelly film, probably produced by Johnson and Gibson again but not for the Taits. Meanwhile, the 1906 film remained in circulation, particularly in rural areas, until at least 1920 when it was withdrawn by Gibson, who had backed Harry Southwell's 1920 production of *The Kelly Gang*. After that, *The Story of the Kelly Gang* disappeared from view, even though many prints must have been struck to cover its distribution in all states and overseas.

For the centenary of the film's production in 2006, the National Film and Sound Archive prepared a reconstruction from surviving footage and stills, and this was issued on DVD with an accompanying booklet that contained both commentary and transcripts of many of the related documents. It is hoped that this will be the definitive work, until more of the film turns up or more evidence about its production comes to light to fill some of the tantalising gaps that still remain.

Ina Bertrand

REFERENCES

Bertrand, Ina (2000) 'The Mystery of the Missing Director', *Film History*, 12, 2, 215–25.

Long, Chris (1995) 'Sorry, Wrong Centenary!', in Ken Berryman (ed.) *Screening the Past: Aspects of Early Australian Film*. Canberra: National Film and Sound Archive.

THE WOMAN SUFFERS

RAYMOND LONGFORD, AUSTRALIA, 1918

The Commonwealth of Australia was founded in 1900 by the federation of the six states and the Northern Territory, with the Australian Capital Territory set aside as the location for the federal parliament. Meanwhile, Parliament met in Melbourne, the financial capital of Australia, which had boomed after the gold rushes of the 1850s. But the hopeful years of the start of the new nation were transformed by international events. Australia still felt a powerful tie to Great Britain, and answered Britain's call to arms in 1914. By 1918, four years of war had devastated Europe, and in Australia scarcely any family escaped without personal tragedy. In these circumstances, a film about seduction and betrayal seems somehow incongruous, but *The Woman Suffers* was released early in 1918, several months before the war ended. It was made in Adelaide, by Southern Cross Feature Films, was directed by Raymond Longford and starred Lottie Lyell.

John Walter Longford was born in 1878, and used the stage name Raymond Hollis Longford over a long career, as both actor and director, first on the stage, then on film. Lottie Edith Cox was born in 1890, and used the stage name Lottie Lyell as an actor on stage and film, in a career cut short by her death from tuberculosis in 1925. Their personal and professional partnership lasted from 1909 to Lottie's death. Longford's first wife was Catholic, so divorce was difficult, but it finally was achieved – after Lottie's death. The Longford/Lyell relationship was well known (in the theatrical and film world at least), but surprisingly no public comment was ever made, no aspersions passed on Lottie's morals or character. Indeed, she seems to have been universally admired and respected, both as a generous person and as a fine actress. Though the public knew her best as a performer (advertisements for the film proclaim her as 'Australia's Film Star'), her role in the Longford/Lyell production team was actually much more significant, and on various films she was credited as actor and writer, and even once as assistant director. But behind the scenes she was also producer, editor, art director and Girl Friday.

After her death, Longford's work suffered and he never again rose to the heights he had achieved during their partnership. The sympathetic interpretation accounts for this situation as the result of his intense grief. A less sympathetic interpretation would conclude that Lottie was the creative genius of the partnership. The truth probably lies somewhere between these two assessments, and it is likely that they each benefited creatively from the relationship, ultimately leaving Longford unable to find the same inspiration without her. They made nearly thirty feature films together, but few have survived, making overall judgement of their work difficult. Only a few scenes remain of their early production, *The Romantic Story of Margaret Catchpole* (1912). Fortunately, however, their masterpiece, *The Sentimental Bloke* (1919) and the delightful bucolic comedy *On Our Selection* (1920) both survive intact. *The Woman Suffers* was made at the height of their careers, and seems to have been one of their most successful collaborations. An incomplete copy was located in Adelaide in 1983, and this was used by Marilyn Dooley of the National Film and Sound Archive as the basis for a video reconstruction – with the addition of titles taken from the script lodged for copyright registration, as well as advertising stills to represent missing sections of the story, and a music score commissioned from composer Donald Hollier.

The film's production company, Southern Cross Feature Films, was registered in South Australia in May 1917. In June that year, American Walter May Plank arrived in Adelaide as the first director of production, with Raymond Longford as his assistant for the first month. After Longford returned to Sydney to work on his own films, Plank achieved very little, and in December Longford was invited to take over as director of production. He returned to Adelaide and began work on the script of *The Woman Suffers*, and Lottie Lyell joined him there in time for Christmas. They employed Arthur Higgins as cinematographer, and finished the film in early March 1918. This was a rescue mission for the Southern Cross Feature Film company, so it was important that the film do well at the box office. All concerned were pleased at how well it played in Adelaide, so they were looking forward to good returns from its release by Australasian Films through Union Theatres in Melbourne and Sydney. However, in the middle of a successful Sydney season, Union Theatres announced it was withdrawing the film from its city venues, and the state government suddenly prohibited further screening pending a review of censorship approval.

Censorship in 1918 was a complicated and multi-layered procedure, operating at both state and federal levels. Under the War Precautions Act (1914), the Commonwealth government was entitled to make regulations for securing the public safety and the defence of the Commonwealth. Military censorship of communications, including films, was quickly introduced, and Australians soon became accustomed to this, accepting it as a necessary response to a national emergency. The war climate made the public more tolerant of censorship generally, including civilian film censorship, which was still a state responsibility. In New South Wales, the responsible authority was the Chief Secretary's department, on the recommendation of the police, until December 1916, when – after pressure from the moral lobby – the state government appointed the first Board of Censors. The board was chaired by the Chief Secretary, and included the Minister for Education, the Under Secretary in the Chief Secretary's Department, the Director General of Public Health, the Inspector General of Police and the chairman of the Art Gallery. It judged by synopses rather than watching every film, and referred doubtful examples to the police.

Other states also had a civilian film censorship system running parallel with the national military censorship, and in January 1917 the state premiers discussed the possibility of a national civilian censorship. In February that year the Commonwealth appointed a three-man censorship board and in March the first regulations came into operation – making a third layer of censorship. Like the New South Wales board, the Commonwealth board did not view films routinely: it judged first on synopses, and only viewed those films that were the subject of an appeal from the distributor, or of a complaint after public screening. Also, as it was established under the federal Customs Act, the Commonwealth board had power only over imported films. This meant that, despite the existence of national film censorship (both military and civilian), local productions like *The Woman Suffers* were still being censored by the state authorities, and in New South Wales there was still some confusion over the powers of the various components of the state system – the police who administered the regulations, the board who made most of the judgements, and the Chief Secretary who signed off on the decisions.

Longford knew this Byzantine system well, and had applied for censorship approval before the release of the film in Sydney. He had received a letter from the New South Wales Chief Secretary, dated 25 July 1918, clearly stating that no objection would be offered, so far as the department was concerned, to the public exhibition of *The Woman Suffers*. However, he received another letter, dated 22 October 1918, informing him that, following certain representations, approval was withdrawn and film screenings must cease pending a censorship review. Longford was incensed. He immediately complained to the Chief Secretary and made sure that the issue was publicised, both in the newspapers and by questions in state parliament. By that time, the board had viewed the film and had unanimously recommended prohibition of further screenings in the state. No reasons for the decision were ever given (nor were they required under the regulations), but it was generally assumed that the objections were on moral grounds.

This situation did not mollify Longford. He was furious that his business was being placed in such an untenable position, particularly as he considered the film to be highly moral, and this was indeed how it had been received elsewhere. He simply did not believe that the certain representations which had convinced the Chief Secretary to take action against the film could have been on moral grounds, and he was sure that this was another phase of his war with Australasian Films, the Combine. The Combine had been formed over the years 1911 to 1913, out of the interests of Amalgamated Pictures, T. J. West, Cozens Spencer and J. D. Williams. The new organisation comprised a distribution wing (Australasian Films) and an exhibition wing (Union Theatres). It had little interest in production and by 1914 the various newsreels produced by the member companies had been amalgamated and soon feature film production within the Combine also ceased, despite the fact that the company controlled the major studios in both Melbourne and Sydney. The power of the Combine seemed absolute. Australasian Films was the major film importer, particularly of Hollywood films, so any exhibitor who wished to keep up with public taste was virtually forced to do business with the company. At the same time, most of the first-release cinemas in the state capitals were either owned by Union Theatres or supplied by Australasian Films, so only imported films had the opportunity for the kind of splashy first release and subsequent systematic distribution that produced big box office success. As a result, local independent film producers found their market drying up, and opportunities for alternative release strategies largely denied to them.

In 1914, Longford had made *The Silence of Dean Maitland*, the first film of a two-year contract with the Fraser Film Exchange, one of the few remaining distributors independent of the Combine. However, as soon as the film began to appear in Sydney cinemas, the Combine started a campaign, threatening withdrawal of film supply or higher contract charges to any exhibitor who showed it. The Combine only needed to act on this threat with one or two exhibitors and the rest soon capitulated. Fraser broke his contract with Longford, leaving him unemployed, with no prospect of alternative employment in the industry. He took the Combine to court (through their nominee, Henry Gee) and lost. In December 1914, *Theatre Magazine* printed Justice Pring's case notes, exposing the machinations of the Combine, despite the judgement being in their favour.

Longford remained convinced of the justice of his case, and in 1918 was still smarting at the decision against him. Even after the ban on *The Woman Suffers* in New South Wales, audiences continued to flock to the film in the rest of Australia. The lack of complaints in the other states tended to support Longford's interpretation of the New South Wales ban as based on industrial pressure rather than moral issues. Nevertheless, the film does openly address issues of morality – and takes a position that was not common for its time.

In one sense, *The Woman Suffers* is a conventional melodrama – a story of love and betrayal, seduction of the innocent and revenge against the seducer. However, it is also unconventional in its moral position: as its title implies (*The Woman Suffers – and the man goes free*) the film exposes the sexual double standard. In this story women suffer from domestic violence, from sexual exploitation and from social sanctions, none of which are inflicted on men. A man uses a woman as the agent of his revenge on another man. The women in this story, however, are still not free to challenge what men do: they can only escape, or resist passively, or wait for the man to have a change of heart.

There are three interlocking threads to the story. The first opens with traumatised war veteran Philip Masters (Boyd Irwin) taking out his frustrations in drunken violence against his wife, Marion. She runs away into the bush, with their infant son Philip (Paul Baxter), but is so distressed that she collapses, and the child wanders away. The two are rescued separately. Marion is taken in by a station owner, Stephen Manton (Charles Francis), cares for his two motherless children and eventually marries him, after recovering her memory and finding out that her first husband is dead and her child cannot be traced. Young Philip is taken in by the Stockdale family (C.R. Stanford and Ida Gresham) and raised with their own daughter. Each family, then, has both a son and a daughter: Ralph and Marjory Manton, Joan Stockdale and Philip Stockdale/Masters.

The second thread takes up the story many years later. When Ralph Manton's (Roland Conway) journey to the city is delayed by floods, he coincidentally takes refuge with the Stockdale family, and casually seduces Joan (Evelyn Black), before going on to his usual carefree city life. The little bush girl waits for him in vain, cannot stand the impending shame, and drowns herself.

The third thread begins when Joan's step-brother, Philip, seeks out Ralph Manton for revenge. However, at the Melbourne Cup he learns that Ralph, too, has a sister, Marjory, so Philip sets out to seduce her in revenge for his own sister's seduction and death. Calling himself Jack Dalton, and avoiding Ralph (who might have identified him), he sets out on a campaign to win Marjory. He succeeds: Marjory falls pregnant, but when Ralph finds out the true identity of Jack Dalton he can do nothing because Philip points out Ralph's own guilt.

The dénouement, of course, reveals that Mrs Manton is the former Marion Masters, and that Philip is her long-lost child. This news persuades Philip to marry Marjory after all – though, for later audiences, just how happy this ending might be is open to conjecture. As Geoff Mayer describes, the film is clearly a melodrama – in both structure and style. The film speaks through excesses of both visual style and acting. Philip's seduction of Marjory is depicted as taking place during a wild storm, when they shelter in a cave: Philip glowering, to represent his determination to take revenge, or gazing gloatingly at Marjory as he delivers her home after the seduction, is pure melodrama, in contrast to Lottie Lyell's restrained performance as the innocent and trusting Marjory. One of the clearest markers of melodramatic excess is the inter-titles, such as (while Joan is deciding to take her own life) 'When torturing anguish Racks the soul and Sorrow points its dart', or (just before showing Joan's dead body) 'When icy death hath Sealed the breath of That dear form of clay', or (when Marjory's secret is revealed) 'Woman-like, she refuses to divulge the name of the man who wronged her'.

These stylistic excesses support a narrative structured around melodramatic coincidence: Marion losing her memory and then (when that has returned) discovering that her violent husband is dead, allowing her to re-marry; young Philip being taken so far away from home that he is not recognised as the missing Masters child (though he certainly retains the name Philip, and is referred to as Philip Masters in the telegram that announces the marriage); both families having both a son and a daughter, allowing each son to seduce the daughter of the other family; Ralph Manton happening to take refuge from the flood in the Masters family home; the survival of the medal and its providential re-appearance at key moments in the story. It is also a highly moral tale, in which virtue is (usually) rewarded and immorality (eventually) punished; like many Australian narratives of the period, virtue is associated with the country and vice with the city.

Unlike most early Australian film melodramas, the film represents class difference, though this is never spelled out clearly in the intertitles. The Mantons own Willaroon, a large station property, with a big house in which the family is waited upon by servants. When they attend the Melbourne Cup, the whole household (including the servants) transfers to their city home, a large, solid-brick suburban mansion, set in beautiful gardens. The Stockdales, on the other hand, are farmers: there are no signs of servants in their modest country home, which is their only residence. When Ralph Manton is depicted living high in the city, he is shown dining and drinking with a loose woman, and gambling with other wealthy young men. Joan's seduction, then, is the fall of a little bush girl, the child of rural battlers, at the hands of a wealthy young man who has been seduced by the evils of city life. Marjory's seduction is a different matter.

The film has been called Australia's first feminist film – probably because it so clearly targets the sexual double standard. Marilyn Dooley describes Lottie Lyell's screen roles as a cavalcade of the demure, the defiant and the daredevil, and comments that she never played a shady lady. Marjory Manton is as near as Lyell ever came to such a character – not the kind of deliberate immorality implied by the term 'shady lady', but still not quite the pure heroine so often portrayed in silent melodrama. However, the complex moral values depicted here do not reduce simply to feminism. Male violence (particularly against women) is deplored – and punished: Philip Masters (senior) loses his wife and child and dies violently soon after driving them away from home. He is, however, also depicted as a war hero – his violence explained (though not excused) as the result of war neurosis. There is no suggestion that women should be given the same kind of sexual freedom as is claimed by men: suicide is presented as a perfectly reasonable (perhaps even inevitable) response to being abandoned by a seducer, and the repugnant idea that one man can take revenge upon another man by seducing an innocent third party is never examined as a moral issue.

Though Joan and Philip are clearly not related by blood, there is a certain implication of incestuous desire in their relationship. When Joan rides on the running board of Ralph Manton's car to bid him farewell at the gate, an intertitle tells us: 'And in Philip's heart smoldered the fires of jealousy.' Philip's distress at Joan's death is excessive – more that of a lover (a rival to the seducer) than of a brother. This is supported by his staring eyes and clenched fist as he declaims in an intertitle 'He shall not live! I swear it!' His complete lack of empathy with Marjory, and his willingness to make her a pawn in his game of revenge, further indicates that his affections remain plighted elsewhere.

Rather than arguing in favour of sexual freedom for both genders, the film seems to be requiring that all sexual transgressors (male and female) should be punished. Sex outside marriage – for both men and women – is clearly a potentially dangerous activity, to be deplored: social sanctions against it are supported rather than challenged. In this world, happiness is not the goal, rather the most important social value is respectability or acceptable appearances. All of this suggests that the morality of the film is not simply feminist, not even particularly modern – indeed it is often thoroughly ambiguous.

For instance, morality is constructed around class as much as around gender. Philip must hide behind a false identity, not only to avoid detection by Ralph but also to be able to move in the kind of social circles that the Mantons comfortably inhabit. Though such matters are never made explicit in the narrative, Philip is not a suitable match for the much wealthier Marjory, and the wedding that will resolve the moral dilemma only becomes possible when he is revealed to be the son of Marion Masters/Manton, and so socially acceptable within the Manton family. Though Marjory clearly loves Philip (seeing him is enough to bring her back from her death-bed!), there is never any convincing evidence that he feels the same: the match between them is not presented as a love match, but as a kind of recompense to Marjory (or even, perhaps, punishment of Philip?) for the seduction. Meanwhile, Ralph gets away with causing Joan's suicide, suggesting that perhaps an equally appropriate title might be 'The battlers suffer: while the upper class goes free'.

With its contrived plot, excessive performances (particularly from the male leads) and a strangely contorted morality, this film often seems dated. However, for its time it was also courageous, and even now we can enjoy the splendid cinematography and some compelling performances (particularly from Lottie Lyell). We will never know whether its problems with state censorship in New South Wales were caused by moral or economic issues. We can, however, be glad that enough of it survived to allow reconstruction for later generations to consider all these issues.

Ina Bertrand

REFERENCES

Dooley, Marilyn (1995) 'Suffering in Silents: the reconstruction of *The Woman Suffers*', in Ken Berryman (ed.) *Screening the Past: Aspects of Early Australian Film*. Canberra: National Film and Sound Archive.

_____ (2000) *Photo Play Artiste: Miss Lottie Lyell, 1890–1925*. Canberra: National Film and Sound Archive.

Mayer, Geoff (1995) '*The Woman Suffers*: as melodrama', in Ken Berryman (ed.) *Screening the Past: Aspects of Early Australian Film*. Canberra: National Film and Sound Archive.

DAD AND DAVE COME TO TOWN

03

KEN G. HALL, AUSTRALIA, 1938

Dad and Dave Come to Town (1938) is perhaps the quintessential 'pre-renaissance' Australian film. Yet since the renaissance of the Australian cinema in the 1970s, most cine-literate Australians who have seen the Cinesound bush comedy have found it awkward, unfunny and a little embarrassing. The 1970s renaissance inaugurated an Australian tradition of well-crafted, good-looking features conforming to accepted international conventions and tending to invite discussion worldwide as 'art', but in the process of elevating the present these worthy films have had the effect of making most of Australia's screen past look scrappy, cheap and second-hand.

In world cinema terms, *Dad and Dave Come to Town* is a run-of-the-mill late 1930s B feature. It was the first Australian feature to play in London's West End, after it had been cut by 19 minutes, under the title of *The Rudd Family Goes to Town*. Adolph Zukor liked it, and it was released in the United States as *The Farmer Goes to Town* (1943). On the other hand, it belongs to the genre of rural comedy – and by 1935, in the United States at least, rural movies were out of fashion. Its years, its production values and its dumb comedy have conspired to make the film even less acceptable to cultivated tastes these days than it might have been on its release.

Down on the farm two young men (Dave and Joe Rudd, played by Fred MacDonald and Ossie Wenban) have set a noose to trap a fox. The eldest daughter of the family, Jill (Shirley Ann Richards), arrives back from a fortnight away. Yelling from off-screen signals that Dad Rudd (Bert Bailey) has been caught in the fox trap. Before long he has also fallen into a gate to avoid a shotgun blast, been caught in an automatic fence, chased by a runaway car and watched one of the farm's haystacks go up in flames. A timely letter tells Dad and Mum (Connie Martyn) that Dad's brother Alfred has died, and they are mentioned in the will. This means a trip to the city – and Dave and Jill come along to look after their parents.

In the city Dad and Dave behave like unsophisticated hicks in matters of traffic, etiquette, rising times and indoor plumbing. Dad finds he has inherited a 'fashion emporium' called 'Cecille's'. As it happens, running a modiste is what Jill really wants to do, and she has a flair for it. However, the current management has conspired with the owner of the frock shop across the street to keep Cecille's from reaching its full potential, and when Dad and Jill learn of this they get rid of the man responsible and determine to go head to head with the competition – which they do with the help of a floorwalker named Entwistle and Jill's love interest, Jim, a publicity agent. Plans are laid for a grand gala opening featuring 'the Farmer Dressmaker', but at the same time a crucial bill held by their rival comes due on the night of the opening. In one room the 'Royal Show of Fashiondom' unfolds, displaying tableaux of garments intended for 'everyone' while in another all the rival's attempts to spoil things are foiled by Dave, Entwistle and a model named Myrtle (Muriel Ford). In the end Dad's worst enemy from back home pays off Dad's debt in the name of 'mateship' and rescues Cecille's from catastrophe. A coda sees the whole Rudd family back on the farm for Christmas. The lights go out and all the youngsters pair off. Finally, Dad and Mum decide perhaps they too should join the movement to 'populate or perish'.

But in a popular film, particularly if it is a comedy, the story usually counts for very little. It is a platform for moments, performances, set pieces and the creation of affect. The best scenes in *Dad and Dave Come to Town* have nothing to do with the plot. One of these occurs when young Bill Ryan comes to ask Dad for the hand of his daughter, Sarah (Valerie Scanlan) and Dad is misled by Dave to think that Bill wants to buy his dog, Sally. The resulting exchange, with Dad's references to 'hopping into anyone's bed', 'the best bitch in the district' may be old jokes, but with Bert Bailey as Dad and Peter Finch as Bill, the humorous banter is sustained.

The funniest sequence in the film sees Dad and Dave on the radio as part of the publicity campaign for the 'Farmer Dressmaker's' fashion show. In a simply edited progression, fuelled by well-written dialogue and perfect comic timing by Bailey and his partner of many years, Fred MacDonald, the planned programme progressively falls to pieces, replaced by 'bad' dialogue delivery ('Good even-ing, Fa-ther'), pronunciation gaffes ('a tailor-made coat trimmed with stables'), personal messages (with cutaways to their recipients) and bickering ('Are you phonin' or are you broadcastin'?'). Just as Dad, relishing the chaos they are causing, seems about to climb down the microphone and into the airwaves, the programme finishes.

The production still of this scene perfectly illustrates the film's virtues. It is an amusing still, quite apart from whatever might be going on in the story at the time. Dad, in the kitchen with Mum, is listening to an egg. This precise moment does not occur in the film. Instead,

Dad casually shakes an egg next to his ear while he and Mum are talking quite seriously about the difficult day ahead, when the debt will be foreclosed and the Rudds will lose everything. The still, like the film itself, makes incidental byplay, not narrative action, into a reason for seeing the movie: it is a figure of how the film wants to be read.

Dad and Dave Come to Town is the third film in a series of four 'Dad and Dave' comedies produced by Cinesound in the years from 1932 to 1940. All starred Bailey and MacDonald as Dad and Dave. All were directed by Ken G. Hall, Cinesound's house director, and at least partly written by Bailey. There had been two earlier films featuring the Rudd family, both directed by Raymond Longford. The Rudds had also inspired a radio serial, *Dad and Dave from Snake Gully*, which had begun to appear the year before *Dad and Dave Come to Town* was released. No doubt the radio skit described above was partly a homage to and poking fun at the serial, which was a precursor of *The Archers*-style drama, in which neither Bailey nor MacDonald had any part.

Cinesound's first 'Dad and Dave' feature, *On Our Selection* (1932), was also its most financially successful. It was based on a 1912 stage play written by Bailey in collaboration with his theatrical partner, Edmund Duggan (and possibly one other), in which Bailey had played Dad and MacDonald Dave. *On Our Selection* had been a theatrical success, which constantly toured, revived and supplemented by other Rudd plays. It had a profitable run in London in 1920.

On Our Selection was, in turn, based on a collection of stories published under the same title by Steele Rudd (Arthur Hoey Davis), but the play took Davis's low-key 'realistic' stories and turned them into knockabout farce spiced with old-fashioned melodrama. The first of Davis's Rudd stories had appeared in 1895, and their popularity in Australia and abroad elevated their author to the stature of exemplary bush storyteller and condemned him to the Rudds for the rest of his life.

The popularity of Bailey and Duggan's *On Our Selection* created a new, specifically Australian, subgenre of rural comedy. The Australian theatrical historian, Margaret Williams, calls this subgenre 'bush comedy'. It is sometimes known as 'backblocks farce' and was called 'farce-bucolical' by at least one critic at the time. This subgenre upended the conventional format of leavening melodrama with occasional flashes of comedy and instead used melodrama – and its narrative line – as an occasional intrusion into a plotless series of broadly comic skits of rural life, exploiting Australian rural dialect, vulgar folk humour and moronic (but nobly stubborn) characterisations of the rural poor.

A theatrical entrepreneur named Beaumont Smith was the first to make a bush comedy film. Smith's name had been included as a co-author in some publicity for *On Our Selection*, although it was gone by opening night. In 1916 he adapted two of Henry Lawson's short stories into a theatrical bush comedy called *While the Billy Boils*. The next year he made his first film, *Our Friends, The Hayseeds*, the initial entry in a series featuring a bumbling backblocks family who were quite clearly based on Bailey and Duggan's version of the Rudd family. There were eventually seven Hayseeds films, each one produced quickly and on a low budget. (Smith was known as 'That'll do Beau' in the trade). Of all of these, only one survives – *The Hayseeds* (1933), the last and most expensive, in which Cecil Kellaway makes his first screen appearance as Dad Hayseed.

Smith's output effectively flooded the market for bush comedy in 1917–18 and again in 1923. *On Our Selection* (1920) and *Rudd's New Selection* (1921), Longford's Rudd films, may well have been prompted in part by Smith's success with the genre as well as Longford's own ambitions for a respectable Australian cinema. They were explicitly made as attempts to correct Bailey and Duggan's vulgarisation by returning to the sense of Steele Rudd's original 'bush realism'. And in their turn, Longford's films would seem to have inspired Smith to return to production in 1921 with a film version of *While the Billy Boils*, only to put the genre aside for nearly a decade two years later.

These dates define bush comedy's 'moment' in Australian film production (1917–23). Two other bush comedies were released in 1918, which were clearly attempts to cash in on the genre. In 1921, after Longford's more serious films, the Australian theatrical producer Kate Howarde made a film version of her popular bush comedy, *Possum Paddock*, in which she seems to have tried to emulate the latter director's approach by suppressing most of her play's vulgar comedy and bringing melodrama to the fore. Smith then replied to all the seriousness with two Hayseeds movies in 1923. We must assume that *Prehistoric Hayseeds*, the last of these, did not attract much business for there are no other bush comedy films until 1932 – when Cinesound effectively captured the genre and turned it into something else.

Cinesound may have initially agreed to make *On Our Selection* only to gain access to another Bailey and Duggan property, a popular rural melodrama called *The Squatter's Daughter* (1933), which they were allowed to rewrite, updating it significantly. Certainly Ken Hall was not overly enthused at the prospect of filming such a tired old warhorse as the Bailey/Duggan play. Moreover, the film itself appears to have been made in an even more slapdash manner than its circumstances as Cinesound's first feature might have led one to expect. Yet *On Our Selection* was an overwhelming box office hit and, ultimately, Cinesound's most profitable picture. Its success virtually demanded a Rudd family series, which etched itself on the memories of a decade of Australian film audiences, but Cinesound's market dominance meant that even That'll do Beau's final Hayseeds film could not compete. The bush comedy genre had been reduced to a series of 'Dad and Dave' movies.

Looking back at the 1932 version of *On Our Selection*, one suspects that its success had more to do with the impact of Bailey's characterisation of Dad than with the bush comedy genre itself. Bailey is a ham of the old school who commands a cinema screen as readily as he does the stage. His performance, raw and bibulous, exudes the familiar charisma of an obstreperous relative whom no one likes but everyone obeys. The dramatic highpoint of the film occurs about a third of the way through, when Bailey delivers a long, emotional speech about what Australians even today recognise as 'the pioneer spirit'. In it Dad Rudd metamorphoses temporarily from a tight-fisted windy patriarch into the Aussie battler who is beaten down to nothing and starts all over again. This speech, which was imported in full from the play, is still one of the defining moments of Australian popular culture. It is what very many of us imagine ourselves to be.

The second of Cinesound's Rudd family films was also based on Bailey and Duggan material. At least in its surviving form *Grandad Rudd* (1935) develops some gaping narrative holes near the end, but the visuals are sharper and continuity is smoother throughout. Bailey's performance is much more controlled and assured. As is the case in most other bush comedy, the screen time given over to set pieces far outweighs that devoted to the narrative. These set pieces include a runaway tractor which Dad stops with a commanding King Canute gesture and a cricket match in which Dad handily – and freakishly – tops any score to which legendary cricketer, Don Bradman, might have aspired. There is no big speech for Dad in this film and he wins out in the end through trickery, not hard work or perseverance.

According to Hall's own testimony, *Dad and Dave Come to Town* was the first film of the series to have been conceived entirely without reference to Bailey's (or even Steele Rudd's) earlier work. However, it is also the one closest to the work of Beaumont Smith (even the title is borrowed from *The Hayseeds Come to Town*, a variant title for the second Hayseeds film). Hall does not mention Smith in his memoirs, but Smith had used the premise of country folk in the city so many times that it was almost a signature. Dad makes a big speech in this film about not being beaten, and he triumphs in the end because of his straightforwardness (even his enemy, Ryan, knows that Dad is a man of his word). That is, Dad is much more respectable, and far more admirable, than he has been before, and Bailey works on being irascible and lovable instead of mercurial and devious. When Dad first appears in a morning coat and top hat the other characters are amused, but Bailey looks so perfectly patrician that the joke is lost.

In the context of the Cinesound series, another noteworthy characteristic of the film is the prominence it gives to Dave. This focus may have been due to the popularity of the radio show (which made no mention of Steele Rudd and gave no family name to Dad, Dave and Mum). In fact, this is the only Rudd family film with the words 'Dad and Dave' in the title. Dave has far more to do on his own here than in any of the other films. He moves from being Dad's principal nemesis on the farm to his principal accomplice in the city, and he gets a chance at a comic flirtation with the very funny model, Myrtle.

'Dad and Dave' took on a life of their own after 1937–38, overwhelming the bush comedy genre as well as the bush realism of Steele Rudd's originals. 'Dad and Dave' persisted on radio until 1953, and 'Dad and Dave' were revived briefly in 1972 for a television series. In 1995, when a thoughtful homage to the characters, the genre and the stories was released in the form of a feature film, it was called *Dad and Dave: On Our Selection*. And the phrase 'Dad and Dave' is recognised by some Australians today.

Cinesound, however, did not use 'Dad and Dave' in the title of the next, and last, Rudd family film. Instead it was called *Dad Rudd M.P.* (1940), moving the spotlight firmly back onto Bailey alone. At the end of the 1932 version of *On Our Selection* Dad had been elected to Parliament, and apparently the idea of making a film about Dad in politics had been suggested shortly after that film's success, but neither of the next two entries in the series contains any reference to Dad's political career. At the same time, there is a distinct, and expected, populist tinge to all three. In addition to embodying the politically-charged figure of the stubborn battler, Dad can always be counted on to champion the cause of the common man against the machinations of the rich and powerful. In *Dad Rudd M.P.* the political implications of this characterisation are made explicit, as Dad decides (for the first time, it seems) to stand as an independent candidate against a greedy neighbour with a posh accent and upper-class lifestyle. The film follows the campaign and climaxes with what is supposed to be a spectacular flood that ultimately ensures a narrow victory for Rudd.

Nowadays if you type *Dad and Dave Come to Town* into a good internet search engine you will get a surprising number of hits (many more than you will for *On Our Selection*, for example). The reason is generally because of Peter Finch. *Dad and Dave Come to Town* was the actor's first film, and virtually every internet site with a Finch biography cites it. Another international star appeared in that film, (Shirley) Ann Richards. In 2004 there were perhaps 81 sites on which she was mentioned, compared to over 24,000 for Finch – but it was Richards, not Finch who was Cinesound's contracted big 'discovery'.

The difference between what was expected of these two actors back then and what we think of them today is partly historical and partly cultural. In the late 1930s throughout the English-speaking world the major movie stars were women. Fan magazines, advertisements, publicity campaigns and the like tended to treat the cinema as women's business, and it was generally accepted that women made the decisions about what films to see and that they liked to see movies featuring women. But in Australia this skewed situation was exaggerated further than it was in Hollywood. There are simply no charismatic, good-looking young men in Australian films until 1940. Even those whom one would expect to register strongly, like Errol Flynn, are directed in such a way as to appear wooden. Peter Finch would play some attractive, magnetic parts in later years, but his role in *Dad and Dave Come to Town* is as a moronic adolescent. In the next film he did for Cinesound, his character is selfish and morally weak.

Richards, on the other hand, played a series of independently-minded women for Cinesound. In *Dad and Dave Come to Town*, Richards' Jill Rudd knows what she wants and how to get it. She is fearless, determined and honest – her father's daughter in every way that counts. Although such characters are not unusual in early Australian films – and there are three others in that film alone – Jill is probably the 'top of the heap'. One of her lines became the title of a pioneering feminist documentary about the treatment of women and women's images in early Australian cinema: *Don't Call Me Girlie* (1985).

Nearly twenty years later, the Melbourne Queer Film Festival featured *Dad and Dave Come to Town* – but not because of anything to do with Peter Finch or Ann Richards. What interests historians of queer imagery in film is the character of Entwistle, the floorwalker of Cecille's. Entwistle is played in a broadly camp fashion by Alec Kellaway (who also apparently 'discovered' Peter Finch for Cinesound). At one point Dad remarks enigmatically of him that 'he would make a good milker', but the film itself not only gives the Entwistle character a lot of screen time, it treats him as the Rudd's ally and friend – in short, as a mate. Entwistle was even brought back in the final Rudd film to manage Dad's campaign for Parliament – this time almost as one of the family.

However foresighted this film may have been in its images of women and of gay men, it was a product of its time. The villain of the piece is Pierre (Sidney Wheeler), the owner of the rival dress shop. His name suggests he ought to be French, but his character, appearance and accent intimate a more sinister stereotype. Many more Australian moviegoers in 1938 would have identified Pierre as Jewish than would have been able to put a name to Entwistle's sexual preference or would have disapproved of Jill's independence.

In the most serious and sustained treatment of *Dad and Dave Come to Town* in the extant literature, the Australian film historian, Bruce Molloy, has pointed out that Dad's metamorphosis from bushman to showman parallels Ken Hall's own career, which makes *Dad and Dave Come to Town* another one of the seemingly endless series of 'double vision' films about film. But if this is the case, the film is also explicitly about how the cinema sees *better*. Twice Dad complains that people in the city leave behind them a twisted trail where there ought to be straight furrows.

From the opening gag with the fox trap *Dad and Dave Come to Town* undertakes to expose to us, the viewers, what is hidden from some other characters. The cinema enables us to see better than they do (when Dad is caught by the trap he is cinematically *wiped* onto the screen). But Dad's own 'Royal Show of Fashiondom' is a series of purely cinematic trick shots in which the cinema leaves off *exposing* the truth, and makes us witness instead to its *display*. That is, this film, like Dziga Vertov's *The Man with a Movie Camera* (1929), can be glossed as a celebration of the power of the 'kino-eye'.

Dad and Dave Come to Town is the quintessential Australian film of its period, because it wears all of this background and potential for interpretation so overtly and yet so unself-consciously. It is an unapologetically popular film from an industry that made nothing but popular films for more than half a century. From *The Story of the Kelly Gang*, the world's first secular narrative feature, in 1906 until Cecil Holmes' *Three Into One* in 1957, not one Australian feature tried to be 'art'. There is not one *Ingeborg Holm* (1913) or *Broken Blossoms* (1919), not even anything that aspires to be *Comin' Thro' the Rye* (1923) – much less *Battleship Potemkin* (1925) or *Citizen Kane* (1941). Since the Australian renaissance, this circumstance has been regarded as a source of shame, when it is noted at all, but it may be a form of cultural resistance.

Australia's aggressively populist, aggressively cheap movies, like Cinesound's Rudd family series, seem to be made in defiance of British conventions of what good art ought to be, which were equally the standard for Hollywood's idea of well-tooled production. Their emblematic badness is not the badness of a failure to make good, but the badness of a *refusal* to make good – not 'can't' but '*won't!*'

William D. Routt

REFERENCES

Hall, Ken G. (1980) *Australian Film: The Inside Story.* Sydney: Summit Books.

Molloy, Bruce (1990) *Before the Interval: Australian Mythology and Feature Films, 1930–1960.* Brisbane: University of Queensland Press.

Williams, Margaret (1983) *Australia on the Popular Stage, 1829–1929.* Melbourne: Oxford University Press.

DAD AND DAVE COME TO TOWN

THE PHANTOM STOCKMAN

04

LEE ROBINSON, AUSTRALIA, 1953

In the 1950s the Australian voice was rarely heard in feature films. Yet nobody, it seemed, cared and few people appeared to want a local film industry – especially not Prime Minister Robert Menzies and his Liberal-National Party Government or the major film distributors and exhibitors (Greater Union and Hoyts). It was basically left to an actor (Chips Rafferty) and a young director (Lee Robinson) to keep the feature industry afloat – although Ken G. Hall, Charles Chauvel (*Jedda*, 1955) and New Zealander Cecil Holmes (*Captain Thunderbolt*, 1953 and *Three Into One*, 1957) should also be recognised for their efforts during this barren decade. Yet ten years earlier, few Australians would have anticipated that the local feature film industry would virtually die and that public indifference, even antipathy, would be so strong. In fact, as Lee Robinson remarked some years later, if the public became aware in the 1950s that a feature film was Australian it usually meant death at the box office: 'To put an Australian tag on it was the worse thing you could do.' In terms of its feature film industry, Australia was relegated to nothing more than an exotic location for British and American films for the best part of two decades.

This was not always the situation, as there was a steady stream of Australian feature films throughout the 1930s. The most successful films emerged from Cinesound under the management of film director Ken G. Hall. Its first production, *On Our Selection*, which was released in August 1932, was followed by a succession of commercially successful films: *The Squatter's Daughter* (1933), *The Silence of Dean Maitland* (1934), *Grandad Rudd* (1935), *Thoroughbred* (1936), *Orphan of the Wilderness* (1936), *It Isn't Done* (1937), *Tall Timbers* (1937), *Lovers and Luggers* (1937), *The Broken Melody* (1938), *Let George Do It* (1938), *Mr Chedworth Steps Out* (1939), *Gone to the Dogs* (1939), *Dad and Dave Come to Town* and *Dad Rudd, M.P.*

Cinesound was established in 1932 by Stuart Doyle, the general manager of Greater Union Theatres, to supply films to his theatres. While Doyle was supportive of Ken Hall's attempts to replicate an American studio-style of production, his successor, accountant Norman Rydge, who was appointed in July 1937, was less enthusiastic. However, Cinesound continued to generate healthy profits, culminating in the fourth instalment in the 'Dad and Dave' series, *Dad Rudd, M.P.*, which was completed in February 1940. This film was a major success in Australia and Britain and while the company suspended production of feature films in June 1940, due to World War Two, it was expected that production would resume after the war. Only nine Australian feature films were released during the war as the local industry concentrated on newsreels and propaganda shorts.

The post-war period began with the worldwide success of *The Overlanders* (1946). Although the film was commonly perceived as an Australian production, as it was filmed around Alice Springs and the Roper River and starred Australia's most distinctive actor, Chips Rafferty, it was not an Australian production. It was developed and directed by British filmmaker Harry Watt who arrived in Australia in February 1944 as an employee of Ealing Studios and a guest of the Australian Labour Government. The decision to send Watt to Australia emerged out of a request from Jack Beddington, the director of the Films Division in the Ministry of Information in the British Government, to Michael Balcon, the head of production at Ealing, to increase public awareness of the Australian war effort in Britain. This, in turn, followed a 1943 request from the Australian Government for greater recognition of Australia's contribution to the war.

Watt arrived in Australia in February 1944 without a film crew and with no specific project in mind. After learning that Charles Chauvel's *The Rats of Tobruk* (1944) was nearing completion he decided against a combat film and for the next six months he researched ideas related to the war but not directly concerned with the fighting. His aim was to project Australia as a 'huge, exciting, hard country' and he settled on a story suggested to him by the Commonwealth Food Controller: the first cattle drive in 1942 from Wyndham on the coast of Western Australia to the Queensland coast, a distance of more than 1,600 miles. This drive, which was part of the Australian Government's 'scorched earth' policy to deprive the Japanese of food supplies if they invaded northern Australia, consisted of 968 cattle and 53 horses and it took more than eight months in barren, rugged country.

Late in 1944 Watt travelled the same route while his assistant, Dora Birtles, who expanded Watt's script into a novel, researched government files and archives. Stylistically and structurally, *The Overlanders* is consistent with Watt's earlier films as a documentary filmmaker with the General Post Office Film Unit and the Crown Film Unit. In films such as *North Sea* (1938) and *Target for Tonight* (1941) Watt, and colleague Alberto Cavalcanti, 'dramatised' the material by emphasising characterisations and the inherent (melo)drama of the stories. This approach was also used in *The Overlanders* with its story of survival and achievement as a small band of drovers surmount obstacles, such as poisoned weed and drought, in the Australian outback. Even a clumsy romance does not weaken the film's simple power as this incident provides the pretext for another obstacle, a stampede, which the small band must overcome. The film's 'documentary realism' is also reinforced by the periodic use of Chips Rafferty's laconic voice-over as he prepares the audience for the next problem facing the drovers.

The film was marketed overseas as an 'Australian western' and when it opened in the West End of London on 3 October 1946 the *Evening News* praised it with the headline 'AUSTRALIA SHOWS HOLLYWOOD HOW'. The review argued that the 'natural thrills of this film make today's westerns from Hollywood look like dude-ranch fairytales. Chips Rafferty makes an ideal sort of hero.' Similarly, the *Daily Herald* praised its 'fresh outdoor flavour, its freedom from heroics, its gentle humour and mercifully incidental romance', while the *Daily Graphic* claimed that it was the 'first film to give an idea of what Australia is really like'. There was a similar reaction in New York. The *Herald Tribune* said that it had 'all the sweep and action of an excellent western film' and the *Tribune* differentiated between *The Overlanders* and the usual Hollywood western by claiming that the 'subject itself, though not new in films, has a freshness about it because the terrain is unusual, the time is the present rather than the past, and the terminology is unfamiliar'.

The Overlanders premiered in Sydney in September 1946 at the Lyceum Theatre where it screened until February 1947. It was also the first Ealing film to receive widespread distribution in Europe, especially Eastern Europe. Ealing's next two Australian films, *Eureka Stockade* (1949) and *Bitter Springs* (1950), both starring Chips Rafferty, were less commercially successful. While *Eureka Stockade* is a poor film, *Bitter Springs* is an intriguing one which anticipates the revisionary treatment of race relations that were evident in a number of Hollywood westerns of that period, such as *Broken Arrow* (1950) and *The Devil's Doorway* (1950). In these films, the moral spectrum is inverted so that the white characters are shown to be the villains and, despite a compromised ending, *Bitter Springs* remains, as film historian Bruce Molloy points out, 'one of the most effective statements about Aboriginal land rights in Australian features to the present time'.

After the success of *The Overlanders* Ealing was keen to revitalise the Pagewood Studio in New South Wales and produce, in partnership with Cinesound, a steady stream of feature films. This proposal was supported by Ben Chifley's Labour Government and it needed only the cooperation of Norman Rydge to succeed. However, even after the success of *Smithy* in 1946, which involved most of the Cinesound production team including director Ken Hall, Rydge refused to resume feature-film production. Hall later claimed that Rydge 'never had any faith in film production. He was a bricks and mortar man ... his background was "play safe"'.

Hall tried to continue alone and in 1951 he formed Kenhall Productions to make a film version of Rolf Boldrewood's novel *Robbery Under Arms*. Hall's project attracted interest from Rank-Ealing and the plan was for Hall to direct and produce the film while Rank would guarantee worldwide distribution and one-third of the production cost. Hall also had guarantees from Australian investors for the remaining two-thirds of the budget. However Robert Menzies' newly elected Liberal-Country Party government effectively killed this project, and others, when the Capital Issues Board of the Department of National Development issued a new regulation that public companies in Australia could not be formed for specific projects with a capital outlay of more than £10,000 – unless it was deemed a purpose of national importance. The production of Australian films was not considered to be of national importance and this decision effectively prevented Ealing, or any other overseas company, from developing co-production deals to produce Australian films. Even worse, Australians were prevented from forming local companies to make feature films and despite a personal plea to the Australian treasurer from Hall, his project was rejected and it had to be abandoned. Although Rank eventually filmed *Robbery Under Arms* in 1957, it was a totally British production with most of the key roles, except Peter Finch as Captain Starlight, filled by British actors.

The Capital Issues Board regulation on the maximum capital outlay also affected the plans by Associated TV Programmes, a company formed by two New Zealanders, Colin Scrimgeour and Cecil Holmes, to make two Australian feature films and a series of television programmes in conjunction with Chips Rafferty. Rafferty, working with the title *The Green Opal*, wanted to dramatise the problems associated with post-war immigration into Australia. Again, the £10,000 restriction imposed by the Capital Issues Board scuttled these projects and Holmes and Rafferty went their separate ways. Both, however, chose an Australian 'western', or bush melodrama, as their next projects. While Holmes directed the socially conscious *Captain Thunderbolt* (1953), Chips joined up with cinematographer George Heath and young documentary filmmaker Lee Robinson for *The Phantom Stockman* (1953). The films turned out to be completely different. *Captain Thunderbolt* is an ambitious political film and Holmes used the genre as a pretext for a critique of capitalist exploitation. It suffered from poor distribution and although it was previewed in January 1953 it was not released in Australia until September 1956. *The Phantom Stockman*, on the other hand, was in profit even before its premiere in Brisbane in June 1953, due to Rafferty's ability to elicit pre-sales from overseas distributors.

The early 1950s was a busy time for Rafferty. After a prominent role in Twentieth Century Fox's large-budget (£800,000) Technicolor Australian western *Kangaroo* (1952), which was directed by Lewis Milestone and filmed in the Finders Ranges, Port Augusta and Sydney in late 1950 and early 1951, he went to Hollywood to play an Australian soldier in *The Desert Rats* (1953), Twentieth Century-Fox's 'sequel' to *The Desert Fox* (1951). In between *Kangaroo* and *The Desert Rats* Rafferty starred in and produced *The Phantom Stockman*. It was the beginning of a partnership with Lee Robinson that lasted until 1959 and through another five films: *King of the Coral Sea* (1954), *Walk Into Paradise* (1956), *Dust in the Sun* (1958), *The Stowaway* (1958) and *The Restless and the Damned* (1959).

Rafferty and George Heath chose Robinson for their first film because of his background directing 'exotic' documentaries in distant locations for the Department of Information. After viewing one of these films, *Double Trouble* (1952) Rafferty settled on Robinson because he wanted somebody who had experience in filming in difficult conditions with little money. When Ealing announced that it was closing down its Australian operations in January 1952, as the Australian Government showed no sign of changing its policy towards the Australian film industry, Rafferty chose the series western as a way of making a feature film for less than £10,000. He decided to base the film on the character he played in his weekly radio serial, the 'Sundowner'. This was acceptable to Robinson as he was one of the writers for the programme, *Chips: A Story of the Outback*.

The small budget, which was raised through the sale of personal assets, including Robinson's house, as well as debentures to friends and business acquaintances, meant that elaborate sets were not possible. Consequently, Rafferty, Heath and Robinson took a small film crew, including experienced radio actors Guy Doleman and Max Osbiston, Aboriginal actor George Murdoch and Sydney model Jeanette Elphick (who achieved fame in Hollywood a few years later as Victoria Shaw), to Alice Springs in July 1952 for a 26-day shoot. The film was a commercial success and consolidated Rafferty's image, both in Australia and overseas, as the archetypal Australian bushman. The storyline, however, was essentially a variation on the familiar series western plot involving the efforts of a saviour hero, the 'Sundowner'

(Rafferty) and his Aboriginal sidekick, Dancer (Murdoch), to prevent a young woman, Kim Marsden (Elphick), losing her cattle property to a neighbour, Stapleton (Doleman), following his murder of Kim's father. Stapleton not only covets Kim's land but also her body and in a deviation from the normally asexual Hollywood series western, he makes a clumsy attempt to sexually assault her after she takes a shower. The Sundowner, of course, saves her virtue.

This is a curious film as it tries to insert European ideas of Aboriginal mythology into a familiar Hollywood-style storyline. For example, the film emphasises the mystical relationship between the Sundowner and the local Aborigines who are able to communicate with each other through the transfer of thoughts. This process forms the basis of the film's climax when the Sundowner is captured by Stapleton and his gang. He organises his rescue by transferring his thoughts miles away to Dancer and the other Aborigines who assist in his escape. Similarly, earlier in the film, the Sundowner, or as the Aborigines call him 'Alchidor', is summoned to the Marsden property in the same way. This provides the pretext for Robinson to include a montage of reeds and branches swaying in the wind, to show the transportation of thoughts; a mystical version of the 'bush telegraph'.

The film is less successful, however, in its use of Aboriginal artist Albert Namatjira. Namatjira, who was the subject of Robinson's first documentary for the Department of the Interior (*Namatjira the Painter*, 1947), is shown in the film sitting on a rock sketching the landscape while talking to the Sundowner. Nevertheless, this scene is revealing as it shows that Robinson and Rafferty were not only interested in exploiting a popular genre, which they used to attract financing and sales, but were equally concerned with other non-narrative aspects such as the beauty of the Australian outback and the significance of Aboriginal culture. Although the formulaic plot and small budget ultimately negate these aspects, it is revealing to compare the Rafferty/Robinson film with another Australian western of the period, *The Kangaroo Kid* (1950), a jointly-financed production by Australian (the McCreadie brothers, Tom and Alec), British (Ealing) and American interests. *The Kangaroo Kid* was directed by Lesley Selander who had worked with most of the important western series stars of the 1930s, 1940s and 1950s, such as William Boyd (Hopalong Cassidy), Buck Jones and Tim Holt. Selander knew this type of film intimately and he brought with him experienced Hollywood personnel, including top cinematographer Russell Harlan, actors Veda Ann Borg, Douglas Dumbrille and stuntman-turned-actor Jock O'Mahoney, plus newcomer Martha Hyer. Local actors Guy Doleman, Alec Kellaway and Grant Taylor were also included in the film, which was scripted by Hollywood screenwriter Sherman Lowe. It detailed the investigations by American Tex Kinnane (O'Mahoney), sent to the New South Wales town of Goldstar to arrest Vincent Moller (Dumbrille). Moller, who is posing as a respectable lawyer, is responsible for a series of gold robberies. While *The Kangaroo Kid* exploits the scenery and wildlife around the mining town of Sofala in New South Wales, the film, like most of Selander's westerns, does not deviate from the genre as it foregrounds the melodramatic basis of its story by moving quickly from one confrontation between Kinnane and the villains to the next. Even when Aborigines are introduced into the film, unlike *The Phantom Stockman*, it refuses to dwell on the distinctive aspects of their culture and treats them merely as another danger facing the hero.

The success of *The Phantom Stockman* convinced Robinson and Rafferty that they could produce profitable feature films in Australia providing that costs could be kept low and that the story was sufficiently generic/universal to appeal to foreign audiences. Years later, Robinson explained his approach by claiming that if an Australian film or television series had an exotic or unfamiliar setting it should have a conventional storyline so as not to alienate overseas audiences. This approach proved very successful with *Skippy* ('the Australian Kangaroo'), the long-running children's television programme which he co-produced in the 1960s and 1970s. Although there are obvious weaknesses in *The Phantom Stockman*, due mainly to budgetary restrictions and the sparse, uninspiring dialogue, the film benefits from George Heath's beautifully composed images of the barren country around Alice Springs and his dramatic use of shadow and light in the interiors, which camouflage many of the film's deficiencies. To sell the film, Rafferty took it upon himself to personally visit overseas distributors and after completing *The Desert Rats* he stayed on in Hollywood to sell the American distribution rights for *The Phantom Stockman* for £35,000. It was released as *Return of the Plainsman*. This immediately brought the film into profit, even before the Australian release, as its total cost was only £10,800. Rafferty then travelled to many other countries, including India, Pakistan, Ceylon [Sri Lanka] and Burma, where he was also successful in selling the rights. The icing on the commercial cake was Britain where he sold the film for £7,500 and the film was released, initially, as *The Tribesman* and later as *Cattle Station*. In the 1954 edition of the *Western Film Annual* editor F. Maurice Speed gave the film a two-page coverage claiming that 'Australia's great outdoors provides the sweeping and majestic background of *Cattle Station*, the powerful drama of an Australian Robin Hood who solves a murder mystery and brings the criminals to justice'.

The profits from *The Phantom Stockman* provided the basis for Rafferty and Robinson's next film, *King of the Coral Sea*, which duplicated their practice of locating a formulaic story in an exotic setting. Again, Rafferty and Robinson bypassed the restrictions of the Capital Issues Board by using the same financing technique they employed on *The Phantom Stockman* where they raised the budget by selling debentures to friends and business acquaintances, including newspaper proprietor Frank Packer. For *King of the Coral Sea*, Robinson and Rafferty formed a new company, Southern International, and they sold £250 debentures to 100 investors giving them a budget of £25,000. This allowed a six-week shooting schedule on location at Thursday Island followed by a shorter period on Green Island, on the Great Barrier Reef for the underwater sequences.

This adventure melodrama was located in the pearling industry on Thursday Island and it involved an illegal immigration racket operated by two locals, Yusep (Lloyd Berrell), a Malay pearler, and Grundy (Reg Lye). A sub-plot involves the tension between experienced pearler Ted King (Rafferty) and the playboy owner of his company, Peter Merriman (Charles Tingwell), over the introduction of new diving methods. While King wants to retain the traditional suit and helmet method of gathering oysters, Merriman favours the use of aqualungs. Rod Taylor as Jack Janiero, King's American offsider, made his film debut and the film also offered an opportunity for Lee Robinson to return to the location of his 1949 documentary *The Pearlers*.

Again, the film's leisurely narrative pace reflects the interests of Rafferty and Robinson in highlighting non-narrative aspects involving Thursday Island and its pearling industry. Eventually, however, the plot involving illegal immigrants takes over and the film's climax sees King, Janiero and Merriman adopt the new aqualung technique and swim underwater with their spear guns to Weekend Island where they rescue King's daughter Rusty (Ilma Adey), who has been kidnapped. Within this dramatic context, the film exploits Australian fears concerning illegal immigration and there is also a vague reference to foreign (read Communist) infiltration of Australia as the film was produced during the height of the anti-Communist hysteria in the early 1950s.

The Rafferty/Robinson approach of producing films with tight budgets in exotic settings again proved successful and within three weeks of delivering the final print, *King of the Coral Sea* had recovered its costs. After its premiere on Thursday Island on 17 July 1954, Rafferty proceeded to promote the film by visiting each state in Australia and organising a 'Queen of the Coral Sea' talent quest. The film's profits were diverted into the next project, *Walk*

Into Paradise, which utilised the same formula – an adventure melodrama with an exotic setting (New Guinea) with Rafferty as Steve McAllister, a district officer who investigates the discovery of oil by Sharkeye Kelly (Reg Lye) in Paradise Valley near the Sepik River. Pre-production was nearly complete when French producer Paul-Edmond Decharme proposed a co-production with two French film stars and a French dialogue director, Marcel Pagliero, to assist the production. Pagliero, a former actor who had worked with Roberto Rossellini, established an effective working relationship with Robinson and both men decided there should be only one director (Robinson) on the set; after Pagliero went through the lines with the French actors he left the filming to the Australian. Pagliero also assisted the Australian actors with their dialogue for the French version as every scene was shot twice, once in French and once in English. Pagliero was given a full credit in the French version when it was released in Paris in July 1956.

In May 1956 Robinson and Rafferty bought the Cinesound studio at Bondi and they formed Australian Television Enterprises although they retained the Southern International title for their feature films. Their next film, *Dust in the Sun*, which began filming in Alice Springs in October 1956, was not a success. Robinson later claimed that the decision not to cast Chips as the star was a mistake as the film suffered in pre-sales compared with their earlier films, as English actress Jill Adams in the lead role was not well known. *Dust in the Sun* did not receive a general release in Australia until 1960, after Southern International's next film, *The Stowaway*, another French co-production. This time, however, Robinson did not have the same productive working relationship with his French counterpart, director Ralph Habib. Unlike the arrangement on *Walk Into Paradise*, Habib directed the French version and Robinson the English one. *The Stowaway*, which was filmed on location in Tahiti and the Society Islands with Martine Carol and Roger Livesey in the lead roles, had a budget of £250,000 and was poorly received when it was released in Paris in 1958 and Australia in 1959.

After the success of *King of the Coral Sea* Southern International was riding high. The seeds of the company's downfall came when they broke away from their formula of small budgets and tight personal control by accepting the French offer. Although Rafferty wanted to continue making low-budget genre films, he was talked into partnership with the French as they offered distribution outlets for Southern International films in Europe, South America and French-speaking Canada. Rafferty, however, was not a businessman. He was an actor and the decision by Southern International to produce films without their key asset in the starring role was a critical factor in the company's demise as he was considered by many, both in Australia and overseas, as the archetypal Australian. This perception gained impetus in the 1940s, especially after *The Overlanders,* and it was reinforced by *The Phantom Stockman* and *King of the Coral Sea*, as well as his outback cop Sergeant Flaxman in *Smiley* (1956) and its sequel, *Smiley Gets a Gun* (1958). When Southern International moved away from low-budget action melodramas based on this persona, they had nothing left to sell and by the end of the decade the company had died. Rafferty and Robinson, through Australian Television Enterprises, were involved in one more (disastrous) co-production with the French, *The Restless and the Damned,* and then the company was liquidated. Rafferty, at the age of fifty, was forced to start again by seeking acting roles in Hollywood and elsewhere so that he could address the severe financial debt incurred by the last two French co-productions. Nevertheless, without Chips Rafferty and Lee Robinson, Australia would not have had a film industry in the 1950s.

Geoff Mayer

REFERENCES

Molloy, Bruce (1990) *Before the Interval: Australian Mythology and Feature Films, 1930–1960.* Brisbane: University of Queensland Press.

Speed, F. Maurice (1954) *The Western Film Annual.* London: Macdonald.

THE BACK OF BEYOND

05

JOHN HEYER, AUSTRALIA, 1954

The Back of Beyond (1954) is an Australian documentary film about a weekly mail run along the Birdsville Track, following its driver, Tom Kruse, through the numerous stations and natural obstacles along the way. Its director, John Heyer, a senior producer with the Federal Government's Film Division (later called the Commonwealth Film Unit, now Film Australia), had been employed by Shell to produce a 'prestige' documentary that would encapsulate the essence of Australia. Seen by an estimated 750,000 Australians in the first two years of its release, and with subsequent television and film festival retrospectives and tertiary education screenings, the film is familiar to generations of Australians. In 1996 *The Back of Beyond* figured prominently in the National Film and Sound Archive's survey of key Australian films. In its year of release, the film won the Grand Prix Assoluto at the Venice Biennale Film Festival; in 1956, it took the first prize in the Documentary and Experimental Section at the Montevideo Film Festival, and a Certificate of Merit at the Cape Town Film Festival.

These circumstances indicate two things. First, the film has been understood locally as essentially 'Australian'. Second, its international reception, particularly the Venice prize, suggests that the film was acceptable to a large variety of international audiences and, at least, made sense to these audiences. A possible reconciliation of these two seemingly disparate readings can be found by taking into account the international discourse of the landscape documentary to which *The Back of Beyond* belongs. The following analysis examines the cinematic education of the film's director, John Heyer, before examining the way *The Back of Beyond* remakes themes and stylistic attributes common to an international group of films which includes *Night Mail* (1936) by Harry Watt and Basil Wight, the films of US New Deal filmmaker Pare Lorentz, and more recent televisual and filmic adaptations of the narrative structure of *The Back of Beyond*.

From his earliest involvement with cinema until his recent death, John Heyer understood himself to be working in a medium that was essentially a network that crossed political, national and cultural borders. In the 1930s and 1940s while working as an apprentice on productions by Frank Thring Sr, Charles Chauvel and Ken G. Hall, Heyer swapped imported books and magazines with young turk Damien Parer. Heyer maintained a connection to the international documentary community through the publications he read with Parer. In an interview with Andrew Pike and Ray Edmondson, Heyer commented on his awareness of the international documentary movement during the 1930s: 'Damien and I were reading *Close Up*, *Cinema Quarterly*, *Experimental Cinema*, we were corresponding with the G.I.K. [State Film School] in Moscow, [and] with Grierson's crowd. When I say corresponding we would make efforts to make contact. I didn't see any great flow of letters there. In fact one of my great disappointments – I was very keen to get into G.I.K. but I never did get a decent answer back.'

Heyer was also directly influenced by the films being brought into Australia by embassies and other cultural organisations. His experience of culturally diverse cinema led to an interest in making available these kinds of films to an Australian audience. He continued this engagement with international cinema through the burgeoning film society movement in the 1940s in New South Wales and Victoria, which had promoted an increased interest in culturally and formally diverse films, in particular documentaries. Heyer also became involved with Alfred Heinz, Alan Stout, Frank Howard, Neil Edwards and Frank Nicholls in the first Melbourne Film Festival held at Olinda in 1952, a culmination of Melbourne's film society movement.

In 1945 Heyer was appointed as the first Senior Producer at the Australian National Film Board, bringing to that role not only a sound knowledge of many facets of feature and documentary film, but also some background in the film societies' alternative to commercial film exhibition. He knew film in an international context and he brought that knowledge to bear on what was basically the production of government propaganda films. This knowledge is apparent in the way that *The Back of Beyond* is clearly related to the host of filmic precursors already mentioned. Ross Gibson has suggested that *The Back of Beyond* 'must have been seen as the last possible film that could be made in the *Night Mail* tradition. It must have seemed a particularly strange mutant of the *Night Mail* tradition. It is about communications, it is about the delivery of messages. But it is also about adaptation. *The Back of Beyond* seems a very peculiar adaptation of *Night Mail*.'

The resonances and correspondences between *Night Mail* and *The Back of Beyond* are both direct and elusive. *Night Mail* was made in 1936 by the General Post Office Film Unit, then headed by John Grierson. It was produced, directed and scripted by Harry Watt and Basil Wright and includes a narration written by W. H. Auden and a musical score composed by Benjamin Britten. It is about the complexities involved in a communications system and concerns a train, the Postal Special, which runs from London to Glasgow transporting mail. The film focuses on the structure of what Richard Barsam calls 'this ordinary process', employing a voice-over in the form of rhyming poetry, which is backed by a military style drum beat that propels the image of the train across the landscape. In a sense of linear narrative movement and homogeneity *Night Mail* celebrates movement and work and clearly illustrates Grierson's notion of 'the creative treatment of actuality'.

The Back of Beyond was made for the Shell Film Unit (Australia) and directed, produced and edited by John Heyer with the research and scenario construction for the film performed by Roland Robinson, a poet and renowned anthropologist. The dialogue and narration was written by one of Australia's preeminent poets, Douglas Stewart, with some assistance from John and Janet Heyer. The film was photographed by Ross Wood, one of the great craftspeople of Australian cinema. Both films set out to achieve a lyrical and poetic rendering of their subjects. Unlike *Night Mail*, which represents a process that never falters and remains confined to the railway track, *The Back of Beyond* provides a variation on the journey motif to take in the stories and characters that surround the mail run. One example of this approach is the inclusion of a story of two lost girls. Stories of people lost in the Outback inform the 'bush' legend and in Heyer's film such a story provides a distinct departure from the narrative drive of the journey across the land. The lost girls' story is embedded in the territory that surrounds the track that Tom Kruse travels. Kruse's truck leaves Clifton Hills, and in its journey across the landscape, featuring car wrecks and graves, Kevin Brennan narrates:

Last of the five stations living along the track, where once there were fifteen. The others have gone, beaten by loneliness and drought and their homes reduced to a windswept grave, a crumbling wall. Proud homes built four square and hard, broken by the relentless cycle of the sun until all that remains is the music of their names. Mirra Mitta, Appatunkna, Killalpapina, Oorawillanni. The people are gone but their stories live on in the tales and the legends of the track. Travelling as they did across the sand and the stones; as the story of the two children whose mother died while their father was away mustering cattle. It was early September, so the story goes…

This narration sets up the story of the two girls amidst images of death, isolation, loneliness and elements such as wind, drought and sand. While the scene has been extracted for use in compilation films and advertisements it also represents much of the concerns of the film. It is a story of a homestead family whose father is away droving when the mother has a fall. The two daughters, Sally and Roberta, set out with their dog, Bosun, to search for help in an arid desolate landscape. The children discover that they are lost after crossing their own tracks, and then leave Bosun tied to a tree, at the mercy of an advancing snake. The narrator says 'two days later their father rode after them, followed their tracks for 27 miles until they disappeared under windblown sand'.

Leigh Astbury has pointed out that the 'topic of the lost child had long fascinated Australian artists and writers', arguing that 'the frequent and dramatic occurrence of the event gave impetus to literary and pictorial renditions of the subject, but what raised the theme to the level of myth in Australian culture was its symbolic value'. For Astbury it was the negotiation by a settler society of 'the nature of the Australian bush' which enabled the pervasion of the lost child in literature and painting. For Peter Pierce, who extends his account to include film and what he terms 'true stories', the lost child motif that abounds in Australia stems from what he terms 'an Australian anxiety' whereby, 'symbolically, the lost child represents the anxieties of European settlers because of the ties with home which they have cut in coming to Australia, whether or not they journeyed here by choice. The figure of the child stands in part for the apprehensions of adults about having sought to settle in a place where they might never be at peace.' Within the schema of the film, the kind of naiveté with which the girls operate contrasts with the awareness and familiarity that enables Tom Kruse to sustain the mail run despite the environmental obstacles he consistently encounters. Further, the death of the children functions as a cautionary tale about the dangers of the Outback.

Stuart Cunningham extends the examination of *The Back of Beyond* in relation to the British documentary tradition exemplified by *Night Mail* by pointing to the kinds of adaptation of that tradition performed by Heyer's film. Cunningham notes that 'within a world where survival turns on the necessity to "tell stories", there is a concerted attempt to delegate authority *from* the God-like narrator *to* the humble storytellers within the film's world (the mailmen, the succession of women who "communicate" [with] Tom and his offsiders by two-way radio to the next station, Malcolm, the Aborigine who retells his past in the area, the Birdsville policeman entering in his diary)'. For Cunningham this adaptation results in a 'delegation of authority' from the Grierson model for narration to the people able to survive and make something of themselves in this harsh world; people such as Tom Kruse and the Afghan camel driver Bejah, whom Tom encounters on the track.

Another primary model or reference point for *The Back of Beyond* is Harry Watt's *The Overlanders*, a film which adapts the Griersonian documentary model to a fictional structure based on an unexpected, episodic Outback journey. Watt's understanding of the 'problems' of the Australian film industry is a direct extension of Grierson's critiques of the industry during his post-war visit to Australia. However, it may have been Watt's pre-production methodology that had a larger influence on Heyer.

Graham Shirley and Brian Adams argue that Watt had been the first of the British documentarists after Robert Flaherty to effectively incorporate dramatic episodes and, also like Flaherty, was prepared to spend months familiarising himself with actual locations and people before developing a storyline based on these experiences. In *The Overlanders* it is possible to see Grierson's aesthetic and social requirement for documentary, and to see traces of the documentary work performed under Roosevelt's New Deal. As with the New Deal documentaries, many Australian films were concerned with an interest in representing the country in a way which would reinforce the idea of nationhood and the role of central government. Like the US in the 1930s, what was most significant about the response of the Australian government to the problems of rebuilding a post-war nation was that it was to alter what Terry Cooney describes, in relation to Roosevelt's administration, as 'the very idea of what "government" implied, the images conjured up by the term, and the effects on people's lives that its use assumed'. Both the Roosevelt administration in the US and the Curtin/Chifley governments in Australia had at the centre of their platforms the promise of social reform. It can be noted that to a certain extent the Roosevelt administration provided a domestic economic model for the Australian Labour government of the post-war years. Both administrations placed an emphasis on the representation of governmental initiatives in a way which posited a sense of regionalism as a component of national unity. In Australia this expression was voiced through the creation of the Australian National Film Board and in Roosevelt's United States through the New Deal photographers and documentary filmmakers.

The opening sequence of *The Back of Beyond* introduces 'the Outback': images of a hawk swooping on a bearded lizard, of dinosaur bones, an invocation of Aboriginal communities, of the explorers Charles Sturt and Edward Eyre, the inland sea, and of settlers and drovers imaged in a manner similar to many shots in sections of *The Overlanders*. Following the opening montage a truck appears over a sand dune and the film introduces Tom Kruse and his associates, Henry and Paddy. The narrator says that the truck contains 'supplies and mail for lonely cattle stations. Stations measured in thousands of miles. Where the man living a hundred miles away is your neighbour and the only link with the outside world is Her Majesty's Royal Mail.' The last shot accompanying this narration is of the track, taken from the cabin of the truck.

In this manner the film sets up a journey and its purpose. However, the journey is forestalled when the mail truck becomes bogged on sand dunes and has to be extricated. The journey proper begins in the next scene as Tom and Henry prepare and load the truck. But as soon as it is established that another journey is about to commence, the film diverts again. Tom waves hello to a figure in the distance and the narrator draws a comparison between the two people: 'Two battlers of the Birdsville track. Tom Kruse, who goes out today in a truck, and Bejah, last of the lords of the desert, who carried out food and water on a string of 50 camels. Old Bejah Dervish, the giant Afghan, who fought the desert by compass and Koran.'

Besides Tom and Bejah other people inhabit the Outback. The narrator says, 'part of a vanishing race, the Australian Aborigine, trading ochre and pituri from the south for the black stone axe of the north. Where the explorers Sturt and Eyre came in search of an inland sea twelve million years too late.'

Ross Gibson has noted that 'the figure of Tom Kruse buys into a whole bushman tradition', but this figure also belongs to the tradition of documentary and social character types seen at work from the beginnings of documentary filmmaking itself. Such types are represented by Bejah, Tom and Malcolm Arkaringa, who journeys with Tom and enables one of the lengthier diversions during which another type is introduced – the dingo hunter, Jack the Dogger. Further, for Gibson, *The Back of Beyond* represents a signpost in the development of a concept of truth that involves a relationship between culture and nature. Gibson maintains that the positioning of the landscape in *The Back of Beyond* is an attempt to present 'one component of a symbiotic relationship': 'There is a society operating on the Birdsville track which puts some of its shape onto the environment but there is also the environment putting some of its shape onto the society. So there is, once again, a blurring of that easy distinction of nature and culture that operates elsewhere.'

For Heyer, one part of this blurring of distinctions occurs at the pre-production stage. Heyer's films are all tightly scripted. In an interview with Martha Ansara he told how, in a reflection of Flaherty and Watt, he 'made three trips to the area … Oh yes, lots of trips. And you must learn the history of the place, read up all about it … talk to people out there.' In this interview Heyer also talked of the storytelling nature of script writing. 'You've got to think it up. You've got to dream it up', which is a departure from Grierson's idealisation of Flaherty's ethnographic method of constructing a story from everyday experiences. In an interview with Gordon Glenn and Ian Stocks, Heyer elaborated what he saw as the relationship between the found story and the script:

> It is crucial to me that I know the subject completely. I slowly make up long lists of categories and items which seem to have potential. I put down everything – weather, life cycles, and so on; as well as the places and ideas I think of that seem to be fertile. Then I try and relate these together ... I make the film in my mind, shot for shot before I start. By scripting a practicable basis, you save a lot of money and give yourself more time to be fluid. I always know that if anything goes wrong, I can shoot what I have written down and it will be alright. Also you need something tangible ... to communicate with, for instance, the cameraman.

Interestingly, a host of Australian television programmes have taken the story of Tom Kruse, and retraced and reworked the narrative in an awkward relationship with the 1954 film. Examples here include programmes screened on Australian Broadcasting Corporation among them an edition of *Countrywide: Birdsville Mailrun* (1986), and an edition of the *Australian Story* series titled *The Postmen* (1996). There has also been the commercial television documentary *Last Mail for Birdsville* (2001). These programmes are interested in providing the kind of closure that *The Back of Beyond* refuses. Paradoxically, at the same time these programmes continue the events documented in *The Back of Beyond* as a way of updating the story, making sure that it goes on and on in endless repetition. In each of these works there is a focus on the figure of Tom Kruse as well as the images that form the opening and closing sequences of Heyer's film. All these programmes seek to decontextualise the character type of Tom Kruse as it is constructed by Heyer's film by disregarding entirely the moments that cinema audiences have celebrated and remembered the film for: the lost girls sequence, the crossing of Cooper's Creek, or the visit of the Malcolm Arkaringa character to a Lutheran mission. The storytelling and the departures from the track are omitted entirely in favour of the equivalence of character and truck on the track.

In other ways *The Back of Beyond* has been intuitively adapted. As Keith Beattie has pointed out, David Batty and Francis Jupurrurla Kelly's documentary television series *Bush Mechanics* (2001) has a relationship with Heyer's film, 'blend[ing] a core of documentary observation and information with moments of dramatic re-enactment in a humorous depiction of the mechanical skills of five Aboriginal "bush mechanics", do-it-yourself automobile repairers who use anything at hand to mend broken car parts'. Each episode in the four-part series traces a journey undertaken by the five protagonists managing to keep their decrepit vehicles moving towards their destination. For Beattie, '*Bush Mechanics* rewrites and "Aboriginalises" the Griersonian mode of *The Back of Beyond* abandoning the stentorian voice of God voice-over and the romanticisation of what Grierson called "upstanding labour" in a narrative which mixes traditional Aboriginal knowledge and contemporary automobile repair "advice" within a representational aesthetic derived from sources as varied as MTV and magic realism.'

As Gibson and Beattie both point out, *The Back of Beyond* acts as a kind of model for George Miller's *Mad Max 2: The Road Warrior*. Aesthetically, the images of Max's (Mel Gibson) petrol-tanker truck in the chase sequence from *Mad Max 2* recall the close-ups of the dented and weather-beaten front grill of Tom Kruse's truck. Also in this film Max is not unlike Tom. Both men are merely surviving, reading the land and moving when they are required to. Like Tom, Max encounters people in his travels and has learnt to adapt to the land. Both films propose a way of living with the land that works against the heroic, conquering mythology of the early explorers.

The Back of Beyond can be seen to employ diverse international influences, in addition to local subject matter. These international influences on Heyer's film posit a reconsideration of the notion of an 'essentially' Australian cinema. The film, in its connection with a host of films from diverse countries, draws on these influences which are then channelled out into local productions that are, in turn, embraced by international audiences. This model proposes that Australian film and television has always been engaged, at some level, with the international movements of film culture.

Deane Williams

REFERENCES

Astbury, Leigh (1985) *City Bushmen: The Heidelberg School and the Rural Mythology*. Melbourne: Oxford University Press.

Barsam, Richard M. (1974) *Nonfiction Film: A Critical History*. London: Allen and Unwin.

Beattie, Keith (2004) *Documentary Screens: Non-Fiction Film and Television*. Hampshire and New York: Palgrave Macmillan.

Cooney, Terry A. (1995) *Balancing Acts: American Thought and Culture in the 1930s*. New York: Twayne.

Cunningham, Stuart (1985) 'The Decades of Survival: Australian Film 1930–1970', in Albert Moran and Tom O'Regan (eds) *The Australian Screen*. Melbourne: Penguin.

Gibson, Ross (1987) 'On the Back of Beyond', in Tom O'Regan, Brian Shoesmith and Albert Moran (eds) *Continuum*, 1, 1, 83–92.

Glenn, Gordon and Ian Stocks. (1976) 'John Heyer: Documentary Filmmaker', *Cinema Papers*, September, 120–2, 190.

Heyer, John (1979) Unpublished interview with Andrew Pike and Ray Edmundson.

_____ (1990) Unpublished interview with Martha Ansara.

Pierce, Peter (1999) *The Country of Lost Children: An Australian Anxiety*. Oxford: Oxford University Press.

Shirley, Graham and Brian Adams (1998) *Australian Cinema: The First Eighty Years*. Sydney: Currency-Angus and Robertson.

JEDDA

CHARLES CHAUVEL, AUSTRALIA, 1955

Jedda (1955) is one of Australia's most famous films. Directed by Charles Chauvel, the film is set on a vast and isolated cattle station in the Northern Territory. It tells the story of an Aboriginal baby from the Pintari tribe, whose own mother dies in childbirth, and who is subsequently taken in and raised by a white woman, Sarah McMann (Betty Suttor). The first half of the narrative deals with Jedda's (Margaret Dingle) childhood, her often fraught relationship with her adoptive mother and her development into a beautiful young woman (played by Ngarla Kunoth). Curtailing the girl's contact with the Aboriginal people who live at the station, Sarah raises Jedda as if she were her own white daughter. She hopes Jedda will one day marry Joe, the head-stockman. The son of an Afghan teamster and an Aboriginal woman, Joe (played by Paul Reynall, a white actor in blackface) appears to have been successfully assimilated. He even speaks English, with the studied intonation of a BBC newsreader.

The second part of the narrative focuses on Jedda's desire to be with her own people and her attraction to a handsome tribal black, Marbuk (Robert Tudawali), who arrives at the station looking for work. Taking Jedda captive, Marbuk forces her to flee with him to join his own tribe. Jedda's journey into the interior becomes a rite of passage in which, for the first time, she sheds the trappings of white colonial civilisation. On arrival the pair find themselves rejected by the tribe for breaking the latter's marriage or 'skin' taboos. Hunted by Joe and the police, and disturbed by a death wish uttered against him by his own people, Marbuk is driven insane. In the tragic ending, Joe begs Marbuk to release Jedda, but Marbuk takes her with him over a precipice. Jedda's fall can be read in several ways: a physical fall, a moral fall and a 'falling back' into the other, so-called 'primitive' culture – the fall which Sarah McMann so desperately tried to prevent.

This chapter argues that behind the heated discussions about assimilation which take place between Sarah and Doug McMann (George Simpson-Lyttle), lies another narrative – one which is submerged, camouflaged by the deliberate staging of debates between the McManns. This unexplored narrative raises the question as to whether or not the McManns had the right to take Jedda in the first place. This question is never raised directly in the film. Instead Jedda's 'captivity' – for that is what it is – is represented in the main not as captivity, but as a tale of Jedda's good fortune. With the arrival of Marbuk, the question of assimilation – and the related but unspoken issue of Jedda's origins as a stolen child – is dropped and replaced by a classic captivity narrative in which spectator interest is focused away from the assimilation issue and onto the drama of the outlaw couple and their flight into the desert.

A close analysis of the film's opening sequences makes it clear that the possibility of re-turning Jedda to her own people is never considered. The film's voice-over belongs to Joe, the narrator, who tells us that Jedda was 'born in the dust of the cattle tracks'. Bulu, her father, wonders if 'one of the lubras will take it' but the film does not depict any of the women coming forward to look after the baby. Felix (Wason Byers), the 'boss drover', and Bulu take the baby to Mungalla, the nearby buffalo station owned by their boss, Doug McMann. Felix says that 'Mrs McMann is *one* woman who understands these people'. The question as to whether one of the other 'lubras' will look after the infant is not raised again. Baby Jedda is, at first, reluctantly taken in by Sarah McMann, wife of Doug, who is away droving. Grieving and embittered over the recent death of her own baby, Sarah at first rejects the motherless black child. When one of the women offers the baby to her she screams: 'Take it away!'

At first the Aboriginal women look after the baby, naming her 'Jedda', meaning 'Little Wild Goose', before Sarah takes over. Conferring on baby Jedda all the benefits of white culture that would have been the birthright of her own daughter, Sarah begins her project of civilising Jedda. She tells Jedda she wants her to be 'like my own daughter'. But Jedda prefers to make animal tracks in the dough during cooking lessons, rather than learn the alphabet. Chauvel emphasises Sarah's rigorous attempts at assimila-tion, even showing the frustrated Sarah snatching the little girl away from her playmates, whom she calls 'dirty black pickanninies'. Ignoring Jedda's expressed desire to be with her own people, Sarah dresses her in clean, dainty clothes, teaches her the principles of Christian living, educates her and, when Jedda grows older, teaches her classical music on the piano. The battle between Sarah and Jedda continues as Jedda grows into a beautiful young woman (played by Rosalie Kunoth who was renamed Ngarla for the film).

Interspersed with scenes of Jedda's development are a number of key episodes in which Sarah and her husband argue heatedly about whether or not Jedda, a 'full-blood' Aborigine, can be successfully assimilated into white culture. Sarah and Doug argue over Jedda's upbringing. Sarah believes firmly in assimilationist policies, in which the indigenous culture is assimilated by the dominant one. 'It is our duty', says Sarah, 'to bring them closer to our way of living'; 'No I'm not going to let the child slip back'; 'It is my duty to try.' Sarah is, of course, motivated also by the loss of her own daughter, but Doug fails to understand the extent to which his wife has projected her loss onto Jedda, who is assigned the task of making good the mother's pain, of taking the place of the dead white child.

Doug argues from an essentialist view of culture saying that Sarah will only change Jedda on 'the surface', that Sarah will not be able to wipe out Jedda's 'tribal instincts and desires'. 'They don't tame' he states with conviction. Doug believes that it is essential to let Jedda join the annual walkabout so that she can breathe again, 'regain her tribal status'. Doug appears to have a deep understanding of racial difference but, in the end, he still believes in the superiority of his own culture. He seems to see walkabout as an interlude in the annual routine of the station blacks; he does not suggest that Jedda should – if she wishes – return to her people. Jedda longs to shed the trappings of white domesticity and proper femininity, to go on the walkabout and to understand the wildness that tugs at her heart. But Sarah forbids her to keep company with 'those naked monkeys'. When Sarah asks her what she will do on walkabout, Jedda replies with a clear suggestion of irony in her voice that she will 'do what all the other monkeys do'. 'The best walkabout for you is to come to Darwin with me next year,' says the uncomprehending Sarah. Her fear of Jedda's 'slipping back' refers to a widely-held racist belief that the non-white races were interstitial, that is, easily able to bridge the gap between species, in this case between human and non-human, human and animal.

Sarah supports assimilation, arguing that it is the duty of white Australians to take Aborigines into their homes, to 'civilise' them, to prevent the Aborigines 'slipping back', while Doug argues that for the 'full-blood' Aborigine, full assimilation is impossible, that 'these people' will always respond to the 'call of the wild' which courses through their blood. This is clearly illustrated in a scene between Jedda and Joe. The couple are lying together beside a lagoon. 'Jedda, I want to marry you', Joe says. 'I want to build a little house for you and me.' 'But you can't see the stars through a roof,' Jedda protests. She tells Joe that she likes it best when she can feel 'wild', and see the stars 'dancing a big corroboree'. Then she can go barefoot with 'not too much dress'.

Never at home in her adoptive culture, Jedda is immediately attracted to Marbuk, who wears only a red loincloth, his beautifully muscled body on display for all to see. Notorious for absconding with the women belonging to other Aboriginal tribes, Marbuk holds a powerful attraction for the Aboriginal women at the station. And for Jedda. Nita, one of the young women, tells Jedda that Marbuk has the power to 'sing a girl to his campfire even against her will'. One night, during a men's ceremony, Marbuk 'sings' Jedda out into the darkness where, mesmerised, she secretly feasts her eyes on Marbuk's body as he dances erotically in the moonlight. Later that night, Marbuk steals Jedda away from Mungalla and takes her to join his own people on their distant tribal lands. Repelled, but yet attracted to her abductor, Jedda is in a state of internal conflict throughout their long and dangerous journey together. Jedda's fate is that because of her 'adoption' by the colonial culture, she becomes a liminal figure, living in two cultures, at home in neither.

**

It is impossible to view *Jedda* now without relating Jedda's plight to that of the stolen generations. The 'stolen generations' refers to the practice by which Aboriginal and Torres Strait Islander Children were forcibly, or by other means, taken from their families and adopted by white families and other bodies in order to breed out the black. In 1951 assimilation was established as an official policy of the Commonwealth Government. In her introduction to a collection of stories by the stolen children, published in 1998, Carmel Bird states the aim of the policy as:

> a long-term government plan to assimilate Indigenous people into the dominant white community by removing children from their families at as young an age as possible, preferably at birth, cutting them off from their own place, language and customs, and thereby somehow bleaching aboriginality from Australian society. This attempt at assimilation was nothing but a policy of systematic genocide, an attempt to wipe out a race of people.

The stolen children, usually always 'half-castes', were taken from their families, 'by compulsion, duress or undue influence'. They were the victims of a white society that tolerated shocking cruelties towards the indigenous owners of the land. They were either placed in government/welfare institutions or adopted by white European families in the hope that they would lose their blackness. Henry Reynolds has described the consequences of the policy designed to 'breed out colour' as tragic, leading to worse acts of racism.

For all their talk about 'civilising' and 'saving' and 'uplifting' the indigenous people, white Australia could not accept Aborigines as equals even when they had grown up in

European society and had received a Western education. The caste barrier was impenetrable. Those who had most reason to assume they could become part of settler society were more rather than less likely to become objects of derision and abuse.

Jedda was in production from early 1952 until its release in 1955. Not only was assimilation adopted by the Australian Government during this period, the West was experiencing the social and political consequences of centuries of imperial rule, slavery and colonial empire-building. The year of *Jedda*'s release was also the year in which blacks in Montgomery, Alabama, boycotted segregated city buses. A year later, Martin Luther King emerged as the leader of the black rights movement in the US. Four years later, in 1960, the Sharpeville massacres occurred in South Africa. During this period of international racial dissent and warfare, Australia lauded the virtues of an assimilation policy whose aim was not to bring about a properly functioning inter-racial society but to eliminate or render invisible the existence of indigenous people in Australia.

Stories of adoption were regularly reported in the newspapers. One of the best-known cases of adoption was that undertaken by the Deutscher family. The *Sydney Morning Herald* of 29 May 1957 ran an article under the heading: 'Family To Bring Up Native Girls.' It read: 'A Melbourne couple plan to bring up three Aboriginal girls, on a footing of equality with their own children, in their 15-room mansion at East Brighton.' The article stated that the girls (Doris, 19; Christine, four; and Faye, two) who came from the Croker Island Methodist mission, 180 miles from Darwin, knew little about their own parents. Mr Deutscher said he believed it was possible 'to integrate Aborigines into white families and should be encouraged'. What pleased him most, however, was the way his own children, Lorraine, 16, and Trevor, 12, 'have accepted them'.

The following day the *Sydney Morning Herald* editorial praised the effort of the Deutscher family: 'This lesson in assimilation has a double value – first, in setting a fine community example … and second, in providing evidence over the years on the capacity of Aboriginal children to develop in the environment of a comfortable white household.' The editorial referred to the slowness of assimilation policies and the problem of the growing segregation of Aborigines even in churches. It concluded with a statement about 'Aborigines as victims of white man's neglect'. This patronising sentiment was expressed more directly in a letter to the editor of *The Bulletin* of 21 December 1955 which stated, 'The degree to which Aboriginal people of "settled areas" are deficient in hygiene or moral conduct is also the extent of our failure as their protectors and mentors.'

Indigenous children placed in institutions were subject to shocking cruelties. In comparison the Deutscher story reads like a fairytale. Carmel Bird's collection of stories makes this tragically evident. In *John's Story* the narrator describes his first encounter with his so-called protectors: 'First of all they took you in through these iron gates and took our little ports off us. Stick it in the fire with your little bible inside. They took us around to a room and shaved our hair off … They gave you your clothes and stamped a number on them … They never called you by your name; they called you by your number. That number was stamped on everything.' The intention of the authorities appears to have been to rob the children of all sense of their birthright, true identity and racial pride. The institutionalised lives of the stolen generations is explored in a recent film, *Rabbit-Proof Fence* (2002), in which Aboriginal children are clearly captives of colonial society.

***

In *Jedda* we see two captivity narratives at work: a classic and a reverse captivity narrative. The classic captivity narrative occurs when a white settler, usually a woman, is taken captive by indigenous people. The reverse captivity narrative occurs in those instances in which an indigenous woman (and sometimes a man) is taken captive by a dominant Caucasian culture. The latter have not historically been seen as classic captivity tales. Rather indigenous captives were viewed as 'lucky' to be taken in by the white culture and given the so-called benefits of European civilisation. Jedda is caught up in a reverse captivity narrative in relation to the McManns, and a classic captivity in relation to Marbuk. In the classic captivity narrative (*The Sheik* (1921), *The Searchers* (1956), *Harem* (1985)) the white female hostage functions as a signifier of cultural boundaries. Historically, in American frontier tales, for instance, stories of a woman's capture by indigenous people would circulate amongst the dominant culture, enabling its subjects to explore the unthinkable (particularly in terms of sexual desire) even deriving gratuitous pleasure from such ruminations, while, in the end, mentally redrawing and reinforcing the moral, sexual and cultural boundaries that separate their own culture from the alien one.

Jedda is black, yet brought up as white; hence, the symbolic meaning of her capture is clear. Like the traditional heroine of the classic tales, she is in danger of losing her innocence and virginity to the eroticised wild male. The anxiety of colonial culture about the theft of white women by indigenes is well-documented; however, the theft of female stations blacks brought up according to the conventions of white culture constitutes a different but related issue. In stealing Jedda, the adopted 'daughter' of the station owner, the daughter who is white in every respect bar the colour of her skin, Marbuk strikes at the heart of white society. To some degree, Marbuk's actions fuel the colonial fantasy of 'black rape of white womanhood', a fantasy historically used to justify reprisals on local indigenous people. In this context, Marbuk's abduction of Jedda, despite the fact that she is also black, follows the conventional pattern of the classic captivity narrative in which the captive is a white woman. Joe and the police set out to capture Marbuk and bring him to justice.

Throughout their journey back in time, Jedda's response to Marbuk, as in many filmic representations of captive white women, is deeply ambivalent. At times she is drawn to him; at other times hostile. As his name suggests, Marbuk signifies the animalistic, primitive wild male – the mythic figure of the classic captivity narrative. He is akin to the Sheik, the Warlord, the wild Chieftain. Those moments of attraction occur when Marbuk performs an act that is coded as primitive or as in harmony with the time-honoured rituals and practices of his people, such as the dance before the fire, and his life-and-death battle with the crocodile. Through the symbolism of flames from the fire, Chauvel makes it clear that Jedda and Marbuk have sex. Some critics have referred to what took place as a 'rape' but my reading is that Jedda actively desires sex with Marbuk. Marbuk evokes or brings to light in Jedda desires which, according to the dominant white culture, are incompatible with progress and civilisation.

Marbuk himself is a doomed figure. Like Jedda and Joe he is a victim of the effects of colonisation. Living away from his own people, working for white colonial bosses, he is neither a station black nor a tribal black. Having broken both white law and black law, Marbuk is doomed from the start, but his punishment and death are brought about by the violation of his own people's law – a problematic narrative device. As Marcia Langton argues: '*Jedda* rewrites Australian history so that the black rebel against white colonial rule is a rebel against the laws of his own society. Marbuk a ('wild') Aboriginal man, is condemned to death, not by the white coloniser, but by his own elders. It is Chauvel's inversion of truth on the black/white frontier, as if none of the brutality, murder and land clearances occurred.' Marbuk could have been depicted as a freedom fighter, a political outlaw who returns Jedda to her people; the film partially explores this theme. Like a shamanistic guide, Marbuk takes Jedda on a journey of re-birth in which she learns the ways of her people: her civilised garb is torn and ruined; she learns to travel barefoot and sleep under the stars as she desired from childhood; she eats snake; she experiences the dangers of living in the bush and near crocodile-ridden swamps; she has her first sexual experience in the wild. How much more powerful would *Jedda* have been if Marbuk had been portrayed not as a thief and outlaw, but as defender of his people?

In the final sequence Marbuk, driven mad by the curse of his tribe, drags Jedda with him over the precipice to their deaths. Joe rushes towards them, pleading with Marbuk to let Jedda go. 'She no good for you,' he cries in typical pidgin English, 'she wrong skin.' It could be argued that Joe is using broken English here in order to communicate with Marbuk, the tribal Aborigine, but the fact that in other scenes Joe dissociates himself from the Aboriginal people suggests otherwise. His voice speaks in many registers reflecting the film's contradictory positions on assimilation. Joe's desperate pleas are in vain. As he stumbles away from the cliff edge, a broken man, the camera pulls up and away focusing on a flight of geese in the blue sky above. At the same time the voice of Joe the indigenous character is replaced by the voice of Joe the omniscient 'white' narrator. 'Was it our right to expect that Jedda, one of a race so mystic and so removed should be one of us in one short lifetime?' he ponders. Suddenly, Joe is identifying himself as 'white', speaking to a white audience in magisterial tones. Jedda is from a 'mystic' race, 'so removed' in time. Joe is essentially 'one of us'. Then, as often happens when a text cannot resolve its own ideological contradictions, the narrative moves into the time-honoured realm of myth. Joe tells us that 'the Pintaris whisper that the soul of Jedda now flies the lonely plains and mountain crags with the wild geese and that she is happy with the Great Mother of the world in the dreaming time of tomorrow.'

In *Jedda*, the narrative of reverse captivity – that is, the tale of Jedda as one of the stolen children – is not properly explored. Instead, the film focuses on the classical captivity tale of Marbuk's abduction and seduction of Jedda. Jedda is a stolen child and a stolen woman – but in both contexts her captivity is subordinated to the imperative of upholding the myth of white superiority that the dominant culture seeks to maintain at any cost. There are moments, however, when Jedda's desperate plea that she should be free to be with her own people drowns out the paternalistic voice of assimilationist rhetoric. It is in these moments that the film earns its reputation as one of Australia's cinema classics. The tragedy is that Jedda's freedom can only be realised in the impossible and essentialist image of the Jedda birds flying high above the cliffs at one with the mythical Great Mother and the dream time.

Barbara Creed

REFERENCES

Bird, Carmel (1998) 'Introduction', in Carmel Bird (ed.) *The Stolen Generation: Their Stories*. Sydney: Random House, 1, 2, 57.

Langton, Marcia (1993) '"Well, I heard it on the radio and I saw it on the television...": An essay for the Australian Film Commission on the politics and aesthetics of filmmaking by and about Aboriginal people and things', North Sydney: Australian Film Commission, 45–6.

Reynolds, Henry (1998) 'Afterword', in Carmel Bird (ed.) *The Stolen Generation: Their Stories.* Sydney: Random House, 184.

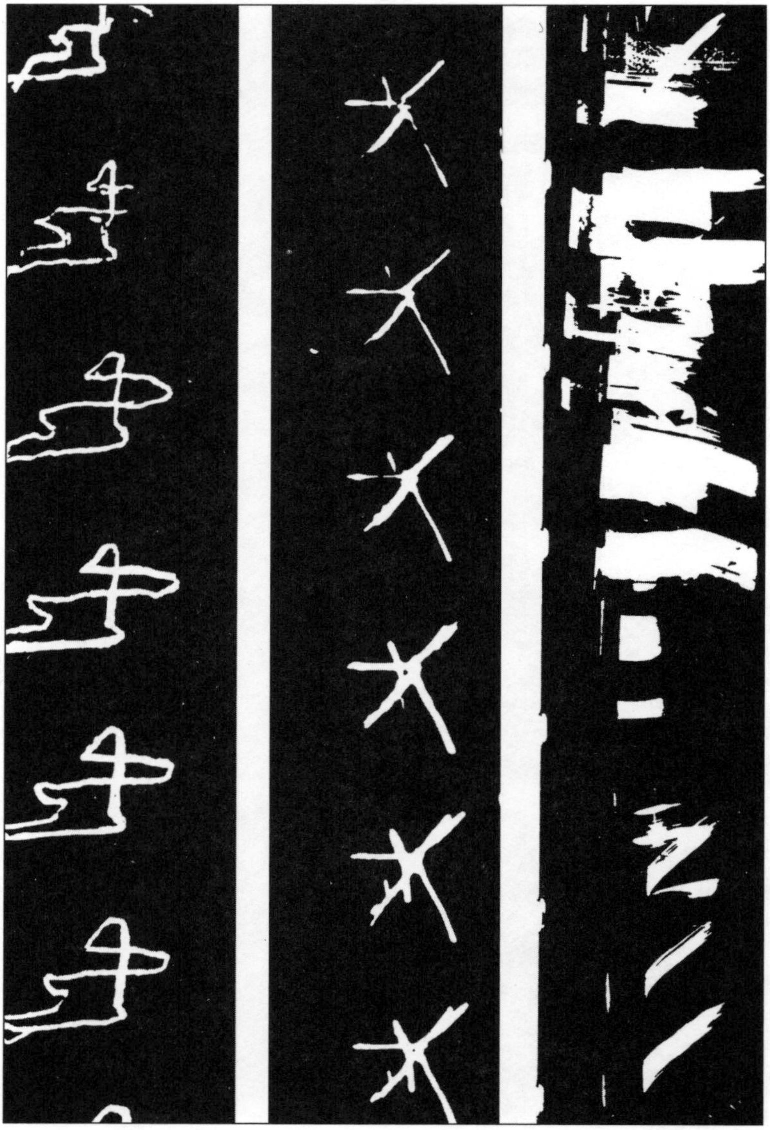

FREE RADICALS

LEN LYE, NEW ZEALAND, 1958

07

Although it is only four minutes long, made without a camera and limited to abstract, white images scratched on black, Len Lye's *Free Radicals* (1958) is such a concentrated and intense film that it packs more punch than most features. Stan Brakhage, the important American experimental filmmaker, summed up *Free Radicals* as 'an almost unbelievably immense masterpiece (a brief epic)'. John Adams described it in *Film Quarterly* as 'the most stylish, condensed, and formal work' in the genre of direct or camera-less animation, adding that 'if proof had ever been needed that Lye, the pioneer in this field, is the real – and for some the only – master, here it is'. Adams' review was written just after *Free Radicals* was awarded the Second Prize of US$5,000 in an International Experimental Film Competition in Belgium, held in association with the World Fair of 1958. The competition had received 400 entries including many of the world's best-known experimental filmmakers. The jury that met in May was a remarkable group – Man Ray, Norman McLaren, Alexander Alexeiff, Edgard Varèse and Lye's one-time producer, John Grierson. Grierson, speaking in the late 1950s in the television series *This Wonderful World*, found *Free Radicals* a 'delight', the work of a 57-year-old filmmaker who was 'young in spirit and experimental as ever'.

The radical nature of *Free Radicals* requires us to think carefully about how we should approach and contextualise it. A tireless innovator, Lye is perhaps the only New Zealander who can be said to have developed not only new content but also new methods of filmmaking. In *Colour Box*, made in 1935 at a time when he could not afford to rent a camera or buy film stock, he came up with the idea of painting and scratching images directly onto celluloid. Historians have unearthed some precedents (not known to Lye or to his early audiences), but it is generally agreed that he deserves credit as 'the pioneer' (to use Adams' term); the filmmaker who developed camera-less animation into a serious genre, demonstrating its potential in such a thorough and sophisticated way that many animators were attracted to it.

Why had others not done so before? Animators had been discouraged from drawing directly on film by the jittery effect caused by the slight differences between one frame and the next. It took a special kind of artist to regard this jumpiness as an advantage, as a display of energy and as a visual equivalent of musical resonance. Lye's interest in this method and the free brushwork of his paintings had prepared him for this new approach to film. Animators of all kinds from Walt Disney to the German abstract artists had sought smooth movement and maximum control. Similarly, the long tradition of tinting film and adding hand-painted areas of colour (by both brush and stencil) had emphasised neatness and precision. Lye was well aware of these precedents but preferred (as Malcolm Le Grice has put it) to work 'with rather than against the "imperfections"'. This approach provides an important context for *Free Radicals* as a showcase for the jumpy energy, the muscularity and vibrancy of Lye's direct imagery.

Lye never rested on his laurels, and continued to experiment with new forms of camera-less animation, employing various types of brushes, stencils, combs and spray-guns. In *Rainbow Dance* (1936) and *Trade Tattoo* (1937) he came up with some highly original ways to manipulate the colour printing process. In the 1950s Lye made painting on film even more challenging by adopting the smaller 16mm format but by then his hand and eye had developed a remarkable precision. In *Color Cry* (1953) he applied Man Ray's photogram method but extended it in new directions by arranging fabrics, stencils and coloured gels on strips of film.

In *Free Radicals* Lye made yet another 'radical' shift by limiting himself to the scratching of white marks on black. Famous for his use of colour, Lye enjoyed reducing the film medium on this occasion to its most basic elements – light in darkness. The idea went back to his first filmmaking in Sydney, circa 1923, where he had drawn some scratches on strips of black leader. During the 1930s he had included scratched as well as painted sequences in colour films such as *Swinging the Lambeth Walk* (1939). A burst of experiment in 1953 had given him tantalising glimpses of a new type of black-and-white imagery that evoked the speed and energy of atomic particles, but until he was invited to enter the Belgian competition he had not completed a film because he found it so difficult to make an image that matched his conception of what he desired of an image.

In 1957–58, with the encouragement of his wife Ann as breadwinner, Lye was able to devote eight months of concentrated work to capturing his 'kinetic figure'. Scratching the images of *Free Radicals* was a complex dance of hand, arm and wrist movements. It took a great deal of precision to work on such a small scale, to scrape vigorously enough to make the images seem bold and energetic while still managing not to tear the celluloid. In the film business at large, accidental scratches were a fact of life, but filmmakers and projectionists were always horrified to see them. A few filmmakers had made conscious use of scratching but in most cases as a special effect only because the method was so difficult to control. Scratching black film so that the light of the projector flashed through the clear celluloid base, Lye created effects as dramatic as lightning in the night sky. With his admiration for the most ancient (as well as the most contemporary) forms of art, he was delighted to think he was cancelling out the thousands of years that separated modern technology from the scratching of designs on cave walls. He haunted second-hand shops in his search for scribing instruments suitable for the 16mm format. The most useful were dental tools, needles and teeth from saw blades, to which he added some Native American arrowheads.

What other contexts can help us decide on the best way to read and discuss *Free Radicals* as a non-narrative, abstract film? A summary of a few of his ideas about film aesthetics provides some of the main principles of his filmmaking. As a teenage art student Lye had decided that movement was the most neglected aspect of art, and the aspect that interested him most. What made movement significant was form or pattern and motion.

Lye's next insight was the extent to which the body as well as the eye is involved in sensing movement. To watch an athlete is to be conscious of strain, weight and balance, and often this makes the spectator's own body tense. His long-term aim was to get more of this physical dimension – this 'body English' – into his art. It was one reason for his interest in the jitter of hand-drawn film images (or motorised sculptures). In Lye's view, most film-makers had yet to come to terms with movement. In his essay 'Is Film Art?', written a year after *Free Radicals*, he saw the medium as 'the Cinderella of the fine arts' still 'waiting for her glass slipper in order to enthrall with her unique kinetic beauty'. Even the best films tended to remain at the level of 'good folklore fun', focusing on emotion and storytelling and paying little attention to the composing of motion, except for the 'roller-coaster sensations' associated with action sequences.

Lye worked across the arts but always showed great respect for the specific, physical properties of each medium. *Free Radicals*, for example, represents a very pure use of film as images on celluloid and as light in darkness. Indeed, the use of film is so specific that it is very difficult to transfer it to video without compromising the rich contrast between the light of a projector and the depth of the black background. A transfer to DVD is likely to lose some of the physicality (the sense of bold scratching) or the subtle movement (every frame of the film being separately drawn, with just enough difference between them to give the images a tense vibration). Finally, for Lye, the best way to combine film images with music was to think of them as a form of dance. The kind of dance that interested him most was jazz or tribal dance.

In *Free Radicals* Lye followed his usual practice of starting to develop a new style of imagery and then looking for suitable music, which he found in a field tape of the Bagirmi tribe. The Bagirmi people are spread through West and Central Africa, today being most closely associated with Chad. The music selected by Lye was a traditional dance piece which might be described in today's terms as a funky four-rhythm performed by a musician shaking a rattle and another beating a pair of drums. As he wrote in a note on dance and film, Lye relished the 'quality of zizz' in the drummer's 'short, sharp, rhythmic figures'. The fact that the piece was somewhat repetitive was helpful to him in synchronising his images. The most distinctive changes in the music were a burst of singing after the opening titles, and a passage of more uneven, syncopated drumming. Lye constructed distinctive visual sequences around these variations. As usual he had the music printed as an optical soundtrack since it helped him to understand the structure of the music and to detect any subtle changes.

Free Radicals can be understood as a set of variations – not on the music but on the visual technique of scratching white marks on black film. Within its four minutes there are nine or ten major variations (though this is a subjective judgement as the variations flow one into another, and sometimes overlap, with a sense of continual metamorphosis). Each variation can be broken down into smaller sequences typically one- to two-seconds long, though there are a few longer sections, and fragments as short as one or two frames. This is the scale on which Lye scratched the film, usually drawing around 24 frames (a second of film) during each pass. As always, he proceeded by trial and error, a slow process. Once he had discovered an interesting 'figure of motion' he would continue for days to make variations on it. Lye was a perfectionist. Eventually the best of the variations would be selected and combined, to make up what the viewer would perceive as a ten- to twenty-second sequence. Slowly the sequences accumulated, and were then juggled and edited tightly to fit the music.

The film commences with one of its principal figures of motion, like the main theme introduced at the beginning of a work of music. This effect is reminiscent of a lightning flash, or the darting, snake-like kinetic sculptures he would later build. After 13 seconds, a vertical line moving sideways across the screen functions as a kind of optical wipe to clear the way for the next section (the title sequence). The hand-scratched titles ('Free Radicals/ Film by Len Lye', etc) have a tense vibration. The letters are constantly on the move like an energetic group of dancers, shifting this way and that to the drum music. Lye had developed this style of scratched words in the early 1950s while preparing to make a poetry film with his friend Dylan Thomas. A line sweeping from the opposite side of the screen clears the way for zig-zag scratches. Then a contrary line introduces a sequence that is carefully structured around a man's singing. His voice is associated with a group of parallel vertical lines that sway gracefully as they keep shifting from side to side and forming new pairs. (Lye described this figure of motion as 'tradeoffs'.) The singer takes three pauses between the four lines of his verse, and those pauses are filled with the sound of drumming. Lye inserts zig-zags as a visual contrast to the parallel lines. This alternation continues throughout the half-minute sequence, though the zig-zags occasionally encroach upon the parallel lines.

After the singing stops, the next sequence consists of a very diverse range of scratched images in brief bursts, mostly only a few frames in length, interspersed with short stretches of black film. Some of the images resemble numbers or letters (7, 3, Z, S, C, L, A, V, W, M, and so on) but they change constantly, and there are also some more complex tangles of lines. All of these white shapes leap and flash out of the darkness as an electric crackle of energy, reinforcing the sharp beats of the drum. It is clear that the black spaces are an integral part of this visual rhythm (as they were in the film's title sequence).

The following section, approximately a minute long, is more continuous, and in some respects it represents the heart of the film. It consists of a wonderful series of turning or spinning movements. Lye found that shapes like letters could be made to pivot or turn inside out, creating a sudden illusion of depth. As a painter himself, he was well aware of the forms of complex, shallow space explored by abstract art. In his filmmaking he was, according to his note on dance and film, 'mixing the dimensional range of visual imagery' to create a fluid, ever-changing sense of space that he described as '3½, 3, 2½, 2D'. In *Free Radicals* many of his shapes appear to perform within the frame as though on a theatre stage. Sometimes they create the impression of a dancer pirouetting or a skater spinning, moving forwards or backwards from the surface of the screen. Then the movement will grow wild again, with the shape flipping upside down or inside out. In this rapid, giddy series of variations it is scarcely possible to tell where a dance (or a strip of film) begins and ends.

The next section is a miscellany of zig-zags, flashes and lines. This includes some tightly structured mini-sequences such as two frames of a flash of lightning high in the frame followed by two frames of lightning lower down. This alternation continues, interspersed with two frames of black. The result is a dynamic effect of flashing. Also, a cluster of scratches moves around the frame like an energetic group of dancers or a flock of birds. Variations on these two ideas turn up several times in the course of the film.

This section is followed by two of the most memorable figures of motion. The first (approximately half a minute long) accompanies a passage of less regular, syncopated drumming. An asterisk shape comes into existence as a number of lines run together from different directions. Once in place, the asterisk struggles to remain intact. It is tugged around the screen as the individual lines engage in an energetic push and pull. A few seconds later there is a brief but beautiful sequence of broad banner or feather-like scratches which curl or whiplash across the screen as though rippling in the wind. This is one of the most striking examples of the shallow but complex sense of depth that characterises the space of the film. After the banner variations there is a brief section of dots, some four rows of six, but with a scattering of dots missing from each frame, so the pattern constantly changes. Then a flurry of rough, vertical scratches functions as a full-stop, bringing the music and the imagery to an abrupt halt.

Lye saw *Free Radicals* as a suitable name for his film in a scientific as well as a political sense. He had felt from the start that the imagery suggested energy particles, like those seen through an electron microscope. In the 1950s he had a growing interest in science, and he was excited by a story in the science section of the *New York Times* about 'free radicals' as atoms or molecules that were highly reactive and unstable because they contained an unpaired electron. He was not interested in the debate about whether free radicals had positive or negative environmental effects, but simply in the fact that they were fundamental particles present in many chemical changes. He liked the description of them as like a compressed spring ready for release. He thought of his title as a colourful analogy – he was certainly not trying to represent such particles literally, and he wanted the film to be approached in the first instance as a pure visual or kinetic experience.

Free Radicals as a whole clearly reflects Lye's long-term involvement with modernist forms of art. From the 1930s he was interested in the most free-wheeling (or 'painterly') aspects of Surrealism such as its interest in automatism, doodling and graffiti as a source of original images. The style of the film has connections with Lye's earlier paintings, such as the repertoire of zig-zags, asterisks, dots, dashes and other 'energy signs' that he shared with the artist Joan Miró. In the 1940s and 1950s, the New York School developed painterly abstraction still further, highlighting the physical textures of paint and the gestural aspects of the painting process. Lye was involved with this group and screened his films at their 'Club' in Greenwich

Village. *Free Radicals* has been described by certain critics as an outstanding example of Abstract Expressionism in film. Not only Lye's imagery but also his filmmaking process were strongly reminiscent of the 'action painting' of artists such as Jackson Pollock through the emphasis on open form, physicality, gesture and the pure energies of the medium.

The fact that the film creates impressions of lettering also opens up the possibility of a semiotic analysis. The scratching may be seen as an indexical sign representing Lye as auteur. (It is interesting to note that his method of direct animation is the only form of filmmaking that literally fits the auteur theory. That theory oversimplifies the orthodox filmmaking process by speaking of films as the work of a single artist, but in the case of *Free Radicals* the distinctive trace of the artist is physically present in every frame.) The scratches are not only indexical but also symbolic (suggesting letters) or iconic (taking the form of lightning, say, or a dancer), but only in an intermittent way. A scratch can have a number of possible readings – interpreted as an atomic particle, a bird in flight, a snake, or purely a vector. A semiotic analysis can draw attention to the complex nature of *Free Radicals*; but clearly such an approach has to be pushed to its limits to come to terms with all that 'sign' and 'signature' can imply in this extremely fluid film. From Lye's point of view, however, there is a danger that interpretations of this kind will tend to privilege what he called 'the New Brain' over 'the Old Brain', diverting too much attention away from the kinetic experience of the film towards intellectual readings. Properly projected, with the images on a large scale and the music pounding, the film is a rich sensory experience that far outstrips any analysis.

Finally, in the context of the present volume, it is relevant to consider whether *Free Radicals* can be usefully related to the New Zealand tradition. While this should be seen as only one way to read the film, such an approach has the advantage of emphasising its points of difference from most American or European examples of experimental filmmaking. And conversely, it forces us to expand or complicate our conception of the New Zealand tradition. For example, Lye's work offers a strong exception to the influential idea that New Zealand's best films represent, according to a documentary produced by the British Film Institute, 'a cinema of unease', since he was an exuberant artist who interpreted happiness as one of the foundations of his thinking about art.

In terms of his 'New Zealandness', Lye was born in Christchurch in 1901 (as a third-generation New Zealander), and *Free Radicals* was one of the end results of a pattern of interests he developed during his formative years as a young artist in the country. He came to see motion as his central interest; arguably, his distinctively physical approach to motion was shaped by the tough, outdoor way of life he experienced (for example in his work as a labourer). Before leaving New Zealand at the age of 23 to go to Samoa, Lye developed a deep interest in indigenous and ancient forms of art, ritual and dance. He studied African, Maori, Aboriginal and Pacific traditions. He shared the Cubist approach to 'primitive art', but coming as he did from the South Pacific he extended this interest in new directions. *Free Radicals* can be seen as a continuation of his 'primitivist' interests in its allusions to African tribal dance, though its imagery is original.

Free Radicals illustrates Lye's lifelong interest in 'lo-tech'. While demonstrating his ability to master the most sophisticated equipment in the production of films and kinetic sculptures, he refused to be overawed by technology and took pleasure in finding new uses for 'primitive' methods. This was sometimes a matter of financial necessity, but he saw it also as his homage to the work of ancient and indigenous artists. Lye could be claimed as a prime example of what Ian Mune describes as the most impressive tradition of New Zealand filmmaking – the line of 'invention' and 'imagination' – made up of filmmakers (from Rudall Hayward to the young Peter Jackson) who have managed to get maximum use out of the minimum of resources.

Lye was always a radical artist, and his radicalism was of the type one might expect from a postcolonial country at the end of the earth where Western culture can seem an alien import. In practice, such extremism is rare, but it does crop up in the work of some of New Zealand's most distinctive artists (from Colin McCahon to contemporary innovators such as Philip Dadson or Merylyn Tweedie). Lye was an outstanding example in his determination to re-invent art and film.

Granted, there are thoughtful critics who disapprove of all attempts to find traces of New Zealandness in Lye, seeing such readings as compromised by an essentialist nationalism. Lye was a rebel who developed his art as much in opposition to the local culture as because of it. And what made him important for the New Zealand artists of the 1960s was precisely his internationalism. In the increasingly global environment of recent years, however, a number of New Zealanders have become interested in reclaiming expatriates such as Lye. There are now more complex, hybrid notions of personal and national identity, and a curiosity about whether New Zealand influences continue to colour international careers. The 1979 re-edit of *Free Radicals* was funded by the newly-formed New Zealand Film Commission, pleased to reclaim Lye as an ancestor. But perhaps Lye's strongest links with New Zealand lie in the future rather than the past since his work is now so frequently screened and exhibited there. Meanwhile, Lye's reputation transcends regional associations. *Free Radicals* continues to command international interest as one of the greatest experimental or (to use Lye's term) 'fine art' films ever made.

Roger Horrocks

REFERENCES

Adams, John (1959) 'Free Radicals', *Film Quarterly*, 12, 3, 58.

Le Grice, Malcolm (1977) *Abstract Film and Beyond*. London: Studio Vista.

Lye, Len (1984a) 'Is Film Art?' in Wystan Curnow and Roger Horrocks (eds) *Figures of Motion: Selected Writings*. Auckland: Oxford University Press/Auckland University Press.

_____ (1984b) 'A Note on Dance and Film', in Wystan Curnow and Roger Horrocks (eds) *Figures of Motion: Selected Writings*. Auckland: Oxford University Press/Auckland University Press.

Mune, Ian (1994/95) 'From Hand-Made Cameras to Hand-Morphed Creatures', *Onfilm*, 11, 11, 13–15.

08

RUNAWAY

JOHN O'SHEA, NEW ZEALAND, 1964

If New Zealand filmmaking in the 1970s was a cottage industry, then previously it had been for hobbyists. Had it not been for John O'Shea and Roger Mirams at Pacific Films and Rudall and Ramai Hayward, there would have been no feature films made in New Zealand between 1940 and 1970. The significance of O'Shea's *Runaway* (1964) within New Zealand's national cinema lies in the fact that it exists at all. It was O'Shea's second feature film and one of only five New Zealand films produced between 1939 and 1972: Rudall Hayward's *Rewi's Last Stand* (1939) and *To Love a Maori* (1972), and O'Shea's *Runaway, Broken Barrier* (1952) and *Don't Let It Get You* (1966). O'Shea describes these sporadic shots at feature filmmaking as sniper bullets that rarely found their target.

Until the formation of the New Zealand Film Commission in 1978 filmmakers struggled in a political environment in which governments were at best disinterested and at worst hostile to film development and a local production industry. Through the silent era there had been sustained film production with both foreign and local investment, but the innovation of sound resulted in a lag in New Zealand film production. By the 1940s local production was limited to documentary, education and government propaganda films made by the National Film Unit (NFU), the single processing facility and only source of equipment in the country. The feature film industry was considered an importation business concerned with distribution and exhibition of Hollywood and British films, rather than an industry that had indigenous cultural value. During the late 1940s and early 1950s O'Shea's company Pacific Films became the only production centre in New Zealand other than the NFU. O'Shea commented in 1992 that by the time he began making films, the idea of an 'industry' had been 'hijacked by film wholesalers and retailers, the distributors and exhibitors. They regarded themselves – in New Zealand at any rate – as the film industry.'

However, during the 1950s and 1960s, and beyond the mainstream and away from production, a film culture was being generated through the establishment of the National Film Library, a Film Institute and a number of film societies. There were a limited number of dedicated film buffs who provided an emerging film culture, importing and exhibiting

European films and enjoying those aspects of an international cinema they could access from a distance. The few people who considered themselves filmmakers were driven by a desire to express and explain what it was to be a New Zealander, and the films of the period explored the country's geographic, social and cultural peculiarities.

New Zealand is a sparsely populated, isolated group of islands in the South Pacific, with an increasingly strained relationship to the 'mother country', Britain, and a strong bicultural tradition involving the indigenous population, Maori. O'Shea wanted to make films that were grounded in New Zealand life and that stylistically referred to overseas films but had local issues at heart. Within this frame he realised that a main source of film drama in New Zealand was the relationship between Maori and Pakeha (British colonials). Conventional genres had to be skewed to cope with the uniqueness of New Zealand concerns. In *Runaway*, a generic category (the fugitive road movie) was affected by the geographical fact that all New Zealand borders are marine. There is no 'next-door state' with more lenient laws in which to hide – in New Zealand there is no Mexico. As O'Shea said in his memoirs published in 1999, 'There is only the sea waiting for the young white man at the end of *Runaway* if he makes it through the snows. It's a notorious fate to die in the mountains or to drown trying to escape the furies.'

Runaway is a strikingly-shot black-and-white film set in 1960s New Zealand. As the title suggests, this is a tale of a fugitive, David Manning (Colin Broadley), a young man in his early twenties who is working as an accountant and living the high life in Auckland. The film is an exploration, in a controlled European interior style, of the existential angst of the 1960s generation. The opening sequences portray David's life of partying and dancing in jazz clubs and boating and water-skiing in Auckland harbour as essentially unsatisfying and morally bankrupt activities. The story begins as the trappings of David's middle-class life are beginning to pall. When David is unable to meet the repayments on his car he attempts to present a stolen cheque from his employer. Faced with legal charges stemming from this action, David runs away north, to the Hokianga, a coastal Maori area. With this dialectic, the corrupt city and the idyllic rural environment, O'Shea established what was to become a significant theme in New Zealand's representational culture.

On his way to the seaside town David is seduced by a rich, bored immigrant, Laura Kossovich (Nadja Regin), with whom he begins an exotic affair. He later meets a local Maori woman, Isobel (Kiri Te Kanawa), and is drawn to her and her family, fascinated by what he supposes to be their peaceful, uncomplicated life. Away from the city David has moments of solace working as a carpenter's labourer, fishing and eating with his Maori workmates, and courting Isobel at the local dance hall. Laura becomes jealous of his attentions towards Isobel, and David, torn between the two women and what they represent – sophisticated European corruption versus rural simplicity – is unable to maintain his equilibrium in such a small community. He baits Laura and they have a vicious mudslinging fight in the mudflats of the town's river. With the relationship unresolved David steals Laura's car and drives away, back towards Auckland. Laura lays a complaint with the police accusing him of assault as well as theft, precipitating the police chase that drives the rest of the story.

David abandons the car, bypassing Auckland, and takes a train to the Central Plateau, where he narrowly escapes police capture and hitchhikes to Wellington. He is next given a ride by Tom (Gil Cornwall) who collapses from a heart attack and dies. David panics and compromises himself further by disposing of the body in a paddock, and then continues south in Tom's car. On the Cook Strait ferry he meets Diana (Deirdre McCarron) and they decide to travel together. David and Diana flee into the hinterland of the Southern Alps where they share a lake-side hut with a hunter, Clarrie (Barry Crump). As the police hunt intensifies, Clarrie reports the fugitives to the police, who call in a seaplane. In a final bid for freedom David and Diana attempt a dangerous alpine crossing, on foot and poorly equipped. It is a hopeless task. Diana slips in the snow and is injured. She urges David to continue without her and the film ends as David abandons her and walks off across the mountains to his own chilly fate. *Runaway*'s last image is of David lost and alone amongst the icy passes.

O'Shea's earlier feature, *Broken Barrier*, was an examination of cultural difference and racial intolerance, in which he took similar risks with the narrative content as he would in *Runaway*. *Broken Barrier*, a story of a young Maori woman who falls in love with a wandering Pakeha journalist, was an attempt to portray Maori beyond the surviving local sentiment of 'noble savages', in which O'Shea wanted to suggest harmonious relations between Maori and European New Zealanders. It was, O'Shea recalled in 1992, 'audacious' and the experience had left him, 'a little breathless'. The production demonstrated that O'Shea and fellow producer Roger Mirams had the requisite skills and personal drive to make feature films even though they lacked the financial investment to sustain continued feature production. Before approaching a second feature, O'Shea and Mirams felt they had to train in the more mundane technical and administrative aspects of the industry and they turned to making tourist films for a local airline, trade documentaries and road-safety films. Pacific Films also had a contract to film every All Black rugby test match from 1956 to 1962. Apart from the significance of this for sporting history, these films developed O'Shea's editing abilities and gave him insights into the construction of action sequences.

In another way, like the culture of film buffs throughout New Zealand in the early 1960s, O'Shea's cinematic sensibility was greatly affected by his access to foreign films through film societies. He also cites his two years as a film censor as influential, because there he viewed numerous imported films through which he learnt about film narrative structure. The National Film Library allowed him to screen internationally produced films in his own home, another potent influence on his career. Looking back, O'Shea listed the principal influences on his career as Carol Reed's adaptation of Graham Greene's *The Third Man* (1949), Ingmar Bergman's published scripts and the French New Wave writers Alain Robbe-Grillet and Marguerite Duras. In *Don't Let It Get You* O'Shea described his 'best films list' for 1947 as *La Grande Illusion* (1937), *Brief Encounter* (1945), *A Walk in the Sun* (1946), *Great Expectations* (1946), the Australian film *The Overlanders* (1946), *Odd Man Out* (1947), *The Southerner* (1947) and *Nicholas Nickleby* (1947). O'Shea's list indicates his partiality for the British/European auteur tradition, particularly those by Carol Reed, whom O'Shea cites as his mentor.

Indeed, *Runaway* bears the marks of British film noir in style and content. The use of shadow as a thematic device, extreme angles and deep-focus cinematography are deployed in the service of a narrative which deals with a self-loathing disillusioned male protagonist as a fugitive from the law, features reminiscent of Reed's noir work. Further, as with Reed's *The Third Man*, O'Shea underpins a combination of elements in *Runaway* with political allegory. New Zealand in the 1950s and the 1960s was becoming increasingly isolated politically and economically from Britain, and *Runaway* is thematically related to this sense of Pakeha dislocation in a changing world. The three female forces in David's life are metaphorical reflections of his identity and through it broader issues of national identity resolutely gendered as male. In his search he is unable to find peace in the idealised Maori woman and is only temporally distracted by the seductive European who ultimately deceives him. And although the ordinary Kiwi girl is willing to go to the ends of the earth for him, she too is unable to assuage his sense of displacement. Not only must David face his spiritual wasteland alone, but he is ultimately undone by the experience.

The theme of 'man alone' had been explored extensively in New Zealand literature in the 1930s and 1940s in the works of Frank Sargeson, Allen Curnow, Katherine Mansfield and John Mulgan. In *Runaway* O'Shea marries the theme to the typically noir conventions of entrapment and fatalism, replacing an urban, criminal setting with a series of austere landscapes. Despite the strong structure that a runaway journey provides, the film's narrative becomes episodic. However, the fugitive genre does allow O'Shea to exploit the symbolism of local landscapes. The latter stages of David's flight take him into the foothills, rivers and mountain passes of the Southern Alps. The wide-shots that sweep across these landscapes create alternately a sense of freedom, and feelings of domination and isolation. O'Shea intercuts the wide-shots with claustrophobic sequences where interiors of motel rooms, huts and cars are shot in tight close-ups, suggestive of the intensity of the relationships and the increasing internal angst of the protagonist.

Runaway achieves dramatic and surreal sequences in its final phases, suggesting that New Zealand films of the era were able to deal with universal themes and, in certain ways, were capable of rivalling the technical sophistication of international cinema. Images of death and impending doom are concisely organised within the film's closing scenes. As David and Diana set off on foot across the mountains, a long-shot across a river valley with a decaying carcass low in the foreground intimates the end of their freedom. The precariousness of the runaway lovers' future is emphasised in a low-angle shot of them struggling across a long swing bridge, followed by a shot of their supply pack lost to fierce rapids. The juxtaposition of high- and low-angle shots emphasises the fugitives' vulnerability to the physical world and the instability of their internal states. O'Shea described New Zealand as a 'surrealist country', suggesting that under a benign surface New Zealand was a politically and socially uneasy country. The notion is reflected in *Runaway*'s final scenes in which O'Shea deploys a series of disturbing images that are at odds with the rest of the diegesis. The final chase sequence includes close-up shots at canted angles of lone shadows cast across rock faces, cracked earth and bleached animal skeletons, and of booted feet splashing through river stones, slipping on scree and breaking new snow. O'Shea contrasts tight close shots of Diana edging precariously around a cliff-face with her point of view – expressed as vertiginous hand-held shots down into a deep river gorge. As their flight progresses, the passage of the pursuers and pursued is interspersed with long shots of heavily-shadowed rock formations where the landscape becomes a cruel and brooding force.

A significant parallel and one which demonstrates the tensions that arise in adopting foreign genres to express local ideas can be drawn between the climax of *Odd Man Out* and the ending of *Runaway*. In *Odd Man Out* the fugitive gunman, Johnny McQueen (James Mason), is hunted by police in a heavy fall of snow and finally trapped at the gates of a wharf.

He dies there, romantically, with his lover in his arms. In the final sequence of *Runaway* O'Shea felt compelled to subvert such an idealistic ending. When Diana falls a last time, injuring her leg, she stays sitting in the snow. She pleads with David to go on without her. As he crouches down to her the two lovers are captured in a final close-up. Unlike *Odd Man Out*, where Johnny marks his final farewell with a passionate embrace, David in *Runaway* turns away without touching Diana, leaving her in the snow to make his escape over the mountains. Diana then whispers his name and presses her lips into the ice, kissing its cold surface briefly.

In an important way this single shot defines *Runaway* as 'a New Zealand film'. It encapsulates the danger and desperation inherent in the landscape, the ultimate hopelessness of both intimate and political relationships, and the emotional intractability of the Pakeha male archetype. In his years at the film censor's office, O'Shea recalls, he got 'fed up with so many movies ending with a fade-out kiss' and wanted to invert the trope in *Runaway*. As the film ends, the police hunting party watch David scale an ice-cliff and, at Diana's insistence, allow him to go on to an inevitable death. Justice will be meted out by nature. The last sequences of the film are dramatic aerial shots across the mountaintops, of David dwarfed in the valleys. The glacial passes press over him as he trudges toward his fate. In the final shot he is a speck engulfed by the icy wasteland surrounding him.

Runway faced the perennial dilemma of a small-nation film – the requirement to find a local audience as well as to attract international attention. O'Shea had invested the film with local themes concerning New Zealand's place in the world, relations with indigenous Maori, and Pakeha spiritual impoverishment. His intention to portray New Zealand honestly is indicated by the poster advertising slogan: 'A daring, intimate drama of a young man in a hungry hurry … set in a New Zealand you know.' The allegory underpinning the narrative – O'Shea saw David's betrayal by his exotic European lover as representative of New Zealand's abandonment, politically and economically, by Britain's entry into the European Economic Community (EEC) – was a difficult one for non-New Zealand audiences to recognise. Further, while the film is technically proficient, the story is overtaken by attempts to incorporate the political allegory within the stylistic conventions of noir. According to O'Shea the allusion, which he had drawn from a documentary he had previously made, was, he suggested in 1992, missed by much of the audience: 'We'd made a film about New Zealand and the EEC before the script – though not the concept – for *Runaway* was written and the allegory was, we thought, fairly direct. So few people got the point I wondered myself whether I'd missed it.' Local reviewers applauded O'Shea's efforts in getting the film made, and praised its cinematography. Though the story was criticised for being dour and the dialogue for being stilted, the fact that the film was unable to find an audience at home was echoed elsewhere. In England O'Shea's original copy of the film was edited, losing twenty minutes, which made the internationally distributed version fragmented and made any allegorical allusions even more obscure.

In the face of the lukewarm reception of *Runaway*, O'Shea progressed almost immediately to a very different project, *Don't Let It Get You*, a musical with established New Zealand entertainers. By 1966 Pacific Pictures had made three feature films, the only features to be made in New Zealand since 1940, but none had found a significant audience. O'Shea continued to make television documentaries, the only source of funding for the independent industry, until the Film Commission was established in the late 1970s. With government financial support now available O'Shea worked within the industry as a producer of various films including *Leave All Fair* (1985), *Ngati* (1987) and *Te Rua*, and as a scriptwriter on *Pictures* (1981) and *Among the Cinders* (1983). As these projects indicate he maintained his interest in, and passion for, making films about, and for, New Zealanders until his death in 2001. He was, with the Haywards, a pioneer in an emerging industry, engaged in key areas of filmmaking for most of his life, and often in straitened circumstances. O'Shea was a key figure in New Zealand cinema, whose career was significant in the lives of several internationally successful New Zealand filmmakers, including Jane Campion, who wrote of him in the preface to his memoirs of 1999, 'his continued vocal support and encouragement to me with successive films has been so generous and sustaining...' It is a sentiment which echoes throughout the New Zealand film industry.

Hester Joyce

REFERENCES

O'Shea, John (1992) 'A Charmed Life', in Jonathan Dennis and Jan Bieringa (eds) *Film in Aotearoa New Zealand*. Wellington: Victoria University Press.

_____ (1999*) Don't Let It Get You*. Wellington: Victoria University Press.

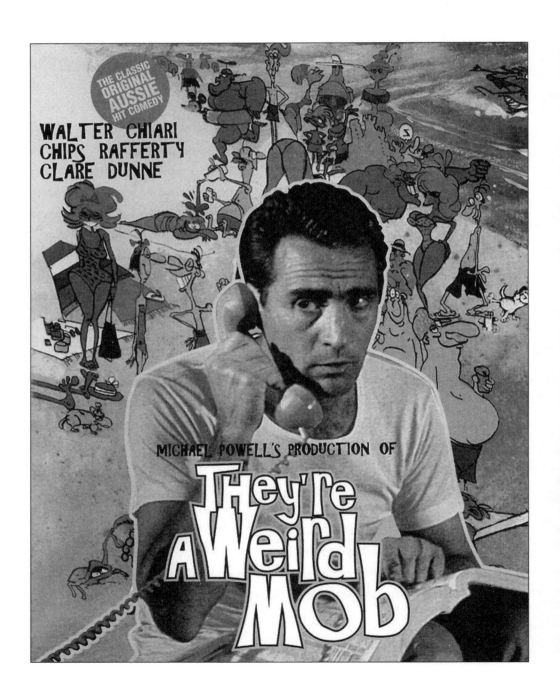

THEY'RE A WEIRD MOB

09

MICHAEL POWELL, AUSTRALIA, 1966

Given the colonial ties between Great Britain and Australia it is not surprising to find a considerable British presence in the history of Australian cinema. What is surprising is to find the eminent figure of Michael Powell – the director of such landmark films in British cinema as *The Life and Death of Colonel Blimp* (1943), *Black Narcissus* (1947) and *The Red Shoes* (1948) – amongst the rollcall of names. The two productions he made in Australia in the 1960s, *They're a Weird Mob* (1966) and *Age of Consent* (1969), were in effect the endgame in Powell's long and productive career in feature filmmaking. That career stemmed back to the early 1930s, and at its best, more often than not, was shared with his long-term collaborator Emeric Pressburger with whom he had formed an independent production company, The Archers. Powell's films deployed such a heightened, stylised mode of baroque melodrama – often with pronounced fantasy elements, as in *A Matter of Life and Death* (1946) or *The Tales of Hoffmann* (1951) – that some critics saw the films as cutting against the grain of British cinema's innate preference for realism. On paper at least, and to a fair degree as a realised film, *They're a Weird Mob* seems an atypical Powell project. However, by the time Powell had come to the production, many of the certainties of his career had been buffeted by the winds of change. As an effective production unit, The Archers had dissolved itself by the late 1950s; his last film of note, the controversial *Peeping Tom* (1960) was both critically savaged by mainstream reviewers and a box office failure. Whereas once Powell could rely on negotiating deals with established studios and distributors – Rank or British Lion, for example – those conduits to finance had slowly dwindled away. Setting off to the antipodes may, at first, have been for Powell a refuge from the old continent, but it was also an escape in the hope of resuscitating an ailing career. And it almost paid off.

They're a Weird Mob was the only Australian-produced feature film made and released in 1966. In his speech at the premiere screening of the film at Sydney's State Theatre, Powell reportedly said that he 'hoped his film would help create an Australian feature film industry'. Indeed, Powell was to set up a second Australian production, his adaptation of Norman Lindsay's novel *Age of Consent*, which in its theme of the ageing artist rediscovering his creative well-spring through the pagan sensuality of a girl (in the figure of a young and luminous Helen Mirren) entering her sexual awakening seemed a story closer to Powell's sensibilities than *They're a Weird Mob*. But *Age of Consent*'s relative failure, both critically and financially, and the eventual lobbying by film workers and policy makers which would result in the revival of the feature film industry in the early 1970s, with the emphasis on an Australian 'national' cinema, meant that 'foreigners' such as Powell would find no long term niche within the industry. For Powell, the possibility of a production oasis in the antipodes had come and gone in the space of a few brief years.

The book *They're a Weird Mob* was a huge bestseller when it was published in 1957. The novel was reprinted many times, serialised for radio, at one point mooted as a television series, and followed by a string of further novels featuring its central character, Nino Culotta. The film was a local success that made approximately $2 million in Australia on its initial release from a $600,000 outlay. Despite also being a hit in New Zealand, it received very limited release or success elsewhere in the world; showing on the second-half of double-bills in Britain in October 1966, struggling to be released in its intended secondary market, Italy, as well as in the United States. The film also went through a long gestation period. It was initially optioned by Gregory Peck in 1958–59 when he was in Melbourne, working on Stanley Kramer's *On the Beach* (he intended to play Nino), then picked up by Powell in 1962, and finally went into production with established Italian actor Walter Chiari in the lead role in 1965. According to *Million-Dollar Movie*, the second volume of Powell's autobiography, Powell travelled to Italy with the initial intention of securing the services of actor Alberto Sordi for the role of Nino. One can see Powell's reasoning: Sordi was at the time one of Italy's most high-profile comic actors and a huge box office drawcard that would have assured more widespread distribution for the film across Europe. Also, in physique and mannerisms, he more closely resembled the character of Nino as described and illustrated in the book. Sordi may have had his own undisclosed reasons for turning down the part: several years later he would appear as the 'migrant-in-a-strange-land' character in the Italian-produced comedy *A Girl in Australia* (1971).

The film tells the story of an Italian sports journalist summoned to Australia to work on the Italian-language magazine called *La Seconda Madre* ('the second motherland'). He discovers, however, that the magazine has gone into liquidation and so finds himself in a foreign country he knows little about and with no work or friends. He eventually finds employment as a builder's labourer and via contact with his Australian co-workers is soon introduced into the customs and social rituals of his new country. The humour is based on the classic comedy premise of the 'accidental' migrant who encounters and must adapt himself to a bewildering range of cultural misapprehensions.

They're a Weird Mob is a film based on a novel written by a Celtic Australian (John O'Grady) posing as an Italian author, Nino Culotta (it is a mock autobiography), directed and produced by a romantic, almost European Englishman, from a script adapted by a Hungarian using an Anglo pseudonym (regular Powell collaborator, Emeric Pressburger, writing as Richard Imrie; he worked on a script first penned by Powell and then elaborated upon by O'Grady), which is itself about the act of translating or understanding another culture. In Million-Dollar Movie Powell has much to say about his experiences in Australia, focusing specifically on the faces, bodies and personalities of the characters he met and the difficult business of finding money and production partners to make films in a country ostensibly without an 'industry'. Much of Powell's discussion of the film centres on the string of journeys he made, respectively, between the 'money' and 'industry' of Melbourne and Sydney, his direct comparison typical of many of the metaphorical readings these two 'competing' cities routinely inspire: 'I went for a walk, city tasting, and decided that if Melbourne was a strong, red wine, Sydney was beer.' They're a Weird Mob constantly foregrounds this liquid metaphor, with beer readily flowing from the opening mock travelogue to the various scenes where it binds together work-mates, classes and even genders. This fixation on a stereotypical element of national 'character' finds its apotheosis in the film's finale: Nino and Kay (the woman he courts throughout the film, played by Clare Dunne) celebrate their impending marriage – and the purchase of a slice of Sydney waterfront – by holding what can only be called a 'slapstick'-style party, in which cartons of beer are tossed around before foaming fountains spurt out from numerous popped bottles.

The book and the film are most significant for being amongst the first mainstream cultural texts to deal with the Italian or ethnic migrant experience in Australia. They're a Weird Mob's largely benign representation of this experience offers a very different set of impressions than the films of the independent filmmaker Giorgio Mangiamele, whose work – The Contract (1953) and The Spag (1962), for example – presents a far more troubled and less populist image of migrant life in the same period. They're a Weird Mob has a lighter, less confrontational tone that in essence explores characteristic or stereotypical Australian traits, rather than a view of the varied ethnic experience of the country. Although in many respects a simple film in terms of its broad, laconic comedy, stereotypes, relaxed tone and reliance upon a very conventional and episodic narrative structure of a visitor confronting, interpreting and to some degree commenting upon the idiosyncrasies of local identity, it nonetheless, as critic Tom O'Regan has argued, adopts the interesting strategy of using the figure of the migrant as a means to 'other' the local culture. The 'weird mob' of the film's title refers not to the migrant but to the very strangeness of Australian culture as perceived via the gaze of the foreigner.

The history of post-World War Two migration to Australia, and its representation in popular discourse – films, photographs, television, novels and theatre – are essentially bracketed by two terms: assimilation and multiculturalism. Assimilation and multiculturalism can be taken as specific social, political and cultural policies dominating and even questioning conceptions of Australian national identity in the post-World War Two period. Broadly speaking assimilationism involves the acculturation of various cultures, subcultures, ethnicities and values into an established singular, monocular or hegemonic cultural model (to form a monoculture), while multiculturalism involves the celebration and incorporation of cultural difference within a more general accepting and shifting conception of identity. Assimilationism was the dominant federal government policy in Australia in relation to immigration and social engineering prior to the 1970s and thus to the period during which *They're a Weird Mob* was made. Multiculturalism is largely the policy or philosophy adopted in principle by the Labour government in the early 1970s and then constituted in institutional practices – as for example, in the establishment of the foreign-language Special Broadcasting Service radio and television network – by the Liberal government in the late 1970s and early 1980s. *They're a Weird Mob* can be considered as an interesting barometer for this debate or policy shift, many of its attitudes arguably reflecting the movement towards a broader multiculturalism in the next decade.

The film does demonstrate some of the benefits of such a multicultural environment even if it often trivialises these cultural influences and differences by embodying them in things like food, music, dance and costume; cultural formations and markings it also relies upon to 'show' the Australian character. As Tom O'Regan suggests, this seemingly more progressive reading of Powell's film runs counter to the common critical response it received in the decades following its release: 'Since the advent of multiculturalism in the late 1970s, *They're a Weird Mob* has acquired a reputation as the apotheosis of the repressive assimilationist policy.'

It is fair to say that *They're a Weird Mob* stands at a kind of crossroads. From one direction it leads the way for a string of much later films including *Moving Out* (1982), *Silver City* (1984), *Head On* (1998), *The Wog Boy* (2000) and *Looking For Alibrandi* (2000), that in their own distinct ways deal more explicitly with questions of ethnicity and cultural difference in relation to European migration or 'migrant culture' inflected themes. From an opposite direction, as an affectionate parody of basic 'ocker' culture, the film's comic tropes prefigure the uses they would be put to by Australian films of the early 1970s such as *Stork* and *The Adventures of Barry McKenzie*.

From its opening comic strip-style sequence, *They're a Weird Mob* tells us much about the way it should be regarded, and possibly by whom. The opening consists of a set of very 'broad' representations including shots of Sydney shown upside-down, images of beauty contestants on a beach, a two-shot of iconic male 'types' expounding in a 'strine'-accented vocabulary while a horse-race takes place in the background, and a brief exchange of shots involving an outback shooting expedition. These images are combined with snatches of 'incongruous' dialogue and a mock-ethnographic voice-over focusing exclusively on the specificity of Australian 'English'. Thus, the film establishes a broad comic tone from the outset. It also establishes a particular mode of address that specifies the ethnographic terrain the film will intermittently encounter, essentially to explain the 'weird mob' of the title.

The opening can also be seen as providing a duel mode of address, attempting to engage both a non-Australian audience ('Like flies on the ceiling they never fall off'), and Australian spectators who will partially see themselves in the broadly comic stereotypes that take centre stage. The opening is also remarkably self-conscious and performative, undermining such stereotypes of nationality through the extremity of their display. The film produces a similar outline or 'cartoon' of identity through its representation of location. The opening sequence plays on the conventional sights of Sydney Harbour, while certain local details are made to signify Sydney – or at least a distinct part of Australia – rather than a holistic 'idea' of the country (as widely reported). The film is quite deliberate in making these distinctions. For example, iconic Melbourne media personality Graham Kennedy is given rough treatment by a 'Sydneyite' when asking for directions in an early scene. At other points, specific aspects of local life are conflated with the national, such as the opening voice-over that states that a certain size of beer glass is called a 'schooner', a colloquialism that is only used in certain parts of the country. Thus, the film's conception of identity is continually shifting and changing shape – despite surface appearances.

They're a Weird Mob has also been used as a staging ground for various arguments about the possibilities and problems of a local film industry and culture in Australia; what it should look like and how it should 'represent' things like nationality. Thus, *They're a Weird Mob* is an object much considered but often in inappropriate ways. The film's 'novelty' and the 'expectations' it created also led to considerable advance publicity for the film (facilitated by the popularity of the book), its production (for example, four or five articles appeared in the national current affairs journal *The Bulletin* during its production and initial release) and its relation to the possibility of a re-emerging film industry: factors which both promoted the film and raised critical expectations. There was also some animosity towards the film simply because it was able to be seen; it received a long-running release in several large cinemas including the State Theatre, Greater Union's flagship cinema in Sydney. The film has also been routinely criticised because it was made by a foreigner, with many accounts of Powell's stay in Australia – including his own – remarking on the stark contrast cast by his dapper, implacable, incongruous English attire.

These positions, aspirations and claims for the film created a set of expectations that placed too much pressure on *They're a Weird Mob*. Many of these expectations were wildly contradictory, too grandiose and faintly ridiculous for a country without a continuous feature film industry; the very well-known source material alone would make one assume that this would be a fairly popular and not necessarily artful entertainment. Nevertheless, this critical and cultural context also helped contribute to both the film's box office success and its general profile (including gala openings, pre-publicity and the raffle of a block of land bought for the film's production). This is a key to why the film has always been wrongly considered or categorised, alternatively, as an Australian or British film; as a Michael Powell film of auteurist statute; as nothing other than a pragmatic film made to succeed and hopefully kick-start the feature film industry in Australia; as something more than a rather broad, somewhat unsophisticated, comedic parody of national type.

The volatile and contradictory critical reception the film received is exemplified by Sylvia Lawson's response to and use of the film in the journal *Nation*. Over the space of three years, in three separate articles, her opinion moves from distracted optimism – linked to the kind of first step for local production she writes about in her seminal article 'Not for the Likes of Us', initially published in 1965 – to lukewarm and damningly accepting, to something approaching outright rejection and disenchantment. Thus, in November 1965, nine or so months prior to the premiere of the film, a report on *They're a Weird Mob*'s production (it was then currently in the middle of its six-week shooting schedule) is buried at the bottom of her review of Jean-Luc Godard's very tardily-released *À bout de souffle* (*Breathless*, 1960): 'Mr Michael Powell and his associates have been commendably anxious to employ Australian performers and technicians as far as possible; they also want the Australian public to regard the final product as, in important senses, ours.'

Therefore, the playing around with terms like 'ours', 'us', 'we're' and 'they're' is central to the things the film, book and the writing generated in response to it, generally do. Lawson's initial response was followed by her September 1966 review of the film that is revealingly entitled, 'They're a Dull Mob': 'it is supposed to be about us ... It isn't, of course. Sydney is there, and that's all; a place rather tiredly glanced at and never really seen ... But with all this, *They're a Weird Mob*, tenth-rate little movie that it is, does give a frustrating glimpse of what it would be like to have our own film industry, and how it might be to have your city given back to you on the screen.' In this review, Lawson opines the failure of the film to recognise and represent the specificity of its Sydney locations beyond a set of travelogue-like conventions and stereotypes. By February 1968 her position on the film has almost totally shifted around from the first. In an article titled 'Co-productions' she states that *They're a Weird Mob* is 'better described for many reasons as a British film made in Australia'. Lawson explicitly undervalues the real contribution of Powell here, who spent a considerable amount of time in Australia, much in pre-production, went out of his way to raise Australian money, attained widespread release and made two films during a very difficult period for the local industry, films that obviously had some relevance to and, in the case of *They're a Weird Mob*, found considerable popularity with Australian audiences.

They're a Weird Mob is essentially about Nino's acculturation, his initiation into a conception of mainstream Australian culture and his confrontation with the Australian idiom (terms such as 'schooner', 'shout', 'scone' and 'Kings *bloody* Cross' abound in the film). But this acculturation should not be considered as directly illustrative of a process of assimilation. For example, the film frowns upon the exclusion of migrants because they fail to take on the ways of the dominant 'local' culture; in one scene set on a Sydney ferry the literal embodiment of this xenophobia – a drunk, ex-digger abusing a non-English-speaking Italian family – is thrown overboard. Nino, in terms of his wish to understand and adapt, to swim between the flags – to follow the metaphor presented in the film's Bondi Beach-set scenes – can be seen as a preferred model. But other possibilities for identity-formation and adaptation abound in the film. Thus, it is a film that strives toward multiculturalism (even if it is not quite there yet). Subsequently, the film might best be seen as occupying a space somewhere between these two states or policies, as exemplifying a new conception or series of conceptions of 'Australia' that emerges from all these varied cultural influences. In this respect it offers a kind of fantasy or wish-fulfilment, in which identity is both stereotypical (for example, observe any of the male types who gather around Nino at work in the film) and a shifting and dynamic formation. Thus, it is also a rather utopian work where 'nationality' can be relatively easily acquired, confined as it is to a command of specific, somewhat detachable expressions, attitudes and values. This 'nationality' is acquired through the mastering of such elements as language, sexuality and behaviour – the positive or utopian aspect of this also residing in the ability of characters to exist outside of this limited nationality – which is, in effect, a self-conscious parody of a narrowly-defined Australianness. Thus, the film can be said to undermine the whole concept of a stable, unitary view of national character, culture or identity by stressing its arbitrary and performative nature. Nino is finally able to shift freely between, and even mix together, the performance of various nationalities and classes across the film. Although obviously middle-class on his arrival he becomes working-class in the course of the film.

In a scene towards the end of the film, Nino looks out over the ocean and down to the shoreline where he dreams of teaching his children how to fish. This somewhat clumsily staged but poetic sequence seems to suggest both a comforting and troubling notion of continuity within national culture (and is Nino dreaming in Italian or Australian here, one wonders?). Nino's 'dream' is predicated on fusing the traditions or clichés of his Italian background with the physical 'realities' of the Australian landscape (and this is one in an endless stream of texts which figures an Australian utopia as an occupation of the land, a dream of home ownership). This scene also presents the only glimpse or expression of Aboriginality we are shown in the film. These Aborigines are revealingly called 'older' Australians by Nino, prior – extinct? – inhabitants who leave marks (a painting of a fish in this case) on rocks to be read (or is it perhaps to be misread so as to avoid confusion?) by 'new' Australians. A basic continuity between Aboriginal and 'newer' Australian traditions and cultures is insisted upon here. Thus, an equivalence or a time-line, a building of one upon the other, is, problematically, suggested, along with the less confusing notions of antiquity, erasure and a heritage built on barely conceivable ruins that we now associate with such approaches. This continuity of inhabitancy is structured around specific concepts of Australianness – for example, suburbia, owning your own home, being able to make of yourself whatever you wish – and a greater universality. In this context, the key unit of continuity between Aboriginal, Italian, Irish and more general Anglo cultures is family, shared tradition, heritage and the simplicity and readability of both actions and signs.

Ultimately, *They're a Weird Mob* seems to vacillate between assimilationism (but to what model of culture one could ask?) and multiculturalism. Nino's impending marriage to the Irish-Catholic in origin, Kay, is both an assimilationist's dream and presents the possibility of an increased, encouraged and rather benign multicultural tolerance. This tolerance is glimpsed inside the insular 'ocker' world that dominates the film, but also in the space the film gives to other possibilities and expressions of identity on its margins (see, for example, the Kings Cross drag queen glimpsed shaving in one of the film's early montage sequences). It is a film of both inclusiveness and exclusion: mundane and visionary, mainstream and marginal, successful and unsuccessful, reactionary and progressive, it is explicitly between worlds. Subsequently, no one is still quite sure what they should actually do with this film, how they should regard it, unsure whether the end result is too weird or not weird enough.

Rolando Caputo & Adrian Danks

REFERENCES

Lawson, Sylvia (1965) 'Godard's *Breathless*', *Nation*, 182.

_____ (1966) 'They're a Dull Mob', *Nation*, 203.

_____ (1968) 'Co-productions', *Nation*, 236.

_____ (1985 [1965]) 'Not for the Likes of Us' in Albert Moran and Tom O'Regan (eds) *An Australian Film Reader*. Sydney: Currency Press.

O'Regan, Tom (1996) *Australian National Cinema*. London: Routledge.

Powell, Michael (1993) *Million-Dollar Movie*. London: Mandarin.

SLEEPING DOGS

ROGER DONALDSON, NEW ZEALAND, 1977

Sleeping Dogs (1977) occupies an important place in the history of New Zealand filmmaking. It was the first 35 mm colour feature-length fictional film made in New Zealand and as such was the first feature made in New Zealand for eleven years. As the first New Zealand film to open in the US, it began a 'new wave' of New Zealand feature-film production: more than one hundred films have been completed and released since then. *Sleeping Dogs* also helped in breaking down the old attitude of 'cultural cringe' that had led to local productions being denigrated or spoken about apologetically. It was a virtually unprecedented experience in 1977 for many New Zealanders to see local landscapes and faces (and to hear local accents) on the big screen. The filming of exciting action in recognisable Auckland city locations was such a novelty that lead actor Sam Neill was actually tackled in Queen Street in the city during the shooting of his character's attempted escape from a police van. *Sleeping Dogs* was also the first feature film for its director Roger Donaldson who, like many other successful filmmakers in New Zealand, has since gone on to a career in Hollywood making mainstream films, among them *No Way Out* (1987), *White Sands* (1992), *The Getaway* (1994), *Species* (1995), *Dante's Peak* (1997), *Thirteen Days* (2000) and *The Recruit* (2003). These subsequent films have frequently been examples of the action film genre to which *Sleeping Dogs* belongs. Donaldson returned to New Zealand temporarily in 2004 to fulfil his long-held ambition to turn his thirty year-old documentary about veteran Kiwi motorcycle racer Bert Munro into a feature film. The result was *The World's Fastest Indian* (2005) and this film has gone on to become the highest box office earner of any local film story.

The plot of *Sleeping Dogs* is clearly that of an action-adventure formula with political themes. The protagonist, Smith (Sam Neill), retreats from a failed marriage to wife Gloria (Nevan Rowe) in Auckland, to live alone on a remote island off the Coromandel Peninsula. His journey there coincides with a deteriorating political situation in the country, as a combination of economic crises and the manipulation of a right-wing prime minister named Volkner produce a form of martial law. Despite his indifference to these developments, Smith finds himself caught up in an armed rebellion, especially when reunited at a Rotorua motel with his wife's lover, Bullen (Ian Mune). Both men flee to Coromandel after the massacre of American-led Special Forces stationed at the motel and they eventually perish in an ambush organised by a political-military leader named Jesperson (Clyde Scott). Smith dies defiantly in the act of helping Bullen (who has joined the dissidents after being caught up in an Auckland riot), thus learning that community is important and that no man is an island.

New Zealand social conditions in the mid-1970s were highly conducive to the emergence of an embryonic film industry. When *Sleeping Dogs* was first released, New Zealand was, in terms of its cultural production, at the end of a period that resembled the late 1960s in the US. There existed a generation of young artists who had witnessed the flowering of the American counter-culture and wanted to achieve something similar in New Zealand; filmmaking was seen as one avenue of such expression. They admired the new kinds of films made in Hollywood, which seemed to work against the studio tradition, films of personal expression such as *Bonnie and Clyde* (1967), *The Graduate* (1967), *Rosemary's Baby* (1968), and *The Parallax View* (1974). In 1977 Donaldson's favourite film was *Five Easy Pieces* (1970), Bob Rafelson's story of an intellectual drop-out concert pianist/oil driller, featuring Jack Nicholson. In terms of politics, the brief tenure of a Labour government (1972–75) had interrupted twelve years of conservative National rule, but this regime was quickly supplanted by the new National government of combative, socially reactionary Rob Muldoon. The country seemed to be taking a step backwards from its earlier progressive direction, when Labour initiated actions such as a nuclear protest by one of its naval vessels against French atomic testing. Such was the environment into which *Sleeping Dogs* was released.

Both the film *Sleeping Dogs* and the novel from which it was adapted (C. K. Stead's *Smith's Dream*) have had a curious history as New Zealand cultural events. The novel was a bestseller and the film was seen by more than 250,000 people in its original theatrical release (and later by an even larger television audience). Every few years in the 1970s and 1980s, both the novel and film experienced a renewal of relevance. For example, they achieved the status of prophetic documents during the 1981 Springbok rugby tour of New Zealand, especially when *Sleeping Dogs* was screened on television in the middle of the tour. People isolated a small costuming detail (the protective riot equipment of the film's Special Police) and in hindsight read it as a prediction of the most lasting visual impression for many New Zealanders of the tour: the menacing anonymity of the Red and Blue Escort Squads. The novel's author, caught up in the civil disobedience events of the tour, was arrested in Hamilton where he spent a widely publicised night in jail. Feeling that he was living inside his own book, he wrote on the cell wall: 'Karl Stead, author of *Smith's Dream*, was here.'

Smith's Dream, written over a period of 18 months, was published in 1971 at the height of the Vietnam War. Stead wanted to relate the Vietnam situation to a New Zealand setting, thus bringing the war home to local readers. He also wanted the book to have a wider relevance; to make some general observations about the political thoughts, feelings and behaviour of New Zealanders. He considered that New Zealanders believed themselves to be immune to political extremism and he wanted to show them that fascism or authoritarianism could exist, as it has elsewhere. Stead attempted to fulfil these aims through a story that wove together the personal and the political. The novel and the film remain similar until Smith's return to Coromandel with Bullen, where the film breaks sharply from the book. In the novel, Smith witnesses an air attack by government forces but, when offered the opportunity to throw in his lot with the rebels, he leaves and strikes out on his own. At the end of the novel he is seated by the sea, a contemplative but socially uninvolved figure. In a second edition of the novel, Stead changed the ending and had Smith shot dead by the Special Police while on the run.

Stead's novel has an emphatic political, social and moral message, but he wanted to sugar the pill by making the story an engrossing one. Looking for examples of exciting political novels, he turned to Graham Greene. Stead has suggested, for instance, that his writing of *Smith's Dream* was influenced by Greene's novel *The Comedians*, which also features an uncommitted protagonist. However, *Smith's Dream* is not just Smith's story. It also traces the impact of political events on the lives of ordinary New Zealanders. Each has their own narrative voice: one narrating the events of Smith's life and the other speaking for the middle-of-the-road New Zealander, who is reluctant to take sides in the political conflicts described in the novel.

Stead sold the film rights for *Smith's Dream* for the modest sum of $5,000. They were bought by Roger Donaldson on the advice of advertising company boss, Bob Harvey. Stead had nothing to do with the script, which was written in 1976 by Ian Mune, with early help from Arthur Baysting. Donaldson was responsible for a number of additional ideas and changes. Although *Sleeping Dogs* plainly suffered from mistakes and naivety in such areas as scriptwriting, they were the natural consequences of inexperience. However, the people working on the film learned quickly, as can be seen from the examples of Roger Donaldson's next film *Smash Palace* (1981) or Ian Mune's *Came a Hot Friday* (1984) which exhibit much tighter scripting. *Sleeping Dogs* also had to break new ground in New Zealand in raising $300,000 (which seemed a huge amount of money at the time) by private investment. The film's producer, Larry Parr, later became one of the country's busiest film producers and directors (though he suffered two major financial failures with his companies Mirage Films and Kahukura Productions.)

Donaldson had been eager to make a feature film after the success of his television drama series *Winners and Losers* (1975), which he made with Ian Mune. He received an unexpected offer of financial backing from a merchant banker (Graham Reeves) who offered to arrange contacts for Donaldson's production company, Aardvark Films, with two large financial concerns: Broadbank and the Development Finance Corporation. Both institutions invested venture capital and Larry Parr was put in charge of Broadbank's interest in the film. During 1976, Mune and Donaldson rewrote drafts of the script.

Some of the backers were unhappy about using the title of the novel, *Smith's Dream*, doubting its commercial potential. Donaldson, quoted in 1986, said he wanted a title that carried a sense of 'unspecified menace', a function of an idea he rooted in the New Zealand character: 'If someone stirred up New Zealanders, he would find them more difficult to control than he might expect. In this sense, the film (while it is pessimistic in the end) is defiant, heroic even. It's optimistic in terms of the New Zealand character because you'd have to shoot every last one of them before you'd get them to say "yes".' The new title also signalled the fact that the screen adaptation was to be a loose rather than a faithful translation of the book. A feature film needs to reach a larger audience than a novel in order to recoup its costs. A first edition of a New Zealand novel in the 1970s would be considered a success if it sold 5,000 copies. A local film at that time would have had to attract close to a million cinema customers to recover even a modest budget. *Sleeping Dogs* cost approximately $450,000 in production and marketing; the production company netted just $160,000 from the New Zealand market.

A good comparison between the film and the novel's political approach to its subject matter can be found in the opening scene of each work. The novel begins with the sentence 'Throughout those crucial months when Volkner was rising to prominence in New Zealand politics Smith's horizons were steadily narrowing.' Smith and Volkner are mentioned together, introducing and foregrounding the two interdependent characters that will run throughout the book. The film tries to do the same thing by editing together shots of Smith watching news stories of industrial unrest on the very day he leaves his wife, but the result is expository confusion. The audience may feel he is fleeing the police rather than leaving his wife and child. While this opening scene presents a mixture of private and public affairs, the rest of the film completely omits the generalised 'we' voice that dominates large sections of the novel.

After the Auckland riot in the film, Volkner is shown conspiring with the Special Police and a group of assassins to fake violent attacks in order to stir up public opinion (reminiscent of the Nazis' arson attack on the Reischstag), thus allowing him to impose martial law. Seen from this point of view, the film is more partisan than the book, where there was indeed an economic crisis which creates a panic situation, but where Volkner does nothing especially vicious. In the film, you even see Jesperson, the head of the secret police, and Volkner together after they have engineered the shooting of the New Zealand soldiers in order to *create* a state of panic. Thus, Volkner in the film is a much more evil figure than Volkner in the book.

Much of the strength of the film's first half comes from the structural device of cross-cutting from Smith's peaceful Coromandel retreat to the violence occurring in the city. This vivid contrast is achieved not just by alternating locations but also by carefully designed contrasts in tone and texture. During the island scenes, the soundtrack carries the peaceful background sounds of birds and the sea. Sudden cuts then take us to the raucous demonstrations in city streets. The city scenes are washed out and grey, whereas the Coromandel scenes are suffused with sunlight and warm colour tones.

The most important change in the film grows out of the altered conception of Smith's character. Whereas in the novel Smith runs away from his comrades at the end, in the film he returns to rescue Bullen. Instead of pursuing his existential dream of being a man alone, his actions in the film contain a new message: that of comaraderie. The intensified personal relationship between the two men alters the intention of Stead's ending in both versions of the novel. This new direction in the film begins in earnest at the point where the two men leave Gloria to head off to Coromandel aboard a sheep truck. When they finally join the Coromandel guerrillas, Smith tries to break free from Bullen's authority. But when the others are strafed by jets and killed, he comes back and saves the wounded Bullen. In doing so, his actions are more admirable than they are in the novel. After Smith rescues the badly-injured Bullen, a protracted sequence depicts the two men staggering over the mountains. Importantly, Smith's commitment here is to an individual (a 'mate'), not to a group or a cause. The two men have forgotten their differences over Gloria and have now become some kind of couple, prepared to die together as they joke and quarrel their way through the rough terrain.

It can be argued that this new idea emerges from New Zealand/Australian notions of 'closeness'. However, another important influence could also be gleaned: that of the Hollywood buddy movie. Financially lucrative in the mid-1970s, the buddy movie celebrated friendship between two men. Finding the same welcoming audience in New Zealand theatres as in America, the genre included *Easy Rider* (1969), *Butch Cassidy and the Sundance Kid* (1969), *Midnight Cowboy* (1969), *M*A*S*H* (1970), *The French Connection* (1971), *Deliverance* (1972) and *Papillon* (1973). *Butch Cassidy and the Sundance Kid* in particular introduced a good deal of humour into the genre that seemed to add to its popularity. The outlaws Butch (Paul Newman) and Sundance (Robert Redford) debate many ways of escaping the law, but the one method they never contemplate is splitting up. American critics during the 1970s attributed the rise of this genre either to a reaction by conservative Hollywood elements to the women's movement of the late 1960s or by seeing it as evidence that Americans wanted to see bravery and comradeship treated positively after the ebbing of self-confidence during the Vietnam War.

A comparison of the endings of *Butch Cassidy and the Sundance Kid* and *Sleeping Dogs* highlights the similarities. At the end of the American film the two heroes are trapped in a room in a small Bolivian town. Unknown to them, hundreds of soldiers have surrounded their place of refuge and are waiting for them to appear. At the end of *Sleeping Dogs*, Smith and Bullen are exultant because they have succeeded in getting across the mountains and appear to have escaped detection, but their elation is deflated by the arrival of the Special Police aboard a helicopter. Bullen is shot yet again. Defying a hail of bullets, Smith drags Bullen behind a tree stump and reassures him that they will get out alive, and jokes that they must be important people to get this kind of attention. Bullen begs Smith to kill him so that he will not be taken alive. Smith holds a gun against his friend's head, agonising whether or not he should shoot, but he is saved from making a decision when Bullen dies. Smith comes out from cover apparently no longer wanting to survive, and in defiance raises his finger to the authorities. He is shot dead, like Butch and Sundance, but when the police approach they find on his face a triumphant smile.

Among the film's other interesting additions to the novel is an extended version of the scene in which Smith seeks permission from local Maori to live on the island, and in this relation the scene depicts two men conversing in Maori, a novelty for films of the time. In an early draft of the script, the old Maori man in this scene was to appear again at the end of the film, as a guide for the Special Police. Enraged when he recognises Smith, he strikes Jesperson over the head with his walking stick, killing him. He then dances and chants in Maori over Jesperson's body in the very last shot of the film. Perhaps the message was that Maoris were New Zealand's 'sleeping dogs' who would finally awaken. This ending was, however, discarded.

Smith's Dream was a mixture of two traditions: that of personal, emotional identification with characters, and of detached political analysis. *Sleeping Dogs* understandably concentrates on the former, with Bullen and Smith placed firmly centre-stage as the active agents. The film works well when the filmmakers are cutting back and forth between action in the streets and stillness in Coromandel. Unfortunately, the later stages of the film are drawn-out. The acting and the scripting are not able to sustain the pressure created by this concentration on only one sphere of action. This criticism should, however, be balanced by commending the general skill of Donaldson's direction and his creation (supported by such key crew members as cinematographer Michael Seresin) of high production values, despite a very modest budget. Since the makers of *Sleeping Dogs* were virtually creating a national film industry with a single feature project, we must not be too harsh in judging their achievements. The film's motifs became part of the popular consciousness of this country, and it helped break down the self-consciousness of New Zealanders in seeing and hearing themselves on the cinema screen. While it used the conventions of international thriller and buddy movie genres, its New Zealand 'voice' was fresh and exciting to local audiences. As New Zealand's first important cinematic literary adaptation, the film may have moved well away from the central concerns and methods of C.K. Stead's Vietnam-era novel. However, as a major stepping-stone in the history of New Zealand filmmaking, it is impossible to overstate its value.

Brian McDonnell

REFERENCE

Stead, C. K. (1971) *Smith's Dream*. Auckland: Longman Paul.

TWO LAWS KANYMARDA YUWA

11

THE BORROLOOLA COMMUNITY WITH ALESSANDRO CAVADINI & CAROLYN STRACHAN, AUSTRALIA, 1981

Two Laws (*Kanymarda Yuwa*, 1981) is an ambitious and complex documentary, concerned with claims to land made by the indigenous population of Borroloola, in Australia's Northern Territory. This theme, and the place of Borroloola customary law in the struggle for land rights, is pursued within a film that combines a vigorous reflexivity with dramatic re-enactment, talking heads, oral testimony and observational sequences. The 'two laws' of the film's title refers to white law and 'the Law' – the system which regulates Borroloola social interactions and relationships with the land. The Borroloola people, who at the time the film was made were involved in court cases over claims to their land, recognised the legal need to document the history of their law as a way of validating their land claims. The necessity for such a document was revealed to the Borroloola people during preliminary hearings of their case during which it became apparent that the white judges dismissed claims which were not supported by historical records of land ownership. Significantly, in *Two Laws* the so-called documentary truth claim and indigenous land claim intersect: for the Borroloola people, the filmic evidentiary truth claim functions in a direct way in support of their historical claim to their lands.

In this way, the potential of *Two Laws* to produce political and legal change is intricately associated with the film's radical revision of filmmaking practices, which have all-too-often constructed or reproduced derogatory cultural stereotypes and assumptions of Aboriginal and Torres Strait Islander Australia. Within these practices, ethnographic film has tended toward prurient studies of Aboriginal 'otherness', while the Griersonian tradition of documentary filmmaking has been applied in a number of depictions of Aborigines as victims. In a similar vein, journalistic reports, such as those undertaken in long-form television news documentaries, have routinely constructed Aboriginal issues as 'problems' to be investigated by white journalists. Fiction filmmaking is also implicated in the practice of stereotyping, as evidenced in Werner Herzog's *Where the Green Ants Dream* (1984), a film which deals with mining operations on Aboriginal land in central Australia. The theme implicates the differences between black and white social and legal systems, yet Herzog's film obscures a rigorous confrontation with the meaning of 'two laws' within a romanticisation of a noble Aboriginal Australia in possession of superior environmental knowledge and an irredeemably venial and wayward white Australia. Contrasting with such filmmaking approaches, *Two Laws* reworks dominant representational strategies and the political positions they encode within a form of filmmaking practice based on *self*-representation, that is, the production of images of indigenous Australians by indigenous Australians. Reflecting the diversity of Aboriginal populations – bush-living people and urban dwellers – Aboriginal self-representations are produced in a variety of contexts, including low-power community-based television services in remote communities, among them those established in 1985 by the Warlpiri Media Association at Yuendumu, in the Northern Territory, and Ernabella Video and Television at the Pitjantjatjara settlement of Ernabella, in South Australia. Opportunities for the production of Aboriginal television were extended in January 1988 with the first broadcasts of the satellite television station Imparja, an initiative of the Central Australia Aboriginal Media Association of Alice Springs. Based in urban areas, the production facilities of the national broadcasters the Australian Broadcasting Corporation (ABC) and the Special Broadcasting Service (SBS) have contributed to indigenous production, in particular through the ABC's Indigenous Programs Unit and SBS's Aboriginal Television Unit.

Further production contexts include self-authored independent productions, and collaborations and co-productions involving members of Aboriginal communities and non-Aboriginal participants. Works in the latter category include *How the West was Lost* (1987), a record of white colonialism and Aboriginal resistance in the Pilbara region of Western Australia made by white filmmaker David Noakes and the local Aboriginal community; *My Life as I Live It* (1993), an autobiography by Aboriginal activist Essie Coffey, made with the assistance of white filmmakers Martha Ansara and Kit Guyatt; *Exile and Kingdom* (1993), a depiction of the Aboriginal communities of Roebourne in the north-west of Western Australia, produced by Frank Rijavec and Noeline Harrison in association with the Injibarndi, Ngarluma and Gurrama peoples; and the close collaborative relationship between white filmmaker Trevor Graham and the Mabo family in the making of *Mabo: Life of an Island Man* (1997). While part of a broad process of indigenous filmmaking, collaboration has frequently been framed within critical assessments as a necessary though anachronistic phase in indigenous media production. Interpretations in this vein typically position indigenous filmmaking within teleological typologies which include an 'early phase' constructed around works by white filmmakers about Aboriginal subjects, which is superseded by collaborative projects in which white filmmakers work with Aboriginal communities, followed by a 'recent phase' of self-authored indigenous productions. Such frameworks, and their implicit critique of collaborative practices, have been productively recast and revised within the understanding that continuing opportunities for collaborative filmmaking contribute to a process of what cultural theorist Stephen Muecke has called a 'respectful appropriation' by black and white Australians of each other's culture, and as such partake of a wider social and political process of reconciliation of indigenous and non-indigenous Australians.

The collaborative basis of *Two Laws* stemmed from an invitation by Leo Findlay, a prominent member of the Borroloola community, to white filmmakers Alessandro Cavadini and Carolyn Strachan to work with the Borroloola community to produce a film documenting the history of the Borroloola people's relationship to their lands. Findlay had seen *Protected* (1976), a collaborative film made by Cavadini and Strachan and the indigenous inhabitants of Palm Island, who re-enact in the film recent events in their struggle for rights to their land. Within the process of collaboration pursued in *Two Laws*, Cavadini and Strachan spent their first two months in Borroloola, in the Gulf of Carpentaria region of northern Australia, learning aspects of Borroloola law, particularly protocols relating to behaviour in Aboriginal society. Collaboration in the making of *Two Laws* involved technical input by Cavadini and Strachan and the verification and authentication of factual content by a broad cross-section of members of the Borroloola community. Each decision made in relation to the production of the film was discussed either at formal meetings or raised in spontaneous, often on-camera, comments by participants. In these terms, collaboration refers to a process of widespread consultation and participation resulting in a film which is most accurately characterised as a collective production.

The process of collective authorship is exemplified in the prologue in which Cavadini and Strachan are introduced to the community by Findlay, not as the film's directors, but as 'Alessandro and Carolyn, they're going to help us make a film, and it's our film, so let's make a good film'. The prologue also foregrounds the importance of Borroloola customary law and its emphasis on the rights of various groups within the community in a scene in which representatives of the language groups around Borroloola – Mara, Yanula, Garrawa and Gurdanjii – announce the chosen title for the film in their own language. The sequence establishes that English is not commonly spoken by the film's participants, and that in this case, 'collaboration' extends to the meeting of people speaking different languages. The decision to make the film in English carried with it an obvious set of difficulties for participants who do not speak English as their first language. However, the decision was based on a desire (which is documented in discussions within the film) to reach a broad audience of both Aboriginal and white viewers. The multiplicity of languages and speech patterns featured in *Two Laws*, and the prominence of female on-screen narrators, move the film away from an expositional form based on a stentorian (typically, male) 'voice of God' narration to one composed of a variety of narrators deployed within an innovative formal complexity that variously combines aspects of exposition, observation, performative reconstruction, reflexivity and interactivity within and across the film's four sections.

Part one, 'Police Times', centres on the themes of dispossession and brutality. The segment focuses on an incident in 1933 when a police constable, Gordon Stott, arrested a number of Aboriginal people for killing a bullock. Through oral testimony and dramatic re-enactment, members of the community narrate the events in which Stott beat those arrested as he marched them in chains from their various lands to the Borroloola township. As a result of Stott's beatings, one of those arrested, Dolly, died on the forced march. The stylised re-enactment of these events avoids an emotive sensationalism and its threat of obscuring the harsh experiences endured by the Borroloola people.

Part two, 'Welfare Times', depicts life for members of the community under the welfare system of the 1950s and includes a re-enactment of handouts of clothing which effectively encapsulates a history of domination and subjection. The scene includes the participants – the women who will play the welfare office and the Borroloola people who will play welfare recipients – discussing the veracity of the scene ('Yes, that's the way they would talk to us, and we would just stand there and look down at our feet, not daring to speak a word', says one Aboriginal woman in response to the re-enactment). While the scene re-enacts the history of welfare times, the accompanying discussions verify the history that the reconstruction evokes. The theme of removal and dispossession which was introduced in part one reappears at the end of part two in dramatisations of the forced removal of the people of Borroloola to Robinson River, to make way for the mining operations of the Mount Isa Mining Company. The loss of lands and the place of Borroloola law in claims to the land emerges in parts three and four as the film's central preoccupations.

The varying ways in which white and black knowledge is encoded in texts, and the validity of differing texts used to document the past, is the core of part three, 'Struggle for Our Land'. The section opens with a stylised re-enactment of a Land Claim Court in 1976 in which the Borroloola people attempted, unsuccessfully, to reclaim large tracts of their traditional lands and the neighbouring sea, all of which were contested by mining and fishing interests. The court scene, staged as a non-naturalistic tableau on a disused airstrip, depicts the differences in evidentiary claims made by the 'two laws', and as such is a crucial focus of the film. Whereas evidence presented under white law includes written documents and maps, Aboriginal evidence is presented in the form of a *gudjika*, a traditional ceremonial song and dance cycle which embodies a history that is not contained in white written documents. The question of the adequacy of written interpretations of Borroloola history had been touched on at the beginning of the second part of the film in two contrasting comments. An on-screen text comments on a piece of white law: 'The year 1953 was the beginning of the Welfare Ordinance. Its aim was to direct and encourage the re-establishment of the Aborigines, that they would eventually be assimilated as an integral part of the Australian community.' Appended by the filmmakers to this statement is the line: 'Which means that they wanted us to be like white people.' The last line is the Borroloola response to the writing of history by whites, a way of 'talking back' to the official white perspective, a strategy which is pursued in a similar way within the performance of the complex *gudjika* and its confrontation with the written evidence presented in the Land Court.

Part three also documents a confrontation between a Borroloola man and a white worker who has chopped down a number of trees of special cultural significance to the Borroloola people. The different perspectives on the incident extend the analysis of the emphasis given to written leases as tangible evidence of claims to the land. In doing so, the scene reworks positions adopted in ethnographic filmmaking which privilege Western points of view and interpretative frameworks. Within this observational sequence the white worker is positioned as the subject of the indigenous filmmakers' gaze, and his arguments concerning land ownership are critiqued within a contrast with Aboriginal conceptions of land custodianship which emerge in Borroloola discussions of the incident. Extending the theme of land rights and land usage, part three contains a scene which dramatically illustrates the outcome of disputes in which control of land is granted to Western interests. A Borroloola man stands next to a river held sacred by the Aborigines as a Rainbow Serpent dreaming site which has been despoiled by effluent dumped by Mount Isa Mines, the successful claimants to the land.

The final part of the film, 'Living with Two Laws', opens with a depiction of a traditional *brolga* dance. The dance connects to the *gudjika* of part three as an assertion of Aboriginal law, and in this context the dance is a ceremony that expresses the history of communal rights to the land. The *brolga* dance is juxtaposed with other culturally important activities, such as an initiation ceremony, a woman's dance and life on the out stations (camps distant from the Borroloola township). Such a positioning, then, places the dance within and against broader contemporary social and cultural activities of the Borroloola people. Part four concludes with a Borroloola woman stating the importance of land rights to the community and the impact that such legal rights have for cultural continuity and assertiveness:

> We've been very weak because we've been hunted and herded around … but with land rights we've got a little stronger … We used to be shoved around and put on government trucks, but now we're not getting on the truck, we're getting off it. We're going to go where we want to go. But Aboriginal people must fight … and we're not going to be pushed around anymore.

The speech moves the film away from analysis of past conditions to a future of active resistance for which the historical experiences of the Borroloola people have prepared them to undertake. It ends with the group of people who opened the film, discussing the meaning of black and white law. As in the prologue, the communal discussion at the end of the film, and the relevance of the discussion to the community, privileges the existence of Borroloola law.

Importantly, this focus on the existence of Borroloola law – an aspect of which is the rules governing social relations in the Borroloola community – is structured into the film itself. Cavadini and Strachan have noted that features of the filmmaking practice, including the position of the camera for each shot and the location of the sound recordist, were determined by the highly structured spatial arrangements of Borroloola society in which, for example, men sit in one position and women in another. Such a spatial distinction does not, however, equate to a marginalisation of women in the filmmaking process. Women figure prominently in the film, whether discussing or interpreting issues or reconstructing events (and acting in the reconstructions), in ways which reflect their prominence within the community, and their central role as custodians of Borroloola history.

Beyond its influence on camera angles and on-screen spatial positions, Borroloola law determined the lens used and the type of shots to be made in the film. The decision to shoot the entire film with a wide-angle lens was made collectively by community members who appreciated the ways in which a wide-angle shot permits a larger number of participants to be framed in each scene, as opposed to the relatively narrow perspective provided by a standard lens. The practice abandons the close-up, and its suggestion that authority is vested in individuals, in favour of shots which include a number of members of the community who are frequently depicted communally weighing evidence and making group decisions.

The evidentiary bases of the film (which are, primarily, established in the form of oral testimony and re-enactments) are accompanied by moments of reflexivity, which function in support of Borroloola law. The pattern of reflexive revelation deployed in the film owes little to Western traditions of filmmaking; few films had been seen in Borroloola and generally the people were unfamiliar with filmic practices. Filmmaking for the Borroloola people is a matter of social function, and in this way the many reflexive moments within *Two Laws* partake of particular social purposes. People talk on camera about aspects of the film's production and look directly at the camera; clapper boards and sound recording equipment appear in the frame; prior to re-enactments individuals introduce themselves and the part they will play in the film and during re-enactments people comment on the historical details relied on in the scene; in one scene a man addresses the camera directly to thank the audience for listening to his speech; and the film documents the discussions and accompanying agreement that the information in the film is correct. The various examples of reflexivity function in support of the film's truth claim by transparently exposing the process involved in the film's production to reveal that the information contained in the film is verified by all members of the community as a correct interpretation of Borroloola law. This is not to suggest that reflexive or deconstructive strategies necessarily guarantee the authenticity of events and information they represent – reflexive sequences can mislead, as their use in so-called 'mockumentary' demonstrates. However, the ability to mislead or deceive an audience stems from an intention to do so. The reflexive sequences in *Two Laws* reveal an interrelationship between ethical intention and representational practice upon which the notions of authenticity and veracity structured within the film are based.

The claim on truth is extended within the film's movement beyond the observational and expositional modes. Ethnographic filmmaker David MacDougall has argued that films made by indigenous Australians tend to rely on an observational showing, as opposed to an argumentative or expositional telling, as the central method of providing information. In contrast, *Two Laws* becomes a document of Borroloola history and law by largely eschewing a realist observational aesthetic within its reflexive foregrounding of the filmmaking process. In this way the 'truth claim' of *Two Laws* is connected to personalised strategies of communal inclusion and reflection, as opposed to depersonalised strategies of balance, bias and neutrality which typically attend the concepts of documentary observation and objectivity. Further, the numerous instances within the film of direct address and 'looks' to the camera by subjects establish a form of interaction between subject and spectator which exceeds the strict boundaries of information exchange characteristic of the expositional mode and its assumption of a spectator who is passively guided by the exposition. In *Two Laws* a self-reflexive and interactive mode invites and licences spectators to 'talk back' to, or interrogate, the film's truth claim. This practice is exemplified in reports of screenings in which Aboriginal audiences routinely discuss the historical experiences depicted in the film and debate the strategies used in the film's representation of history.

The various distinctive formal features of the film point to a work which connects to and reworks aspects of documentary, ethnographic and avant-gardist filming practices. Critical reactions to the film, however, tend in the main to position *Two Laws* within the tradition of ethnographic filmmaking. Certainly, within this context the film addresses the questions central to ethnographic discourse – who speaks, on what terms, and for whom? – through its privileging of indigenous testimonial voices of authority within a collaborative work of political and historical documentation. In doing so the film contributes to the struggle against the legacy of silence, disenfranchisement and domination of indigenous cultures imposed by colonising European societies. While the outcome of such a struggle is far from assured, the struggle itself points to the existence of enduring communities capable of speaking for themselves in vibrant and resistive ways.

This situation contradicts those assessments in which indigenous cultures are interpreted as 'precarious', and indigenous people cast as victims of a dominant culture. The contrast between resistance and victimhood implicit in many characterisations of indigenous cultures is a structuring presence within assessments of postcolonial political and social experiences, and one that is echoed in certain descriptions of indigenous media. The American ethnographer Faye Ginsburg argues that indigenous film and video producers confront a 'Faustian dilemma': one on hand, media technologies constitute tools for cultural expression and survival yet, on the other, such technologies threaten indigenous communities with disintegration through the introduction of Western ideas which are incompatible with traditional or non-Western ways of life. All too frequently the emphasis within the 'dilemma' sketched by Ginsburg is on erosion, disintegration and loss of culture, as opposed to cultural survival and communal assertiveness through the use of film and other media. *Two Laws* is, in both content and form, a contribution to the latter process.

By presenting itself as a legitimate record of Borroloola law the film constitutes a legal document which can be used as evidence in support of the Borroloola claim to their land. Importantly, the presentation of evidence is achieved within a form communally devised by the Borroloola people based on their cultural needs and contingent on Borroloola social structure. The resultant documentation of Aboriginal law and community 'decolonises' the image of Aboriginal Australia circulated within ethnographic cinema, television journalism and fiction film within a collective process of self-representation undertaken for socially useful ends.

Keith Beattie

REFERENCES

Ginsburg, Faye (1991) 'Indigenous Media: Faustian Contract or Global Village', *Cultural Anthropology*, 6, 1, 92–112.

MacDougall, David (1992) 'Complicities of Style', in Peter Crawford and David Turton (eds) *Film as Ethnography*. Manchester: Manchester University Press.

Muecke, Stephen (1992) *Textual Spaces: Aboriginality and Cultural Studies*. Sydney: University of New South Wales Press.

THE YEAR OF LIVING DANGEROUSLY

PETER WEIR, AUSTRALIA, 1982

Although the Asia-Pacific region has supplied exotic locations for Australian filmmakers at irregular intervals since Chips Rafferty, Lee Robinson and their French investors exploited the South Seas adventure-action genre in the 1950s, most Australian attempts at regional filmmaking (with the exception of World War Two and Vietnam War films) have conformed to the rite-of-passage genre. More prominent in Australian literature than film, the genre features the naïve Australian, eager for experience, coming-of-age in exotic, mysterious and threatening Asia. Film versions of the genre include *Turtle Beach* (1992), *Traps* (1994) and *In a Savage Land* (1998). However, until Jane Campion's *The Piano* won the Palme d'Or at Cannes in 1993, Peter Weir's *The Year of Living Dangerously* (1982) set the benchmark for successfully combining Australasian settings and stories with Euro-American talent and finance.

Weir's film quickly gained international recognition (including an Academy Award for Linda Hunt as Best Supporting Actress). However, there remains a lingering uncertainty about its place in contemporary cinema. This uncertainty arises partly from its hybrid status as an Australian auteur film, financed and distributed as an American love story and political thriller based on a historical event. The film is set in Java in 1965 during the volatile months leading to the military coup against President Sukarno, followed by the massacre of half a million supporters of the PKI (Communist Party of Indonesia). Questions arise about the way this traumatic postcolonial event has been translated into a transnational film starring Mel Gibson, Sigourney Weaver and Linda Hunt; financed and distributed by MGM/UA; based on C. J. Koch's 1978 Australian award-winning novel of the same name; co-scripted by leading Australian playwright David Williamson (with Weir and, contentiously, Koch as co-writers); produced by the Australian team of Hal and Jim McElroy; shot on location in the Philippines (until protests by Muslim activists drove it back to Australia), and featuring an Asian-influenced musical score by French composer Maurice Jarre. The problem of how to interpret the film as a transnational hybrid is exacerbated by the eccentricity of its narrative structure. For two decades critics have puzzled over Weir's use of Hollywood genre conventions to represent 'a very real situation', only to render the political situation 'hallucinatory' by adopting the Javanese *wayang kulit* as the film's central compositional device.

Critical responses to *The Year of Living Dangerously* have been marked by fascinated ambivalence. Comparing it to similar political thrillers, Don Shiach argues that although the film is 'something of a puzzle' it is 'overdue for reappraisal' as one of the best films of the 1980s. For Shiach the 'puzzle' of the film lies in its mix of genres, notably the political thriller, the love story, the journalist abroad and the social problem film. Taking an auteurist position, Jonathan Rayner argues that in *The Year of Living Dangerously* and *Gallipoli* (1981) Weir achieves 'the maturation of his heterogeneous film idiom', particularly evident in the film's 'visual polyglot' combining 'the innocence … of generic constructs from past cinema and the parables and symbolism of the Wayang'. For Michael Bliss, Weir's entire body of films is defined by the 'infinite attraction of unresolved, antithetical forces'. While appreciating *The Year of Living Dangerously*'s concern with 'the nature of illusion and reality' in romantic love and politics, ultimately Bliss sides with those critics who berate the film for 'the absence of a coherent and informed political subtext' resulting in 'little more than a love story'. From this perspective the film's ending is seen as implausible and Weir stands accused of 'privileging feelings and disparaging ideas' in a characteristic split which Bliss finds 'fascinating (and at times frustrating)'. It is the disparity between Weir's 'heterogeneous film idiom' and Koch's metaphysical ideas that ultimately makes the film a 'puzzling' kind of love story.

The theatrical trailer released in 1982 gives equal weight to the love story and the political thriller. The trailer draws a parallel between Guy's (Mel Gibson) betrayal of Jill (Sigourney Weaver), in order to score a journalistic coup, and Sukarno's (Mike Emperio) betrayal of the Indonesian people (felt most bitterly in the film by Billy Kwan (Linda Hunt)). Through its motifs of escalating violence, personal and political betrayal, and the outsider compelled to take a moral stand, *The Year of Living Dangerously* has much in common with several films of the 1980s featuring Western journalists caught up in postcolonial struggles, notably *Circle of Deceit* (1982), *Under Fire* (1983), *The Killing Fields* (1984) and *Salvador* (1986).

However, unlike these films, *The Year of Living Dangerously* does not focus on the ethical dilemma of the journalist forced to take sides between a progressive people's movement and a proto-fascist militia (the latter often backed by the journalist's own country). Instead, Weir's film splits the protagonist's role between Billy Kwan and Guy Hamilton, both of whom prove to be unreliable witnesses to the political events unfolding before their eyes. Alongside Guy and Billy, a number of minor characters represent Australian, British and American involvement in the central drama. But these outsiders are confined to the expatriate circuit of embassy receptions, pool parties and press conferences from which they recover in the Wayang Bar located in Jakarta's only air-conditioned hotel. Despite their professional status as paid observers of postcolonial conflict, these urbane diplomats and cynical journalists are deceived by their privileged vantage point. Like the film viewer, they have no direct access to the political crisis whose provenance ultimately remains outside the purview of Weir's film, if not Koch's novel. The Indonesian characters in the film are restricted to those who come into contact with the expatriates, notably Guy's office assistants Kumar (Bembol Roco) and Tiger Lily (Kuh Ledesma), both of whom are members of the PKI, his nervous driver Hartono (Domingo Landicho) and Ibu (Norma Uatuhan), the widow who loses her young son to disease despite Billy's attempts at charity. Of these characters, only Kumar is given a political voice while Tiger Lily (although she is higher up in the PKI than Kumar) is cast in the role of the threatening Oriental beauty.

Although these characters and settings have become standard in Orientalist cinema, Weir took them into different cinematic territory from similar thrillers of the 1980s. In line with the marketing of such thrillers, the front cover of the 2002 DVD release of *The Year of Living Dangerously* bears the tag, 'A love caught in the fire of revolution'. The full-blown, pulp-fiction images of the two stars, Mel Gibson and Sigourney Weaver, evoke a bygone era of glamorous Hollywood lovers in the Bergman/Bogart mould epitomised by *Casablanca* (1942). Jonathan Rayner mentions that to reprise the star quality typical of 1940s melodrama, Weir used clips from Hitchcock's *Notorious* (1946) to show Gibson and Weaver how to kiss for the film. But while their love scenes (enhanced by tropical downpours and Jarre's stirring musical theme), give the film its intense libidinal charge, the less conventional 'gender-bending' performance of Linda Hunt in the role of Billy Kwan is the key to unravelling the film as a metaphysical rather than political thriller. In other words, it is the moral question of *action*, posed by Billy at the beginning of the film, that generates acts of love and betrayal. This reverses the usual terms of the political thriller where escalating political acts of violence force the cynical outsider to take a moral stand.

The exclusion of key political events from the *mise-en-scène* of the film poses problems for many critics who comment on Weir's characters as outsiders who cannot see into the world of Indonesian politics. But critics of Koch's book readily grasp the author's metaphysical and moral motivations for casting his characters as observers whose field of vision is limited and illusory. Although Koch's account of the political story is obscured by

Weir's hallucinatory vision, the film's allegorical impulse has its source in Koch's desire to interpret the Javanese political events of September 1965 from a conservative, Australian perspective based on Catholic humanism. This Cold War moral and social conservatism was given voice in Australian literary culture by the journal *Quadrant* which included Koch in its coterie. Although Koch worked on the first draft of the screenplay, subsequent drafts were completed by Williamson and Weir without further input from Koch.

Whatever the extent of Koch's imprint on the final screenplay, Weir's film relies heavily on Koch's motif of the shadow-play as the film's central compositional device. Explicit visual and verbal references to the *wayang* imply that the film should be read as an allegorical rather than political thriller. Unlike the investigative reporters in similar political thrillers, Weir's characters are like the *wayang*'s backlit puppets caught up in the shadow-play of events whose origins are invisible to players, observers and puppetmaster. Like the god-king Sukarno, balancing the left against the right while holding the people in the palm of his hand, both Guy (cast as the flawed Prince Arjuna) and Billy (as the helpful dwarf Semar) are blinded by desire. Even the self-possessed Jill, the putative object of exchange between Billy and Guy, is unwittingly cast in the role of the headstrong Princess Srikandi, adding a further dimension of love and betrayal to the film's allegory.

In order to understand Weir's 'polyglot vision' as allegorical – that is, as expressing a moral and spiritual crisis through a political crisis – it is necessary to look more closely at how moral ideas (expressed through Billy's words and images) generate libidinal sensations (expressed through Guy's action and desire) and lead to a metaphysical ending. The moral idea which generates action in the film comes from Billy Kwan in his first encounter with Guy during a walk through the slums of Jakarta. Noting Guy's shocked return to the intensities of childhood, Billy slyly chooses that moment to ask the question, 'What then must we do?' Metaphysical conversation is Billy's avenue to intimacy with Guy, whose professional scepticism is shaken by Java's slums. Observing Guy's disquiet, Billy cites Luke's gospel and Tolstoy, using their words to provoke in Guy a moral rather than journalistic response to suffering.

Although the film trailer focuses on the romance between Jill and Guy, the key relationship in the film is between wordsmith, Guy Hamilton and 'his eyes', Billy Kwan. Their relationship is established economically in the film's opening sequences. Billy (in his role as cameraman) declares that he will provide the images to match Guy's words, but it is Billy who is both scribe and seer, writer and image-maker, while Guy is the man of action. The film opens with Billy at his typewriter surrounded by his photographs of slum-dwellers.

This scene is cross-cut with images of Guy taking in his new environment. But it is Billy's intimate voice-over that orients the viewer, turning Guy into the naïve observer who is being secretly observed. Guy's initiation into the rivalrous camaraderie of the foreign press corps sequestered in the Wayang Bar and his first encounter with the poverty and hostility of Java's slum-dwellers is narrated by Billy. However, the opening narration is not linear but circular, establishing that Weir's film is concerned with metaphysical questions of time, with 'the wheel of life' and the vainglorious ambitions of young men vying to be heroes through action. Although Billy's voice-over begins as a conventional exposition addressed to the audience, it is made clear at the end of the sequence that the narration we have just heard is being written the day *after* the events we have just seen. Billy's voice-over ends with a question addressed to Guy: 'Could you be the unmet friend?' This is the first indication that the narrator, Billy, who compiles dossiers on his many friends and acquaintances, is prone to the same blinding desires which cloud the vision of his new hero, Guy, and his idol, Sukarno.

Departing from Koch's novel by making Billy the narrator, Weir's film shows how the narrator's perspective itself is bound up with moral and metaphysical problems of vision and blindness. These problems are expressed most vividly through the dossiers and voice-overs of Billy in his self-appointed role as Semar, the dwarf whose words are deemed wise by the god-king. Whether Billy is a dwarf is never fully established in the film, but his diminutive size, Chinese-Australian background and unusual physiognomy set him apart from his peers in the press corps. His 'basic Indonesian' dwelling and his desire to record the suffering of Jakarta's slum-dwellers in black-and-white photographs also distance him from the journalists of the Wayang Bar who exploit local women and boys for art, pornography and sex. But whether Billy can truly find a place for himself as Semar is one of the central stakes of the narrative.

In contrast, Guy's relation to words and images is ruled by a professional ethic of non-involvement and his personal ambition not to return to the 'graveyard' of the Sydney newsroom. Although Billy adopts Guy as a 'man of light' it is clear that Weir cast Mel Gibson as a man of action, drawing on Gibson's established screen persona as Frank in *Gallipoli* and the road warrior in George Miller's *Mad Max* and *Mad Max 2: The Road Warrior*. For Guy, action consists of getting the story and getting the woman. His first broadcast is criticised by his editor as 'travelogue'. His second story, based on an interview Billy sets up with the leader of the PKI, provokes envy and derision in the Wayang Bar where his peers berate him for taking his source at face-value. Guy's third story on the famine in Lombok is described by Jill as 'melodramatic', although for Billy it is this story that justifies his claim that he made Guy 'see things', 'feel things'. But Guy betrays the trust of Jill and Billy in order to pursue his fourth story, based on confidential information conveyed by Jill at the risk of her own career. In the act of pursuing this story, Guy comes closest to his alter ego, Curtis (Michael Murphy), the ambitious and morally degraded American correspondent with whom Guy shares a drunken visit to the notorious Cemetery, a sexual graveyard for Indonesian women.

Blinded by the desire for action, physical and sexual, Guy repeatedly runs into obstacles – closed doors, angry demonstrators, tropical downpours, the cold shoulder, roadblocks, armed guards, the brush-off. But these obstacles do not give him pause. Rather they incite him to sensational acts of bravado which allow a welcome release of libidinal energy, a release enhanced by Jarre's pulsing musical score. The excitement of beating off a violent mob of demonstrators with Billy or running a roadblock with Jill after curfew offers some relief from the stasis of the Wayang Bar and the stuffiness of the British embassy crowd. So it is paradoxical that the sequence where Guy leaves behind the blocked streets of Jakarta for the open road is also the moment when his view of frontline reporting, as a fearless act of bravado, begins to falter. Leaving the city, Guy has been warned that his search for a witness who can confirm Jill's top-secret information will put him on the PKI death list. With Kumar and Tiger Lily he stops off at a Dutch villa in 'Old Java' where the ominous silence and the oppressive heat bring a halt to his quest. Overcome by lethargy, Guy falls into a classic Orientalist dream of being seduced and drowned by Tiger Lily. He awakens sure that Kumar and Tiger Lily are PKI members. Guy's intuition marks a turning point. This man of action, who 'can't afford to get involved', has been drawn into a world of shadow-play. Using Kumar's silence to confirm his story, Guy is now aware that, like Billy watching the shadows not the puppets, he too can 'shuffle like cards the lives that [he] deals with'. Whether this knowledge will lead to Guy's moral demise at the Cemetery or to salvation through love, is the final stake of the narrative. However, for many critics, the film fails to find a convincing resolution to Guy's moral and spiritual crisis.

After Guy's dream, further action is blocked. Jill has retreated to the barricaded British enclave, Billy is alone with his dossiers and photographs of 'people who will become old, betray their dreams, become ghosts', and Guy, after filing his story, has nowhere to go except the debauched underworld of the Cemetery. Leaving Guy in a state of impasse, the film cuts back to Billy in his 'basic Indonesian' hideaway where images and words finally drive the scribe, the man of words, to action. While the failed PKI coup and the ascendancy of the Muslim generals take place off-screen, the last scenes of *The Year of Living Dangerously* return to Billy's earlier moral question, 'What then must we *do*?' This return to the metaphysical question of action leads to an ending which some critics have found puzzling and unsatisfactory.

Billy's answer to the moral question of action is to hang a white banner painted with red words from the high-rise window of the Wayang hotel where the journalists and the embassy crowd await Sukarno's arrival. The banner reads 'Sukarno, feed your people'. Ironically, only the Betjak drivers across the road see the banner (which they cannot read) before Billy is pushed to his death. The action-image (of the banner and of Billy's fall) is more powerful than Billy's words which appear to address no-one, but even his action is quickly erased. As Billy's body is surrounded by officials, a car carrying Sukarno passes. Gazing out the window, the 'great puppetmaster' sees nothing, extending the film's metaphor of clouded vision. Only Guy is able to break through the crowd to reach Billy. In the film's most ineffable moment, a flicker of light passes over Billy's serene face as he looks at Guy for the last time. How then are we to make sense of Billy's final look?

Throughout the film oversized posters of Sukarno have dominated the cityscape. When Ibu's child dies from the infected canal water Billy pauses beneath one of these ubiquitous posters, awakening to the nature of illusion as he begins to see the reality behind Sukarno's words to the poor, 'Eat rats'. Until this moment Billy has been able to admire the 'great puppetmaster' by invoking the *wayang*: 'In the West we want answers for everything; everything is right or wrong, good or bad. But in the *wayang* no such final conclusions exist.' But after watching Ibu wash the body of her dead son Billy reprises Tolstoy's question from Luke's gospel, typing over and over again, 'what then must we do' while 'September' from Strauss's *Four Last Songs* plays on the soundtrack. Although Billy has been the cultural translator in the film, standing between East and West, Hindu myth and Christian duality, his final resort to action can be interpreted as a return to Christian humanism in the face of Hindu fatalism. When Billy repeats the words of Luke's gospel, his act of repetition, of typing the words over and over again, generates an action based on Christian love rather than the *wayang*.

Critics have taken issue with the film's dramatic climax, claiming that it is inconsistent with the *Bhagavad Gita* from which Billy has drawn inspiration. Michael Bliss points out that in the *Gita* sacrifice is a form of self-realisation beyond the attachments of ego. In a reading of Hindu philosophy in Koch's novel Sathyabhama Daly argues that 'Billy finds Krishna's philosophy of detachment impossible to follow since he is unable to separate his ego from the sufferings of those around him'. Going against the compositional principle of the *wayang*, the film's climax has to be understood in the Christian sense of love as self-sacrifice: Billy dies to expiate the sins of others. If Billy's action is Christ-like, and therefore meaningless to Sukarno and the Indonesians, it nonetheless motivates Guy to commit himself to love in a moral and spiritual sense that has been beyond him until now. However, this new commitment to love does not explain Guy's senseless act of trying to enter the Presidential palace after the coup, even though he has promised to leave the country with Jill. Unable to resist a final act of bravado, Guy tries to bluff his way through the barriers. For his hubris he receives a karmic blow to the eye which detaches his retina and threatens to blind him if he does not lie still for ten days. Michael Bliss believes that this injury 'works as a fine example of the film's vision metaphors' making Guy 'one of the Platonic cave dwellers, unable to distinguish friend from foe'. At this point the *wayang* is revived for the final time. Deprived of the capacity to take action, Guy hears Billy's words again, quoting Krishna to Arjuna: 'all is clouded by desire ... it blinds the soul.'

From within his cave Guy decides to risk his eye in order to join Jill on the plane. Freed from the Platonic shadow-world by the decision to act, he endangers Kumar's life but succeeds in bluffing his way past the checkpoints one last time. He leaves behind only his tape-recorded words which turn to gibberish in the hands of airport officials. When Guy embraces Jill in the doorway of the plane (in a long shot rather than a romantic close-up) a circle of darkness closes in on the couple and the world of the film is lost to view. Sathyabhama Daly argues that Koch's novel, which also ends with metaphors of light and darkness, 'provides a brief glimpse into the sacred space that is the other of the profane world. But ... the contemporary character can no longer become immersed in the sacred mythical world; history and time intervene.' For the film's detractors it is the love story that intervenes, and history that has gone missing from Weir's adaptation, despite the 'maturation of his heterogeneous film idiom'. The film ends in retreat from allegory, unable to find a truly persuasive action to resolve Guy's moral and spiritual crisis. Instead, what lingers in the mind is the jaunty quality of Mel Gibson's jog across the tarmac, undaunted in the end as he was in the beginning. Gibson's jog makes it impossible, finally, to attribute a spiritual intention to his retreat from the political playing field. Despite the film's achievements, the manner of Guy's retreat leaves a question mark over the ending, returning critics to the puzzle of the film's mixed origins, its transnational identity, its uneasy fit within Hollywood genres and its play with political and metaphysical allegory.

Felicity Collins

REFERENCES

Bliss, Michael (2000) *Dreams Within a Dream: The Films of Peter Weir*. Carbondale: Southern Illinois University Press.

Daly, Sathyabhama (2002) 'The Metaphors of Quests, Labyrinths and the Dance of Kali in Christopher Koch's *The Year of Living Dangerously*', *Etropic: Electronic Journal of Multidisciplinary Studies in the Tropics*, 1, 2, http://www.jcu.eddu.au/etropic.

Rayner, Jonathan (1998) *The Films of Peter Weir*. London: Cassell.

Shiach, Don (1993) *The Films of Peter Weir*. London: Charles Letts.

VIGIL

VINCENT WARD, NEW ZEALAND, 1984

Within the new wave of New Zealand cinema, stretching from 1977 to 1986, Vincent Ward's *Vigil* (1984) stands out as a remarkable production and one of just a few feature films that could be regarded as part of an art cinema. Other films include *Angel Mine* (1978), *Strata* (1983) and *Trespasses* (1984) (and arguably *Pictures* (1981)), productions made at a time when New Zealand cinema was dominated by mainstream commercial filmmaking, and led by tax breaks (for a period). As an emerging cinema, with a small domestic audience, the New Zealand film industry needed international distribution, which in turn dictated imitations of Hollywood-style narratives, especially those associated with the action movie. Overseas recognition of New Zealand film was also important for validating the new wave. As such, *Vigil*, the first New Zealand film screened in competition at the prestigious Cannes Film Festival, can be seen to mark the maturing of a national cinema.

Of the festival invitations that followed, *Vigil* was chosen for a gala screening at the Montreal World Film Festival and special selection at Prades, in France, which honours 'distinguished new filmmakers'. At the Madrid Film Festival it won the Best Film Award. Within a year, the film had been released on the cinema circuits in Britain and France, followed by Germany, Italy and Canada. Strangely for a New Zealand movie, the New Zealand premiere of *Vigil* (in New Plymouth, where it had been shot) was after the film's release in many overseas markets, and it was not screened on the South Island until late 1985. A year later, in August 1986, *Vigil* was released in the US, where it continued to gain critical acclaim. Ted Mahar, writing in the *Oreganian*, said that *Vigil* 'is a photographic masterpiece'; Deborah J. Kunk of the *Los Angeles Herald*, described the film as 'pure cinematic magic'; Ed Kaufman, of *The Hollywood Reporter*, declared the film to be 'utterly compelling'; whilst Kevin Thomas of the *Los Angeles Times*, said Ward 'was the most gifted and original of New Zealand's filmmakers'. The reviews echoed previous responses, with critics such as Tom McWilliams of New Zealand's *Listener* suggesting '*Vigil* may be a turning point in New Zealand Film'. Nick Roddick, writing in London's *Time Out*, said 'the real joy of *Vigil* is that every shot and every inch of the soundtrack testifies to the kind of care that only a filmmaker with a genuine vision can bring to the cinema', while Ron Base, of Canada's *Toronto Star*, wrote '*Vigil* marks the spot on the map of world cinema at which a major new talent has arrived'.

Vigil was Ward's feature debut, following his acclaimed featurette *State of Siege* (1978), and the documentary *In Spring One Plants Alone* (1980). A meticulous filmmaker who has been hindered by financial and industrial decisions, Ward has made, in the 21 years following *Vigil*, just four feature films: *The Navigator: A Mediaeval Odyssey* (1988), *Map of the Human Heart* (1992), *What Dreams May Come* (1998) and *The River Queen* (2005). Ward's films reveal the style of an auteur, one who has continuously returned to a series of themes and approaches, many of which can be traced back to *Vigil*. Landscape and location are central to Ward's narratives, with isolated communities and individuals struggling to maintain or advance settlement in an unforgiving or challenging place. In these psychological explorations, identity, function and belonging are developed in relation to an unfamiliar land, with distinct passages of symbolic voyaging in a search for acceptance or resolution. Outsiders or travellers appear as figures of disruption, acting as a catalyst for disorder and community instability. Ward has a unique style, taking inspiration from an environment that has been a striking influence on others and, as such, engaging with recognised cultural subjects – the Kiwi Gothic, remote and impaired settlement and the power of the land.

The location for *Vigil* is an unspecified and remote sheep farm in a storm-drenched valley. Near the film's beginning, Toss (Fiona Kay) experiences the dramatic loss of her father, Justin (Gordon Shields), when he climbs down a vast cliff face to free a sheep wedged in a crevice, but in his struggle falls to his death. The body is brought home by a passing poacher, Ethan (Frank Whitten), who – against the wishes of Toss's mother Liz (Penelope Stewart) – is hired by Toss's grandfather, Birdie (Bill Kerr), to help with the farm labour. Ethan's presence is also opposed by Toss, who views him with fear and mistrust. She takes frequent refuge in an abandoned car at the foot of the cliff where her father fell and where she has built a shrine. Later, she befriends Ethan in the belief he can work magic and bring her father back. But upon seeing her mother and Ethan develop a relationship and witnessing them engaged in sexual activity she withdraws into Birdie's hut, locking themselves inside. It is here that Toss believes she is dying, when she experiences her first menstruation. Against Birdie's wishes Liz sells the farm, Ethan is given his notice and leaves, and the family move on, with Birdie towing his hut with his tractor.

The story for *Vigil* is beguilingly simple. Rob White, writing for New Zealand's *Christchurch Star*, described the story-line as 'thin', but also wrote that the film is 'all about images' and around the story 'Ward has swathed a thick coat of … fantasy and eroticism'. Critics stressed the vision, style and symbolism of *Vigil*, noting the lack of dialogue, and the unsettling or abstract soundtrack (the work of photographer Alun Bollinger and composer Jack Body was often given individual praise). Of the small cast – other than a funeral scene with assembled mourners there are just five characters – 12-year-old Fiona Kay drew the most attention, with the *Chicago Reader* seeing her central performance as 'a disturbingly authentic child' as the film's cornerstone. In a film concerned with perspective (often filmed as subjective), it is not just the imagination and experience of a child that is revealing of the challenges presented by isolation and a harsh landscape. Toss's father, mother, grandfather and the itinerant hunter Ethan endure their own personal conflicts in this difficult environment. These individual experiences, and the nature of the environment, dispel any notion that the story-line is reductive. On the contrary, *Vigil* establishes a series of complex and intense relationships, integrating a striking figurative and expressionistic visual display with an existential conception of colonisation and human endeavour.

Ward himself grew up on a sheep farm in an inhospitable landscape with distinct similarities to the untamed environment of *Vigil*. In fact, the degree to which comparisons can be made between *Vigil* and Ward's childhood experiences present a film that could be viewed as semi-autobiographical. In creating *Vigil*, he constructed what he described as 'a world of shadows that had become as real as my actual childhood'. Ward writes that his 'childhood was not extraordinarily eventful. It's the emotional intensity with which I viewed the world that dominates my memories … In *Vigil* I wanted to recreate my childhood experience of the world I had inhabited'. This recreation was extensive and both conscious and unconscious, with some of the characters a compound of people within Ward's life. There is within Liz part of Ward's mother, a German-born Jew who had fled in the 1930s to Haifa, in what was then Palestine. There, working as an ATS girl in support of the British army, Ward's mother met and married his father, a soldier, whom she accompanied back to his home in New Zealand. As Ward writes of his mother's journeying away from Palestine, 'co-writer Graeme Tetley and I developed a woman [in Liz] whose estrangement from the land echoed my mother's sense of isolation and frustration at this strange new country'.

The character of Toss is a more tangled composite. Ward sees her as the play-friend or childhood companion he never had: 'I could remember fantasising [when I was young] about having a female companion, one I could play with or go hunting with. Perhaps those relationships you miss out on in childhood are those you search for as an adult, and I was giving form and flesh to my imaginary friend.' Ward believes that Toss was also created 'from parts of my sister and girlfriend', and could also be himself. He writes of searching 'several hundred schools' looking for the girl to play this tomboy figure and that his eventual choice amused the women on the set as 'it seemed to them that Fiona [Kay] bore more than a passing resemblance to me. And I wondered if I had really scanned the faces of 40,000 schoolgirls unconsciously searching for my clone'. Ward was delving into his self-identity, his past and his own familial relationships through the process of the film's construction. There is even the fascinating casting of Ward's father as a mourner at the funeral for Toss's father, Justin. Ward's father, who visited the set during production, 'always had a fondness for funerals'.

The desired landscape for the film was also a composite. Looking for a landscape that 'was composed of many different places' led to significant challenges. In a film where the landscape is so important, considerable time was spent exploring possibilities within rural New Zealand, with Ward writing that he 'travelled 18,000 miles to try and find this product of my imagination and it seemed that I had driven along every road and track in both islands'. The location that was eventually chosen was a 'horseshoe-shaped valley' in Taranaki, near Uruti and Pukearuhe. 'The hills were burnt, eroded by time, primitive looking and yet not so large that they would dwarf the actors below. The valley had everything I needed to tell the story', wrote Ward. Reading Ward's accounts of the attempts of his own father, mother and grandfather at settlement, it would appear that his search for a location for *Vigil* – a sodden, cold and 'burnt' landscape – was similar to that experienced by his family.

The land in *Vigil* defies control. Justin, the paternal figure who displays knowledge and an awareness of the dangers of the valley, is abruptly taken, or thrown from the land, when he falls from the cliff (a dramatic fall is a recurring feature throughout Ward's work). At points in the film, Liz accepts defeat in her attempts to try and tame or domesticate the space, finally making the decision to abandon the land. Consequently, Ethan drives away at speed, crashing through the main gate (which he said he would fix), exiled, it seems, with some haste. In contrast, when Liz, Toss and Birdie leave, they part in silence, like a train of refugees, carrying all they possess (including Birdie's hut), in search of a more hospitable land.

Within the valley, these settlers are cramped by the surrounding hillside, which threatens to engulf the family: 'We can't stop the hills caving in on us', declares a conquered Liz. The land itself appears broken, a deforested, torched and creaking enclosure where the remaining trees are crooked, withered and defoliated. Moreover, it is suggested that this is a land on a collision course, drifting and unchained – in Birdie's first utterance he says 'the more I think about it, the more I reckon we are heading towards the South Pole'. Justin is first introduced as a farmer burning animal carcasses and detritus from the land, the valley filmed through the haze of the heat of the flame, which disrupts and obscures the image. The alien nature of this land is capable of feeding fertile imaginations of fantasy and fear. Following the loss of her father, Toss carries a large talismanic pole with a twisted branch at one end. This is used as a support, as a standard marking the presence of the smaller Toss within the landscape and as a device for engagement when, from a distance, an offering of an apple placed on the end of the pole is presented to Birdie. The apple, which appears ripe and fresh, is accepted by Birdie who takes a bite. Repulsed, he spits the fruit out and immediately takes a swig of water to cleanse his mouth. In a land of dull greens, browns and greys, this bright green apple is incongruous and seemingly too rich or pure for someone more used to an insipid or stale experience.

Toss, the tomboy, is clearly closest to her father. But from the beginning the land seeks to separate the two. Atop the surrounding hills, even before Justin's tragic fall, Toss is removed from her father within the thick fog that envelops them. 'Thought I lost yer', declares Justin on being reunited with Toss. At the foot of the cliff where Justin dies, Toss builds a shrine in the wreck of a car and fills it with a mirror and collected fragments: photographs, sketches and depictions of hellish omens from a bible. Near to the car she plants a tree, which she waters with animal blood and fertilises with a plate of cut meat, pressing it into the surrounding mud. This symbolic tree is fed with its own portion of an intended family meal, but its presence is forced and, like the farming settlement, it is unable to take root and is finally blown away in a windstorm that sweeps through the valley.

Modernity and settlement are rebuffed in this landscape. The land often appears pre-industrial, or post-apocalyptic. Farming occurs with the implementation of simple tools, and despite the presence of a tractor and two cars, it is still difficult to connect this environment to a period of mechanisation. One of the cars is a shell of a vehicle that somehow managed to rest at the foot of a cliff far from any roads. The second car, which belongs to Ethan, is a beast of a machine that roars into and out of the farm and is not too distant from the ferocious vehicles of the futuristic *Mad Max* films, in which collapsed civilisation is depicted. Birdie's tractor sits motionless and exhausted throughout much of the film, with only Ethan capable of breathing life back into its metal lungs. On the first occasion the tractor starts, after the sharp turn of a crank handle, it chugs and splatters before charging down the valley in an escape that lands it in a lake, where it bubbles like a partly submerged creature. 'Got a mind of her own', says Birdie, 'that tractor's been sitting out there watching … waiting.' 'You mean the tractor's alive', says Toss; 'it stands to reason', Birdie concludes.

Birdie and Toss unite in moments of oddity such as their rebellion against Liz and Ethan where, locked in Birdie's hut, communication is largely through the blasting of notes on a tuba. Ethan and Birdie bond over moments of Kiwi masculinity such as the fixing of the broken tractor (which on the first occasion drowns), or the construction of a giant pumping or drilling machine (which promptly keels over with a deep groan). Whilst Birdie is hindered by age, Ethan and Justin are strong and confident men. Yet they are continuously defeated by a land that they cannot master. Both are ejected from the valley after failed attempts to assert their authority. The more sedate Birdie, who has a hopeless attachment to the farm and a naïve and romantic vision of how it may be used, is forced to leave too, with his house tugged tortoise-like behind on his tractor, after his daughter sells the land. These are views of masculinity in crisis. The 'Kiwi bloke' is, according to Jock Phillips, one of antithetical pulls, a conflict between two traditions where the male is the itinerant loner or the pioneer settler. In *Vigil*, there is both the itinerant male (Ethan), the man alone who is on the move yet in this situation desires settlement (with Liz and her family; she warns him, 'I wouldn't get too settled here if I was you'), and the settled male (Justin), the family man seemingly of a fixed abode. In presenting these paradigms of Kiwi masculinity as failed, Ward is able to stress the brutality and dominance of the land.

In fact, Liz is shown labouring the hardest on the farm, hauling hay bales and large branches across the boggy land. She has a complicated relationship with Toss, who desires the outdoors over the domestic spaces of the home and who on several occasions dashes outside – against her mother's wishes – to be with her father, or Ethan or Birdie. Toss's attire is one of combat, protection and disguise. Throughout much of the film, she wears a balaclava and heavy drab clothes which will save her from the harsh weather, but they also obscure her gender. Liz fixes a tutu for Toss and provides her with a ballet lesson. Toss similarly copies her mother when, standing in front of a mirror, she combs her hair and applies make-up. These moments are brief, and if in this space masculinity is in crisis then femininity is suppressed. Toss is confused by her own emerging sexuality and unable to understand her menstrual bleeding. Birdie is too detached to offer advice and Liz at this point has formed a sexual union with Ethan. This relationship is borne out of psychosexual frustration and despite the needs of both Liz and Ethan being met, it can only be temporary in a landscape that demands isolation.

Despite the relatively connected spaces of the immediate farm, the buildings and the land function to separate and seclude individuals, with emphasised spaces of darkness or light extinguishing notions of a home and of harmony and warmth. Within the bathroom, Toss takes a bath in which she huddles at one end in the expanse of the tub exposed against a room of cold white design. In the film's first scene the gathered family can be observed within proximity of each other, but they are clearly detached – Birdie within the dark corner of the room, Toss at the table, Liz at the kitchen sink framed by a narrow window giving restricted daylight, with Justin outside seen through an opposing window frame. There are many shots within the film where individuals are separated between the inside and the outside. From inside, characters stare motionless at the restless valley, the passing clouds reflected on the windowpane. Windows are surfaces through which those inside or outside can observe others within this small settlement. It adds to the feeling of claustrophobia and to the hypnotic and haunting space of a farm that is watched over by its own sentinels.

Vigil is very much part of New Zealand's cinema of a perilous paradise (where I have argued for the existence of a Kiwi Gothic). Here, there have been frequent depictions within New Zealand film and literature of individuals appearing trapped and isolated within a dominant landscape that is seemingly 'alive'. Settlement ends in loss and retreat, where there is a constant struggle to maintain a domestic space, and where strangers or outsiders are viewed with suspicion and fear. In *Vigil*, Ethan the poacher is compared by Toss to figures of death in images of chaos that she sees in a bible. Moreover, as a poacher, he is associated with the hawks that prey on the land. Hawks, in particular, are a threat to grazing sheep and Ward writes that 'once I saw a hawk dive out of the sky and pluck the eyes from a live lamb. I was not surprised because like most children growing up in the country, I accepted the farm's casual violence.' Toss, the child who was abandoned by her father the shepherd as he attempted to free a helpless sheep, becomes an innocent prey who sees in her nightmare Ethan as a figure of fright. In a shearing shed where paddock doors violently swing shut by themselves and electric shears come alive, Ethan emerges in Toss's nightmare, and holds her as if she was a sheep in preparation for a shearing.

The haunting does not cease when Toss is awake and lying on her bed. She is oppressed by the wind that gusts around the home and violently blows open the windows and curtains of her bedroom. Despite the isolation, the landscape is never silent and is forever reminding that it is alive: the wind that is at times whispering or howling, the distant boom of the valley as a rifle is fired, or Birdie stamping to emphasise the hollowness of the ground. The abstract score adds to the sounds of this unfamiliar land where there is a feeling of vulnerability in reaction to a sense of place.

Ian Conrich

REFERENCES

Conrich, Ian (2005) 'Kiwi Gothic: New Zealand's Cinema of a Perilous Paradise', in Steven Jay Schneider and Tony Williams (eds) *Horror International: World Horror Cinema*. Detroit: Wayne State University Press.

Phillips, Jock (1996) *A Man's Country? The Image of the Pakeha Male – A History*. Auckland: Penguin.

Ward, Vincent (1990) *Edge of the Earth: Stories and Images from the Antipodes*. Auckland: Heinemann Reed.

IN THIS LIFE'S BODY

14

CORINNE CANTRILL, AUSTRALIA, 1984

In This Life's Body (1984), an independently produced autobiographical film, documents the life and times of a significant Australian artist, Corinne Cantrill, who has been contributing to film culture for over forty years. It is an important film because it is Corinne Cantrill's film but also, because of the way it uses still photographic images to tell its story, it raises many questions not only about its own form but also about the complex relationship between photography, memory and loss. The film is the culmination of many years of creative work during which Cantrill has been making films in collaboration with her husband, Arthur Cantrill.

The Cantrills are amongst the most active and prolific avant-garde filmmakers in Australia. They began making documentaries in the early 1960s, but soon moved to working primarily in experimental filmmaking. Much of their work is distinguished by their interest in the materials, methods and processes of the cinema. Their many cinematic experiments have included multi-screen projection, film-performance and landscape filmmaking. This interest in the materiality of the cinema is evident in films such as *Reflections on Three Images by Baldwin Spencer* (1974) and *Three Colour Separations Studies: Landscapes* (1976). It is also apparent in their landscape studies such as *At Uluru* (1976–77) and *The Second Journey to Uluru* (1981). The Cantrills have also remade and reworked their earlier films, often presenting them as performance pieces, such as *Fields of Vision* (1978), *Grain of the Voice* (1979–80) and *Projected Light* (1988). Another strand of theirs is concerned with biography, including the films *Robert Klippel* (1963–65), *Charles Lloyd* (1966*), Will Spoor* (1969) and *Harry Hooton* (1969).

As well as being filmmakers, the Cantrills also produced an important journal devoted to avant-garde film culture, *Cantrills Film Notes*. This quarterly journal began in 1971 and remained in production up until 2000. The aim of the journal was to document work at the fringes of film culture that had largely been ignored by the mainstream. This focus included work in Super-8 and 16mm film, animation, video, digital art, installation, sound and performance art. The journal also featured many interviews and articles that gave artists a chance to discuss their work. For example, it was in *Cantrills Film Notes* that she first published her 'Notes on *In This Life's Body* by Corinne Cantrill' in which she presented her reasons for making the film, and what she went through in its creation.

A personal medical crisis in 1982 had originally motivated Cantrill to begin working on *In This Life's Body*. She decided to work with still photographic images because she realised it was only through photographs that she could trace her early memories, given that 'there is now nothing to show in the way of material artefacts, from my early years – no clothes, no toys, just a few books. Only photographs, which take up little space, survive: so much information compressed into little pieces of bromide paper.' She gathered together as many photographs as she could: 'Many genres of photography are represented: snapshots, studio portraits, school photos, candid camera shots and street photos, studies by aspiring amateurs, press photos and work by other professionals, film stills and mirror self-portraits.'

Looking, sorting, studying and deciding which photographs to use allowed her to reflect on her early memories, family conflicts, school years, travels to England and Europe, her work as a botanist, artist's model and filmmaker, her early love affairs, motherhood, bringing up an autistic child and confronting the prospect of her own death. The photographs also allowed her to reflect on her relationships with her immediate family and relatives, her friends, mentors and lovers, at the same time as it allowed her to share her thoughts and feelings about her triumphs, difficulties and despairs.

The photographs are presented as slides, fading to black between images, and are free of film techniques such as zooming or panning. The different stages in Cantrill's life are represented in the film as different segments, and at the end of each segment she creates tableaux that become increasingly complex as she overlays and juxtaposes images of herself and various family members at similar stages in their lives. At other times Cantrill's voice-over unravels the many layered meanings an image may contain; this voice-over is both descriptive and interrogative. Beginning in the first-person she describes what she sees and understands. She later changes to the third-person as she reflects on the images and how they represent her own life, as well as her means of production and the processes of photography and filmmaking.

The film was first screened in May 1984 as a work-in-progress at La Mama theatre in Melbourne with the title *Journey Through a Face*. In this earliest version only original photographs were used and Cantrill provided live narration but found that 'there was a real sense of the second part of the film being less interesting than the first part; the range of images was too thin.' She therefore decided to seek out additional images. 'To compensate for the absence of photographs from the past twenty years, we made stills from films (such as *4000 Frames* [1970]) in which I am seen, and copied on an optical printer various film footage sequences of me – Super-8 and 16mm home movies, parts from *Harry Hooton* and *Skin of Your Eye* [1974–76]…' The final version of *In This Life's Body* includes the complete selection of all these images.

The story of Corinne Cantrill's life presented in the film is one that spans important Australian historical and cultural events. She was born in Sydney before the Great Depression. Her mother was of Anglo/Irish and German origins and her father was Jewish, whose family originated from Baghdad. Her parents had a difficult relationship and her childhood memories are coloured by this conflict. In the film she tells us that there were two things that added to her childhood despair. One was her father's unemployment and the other was the arrival of her sister. The house she describes, however, was full of ideas, philosophies and colourful people. As a young girl, she went to Campsie Primary School in Sydney, won a bursary to Fort Street Girls' High School, and was involved with the Theosophical Society and Bishop Leadbeater's Liberal Catholic Church. These experiences project the social, cultural and historical times she lived through and add depth and richness to the imagery.

By her own reckoning she was a good student but left school after her high school Intermediate Certificate. She told her principal that she was upset by the break-up of her parents' marriage but confesses that she really wanted to explore the world of sex and love. Yet, despite leaving school at a young age, she did proceed to study botany at Sydney University. During this period she also worked as an artist's model and became involved with a bohemian crowd. At 19 she followed one of her lovers to London, and stayed overseas for five years. From London, she moved to Paris and then travelled through Europe. In Paris she became involved with the photographer Bernard Poinssot, and included his photograph in articles she wrote for an Australian newspaper on the topic of living abroad. She moved to Rome, and then Yugoslavia where she worked in an International Youth Brigade, before returning to Sydney in 1953 at the age of 24.

On her return to Australia, Cantrill lived in Sydney's Kings Cross and worked with a number of photographers. During this period she met many people who proved to be important in her life. They included the eminent philosopher Harry Hooton, who impressed her enormously, and Mary Matheson, through whom she started working for the Children's Library and Crafts Movement. At this time she met and fell in love with a Jewish man, Jacob, with whom she had her first child, Aaron. She followed him to Brisbane, but the relationship was difficult and they soon separated. In Brisbane, at the Children's Library and Crafts Movement, she met Arthur Cantrill, who became her life partner. With Arthur she had another child, Ivor, who was diagnosed as autistic.

In This Life's Body provides Corinne with the opportunity to document her filmmaking collaborations with Arthur. Their work as filmmakers took the family around the world. In 1965 they travelled to London, returning to Australia in 1969 to take up a Fellowship in the Creative Arts at the Australian National University in Canberra. In 1970 they set up the Maze, a space run by artists in which they held screenings, and started to tour with their Harry Hooton film. In the early 1970s Arthur was invited to the University of Oklahoma to take up a teaching position. Returning to Melbourne in 1975 they filmed places like Uluru in Australia's Central Desert. In 1982 they screened *The Second Journey to Uluru* at the International Forum of Young Cinema and were delighted to discover city billboards advertising the film. It was the kind of acknowledgement they had not experienced before in Australia.

Critical writing on *In This Life's Body* has situated the film in a tradition of independent cinema and feminist filmmaking. It has also been discussed as a striking example of women's autobiography. Freda Freiberg, for example, acknowledges that Cantrill does not actively polemicise for feminism, and that she is more committed to 'personal avant-garde practice'. Freiberg adds, however, that there are many things that make this film a feminist film: 'The irruption of the singularly feminine voice of a woman who has struggled all her life to survive many obstacles, who has worked and battled to live according to her own rigorous standards, identifies this film as one that is of particular interest to feminists.' Freiberg argues that the film raises many feminist issues, including 'the female child's obsession with the imperfection of her body; the domestic exploitation of daughters; the adolescent girl's abandonment of higher education in favour of the search for sexual fulfilment; limited job opportunities for women in the early post-war era; balancing the work of childcare – made more onerous in the case of a handicapped child – with the work of filmmaking; orthodox male medicine's mistreatment of women's bodies.'

Kate Sands finds in the film an example of the 'nexus between documentary (documentation), fiction and autobiography [located] in several of the recent Australian films made by women'. According to Sands, *In This Life's Body* and another Australian experimental documentary, *A Song of Air* (1987), 'rely on extant material as their basis, which the filmmakers take and mould within the context of their enquiry into self, identity and the construction of a life story.' Such works, according to Sands, explore 'a feminine aesthetic' and 're-enact and reshape the genre of autobiography'. For Meredith Seaman the film emphasises personal identity where the self is performed through self-portraiture 'as the filmmakers step not only onto the screen as subjects but in front of the mirror to view the reflection of their own image'. Seaman is also interested in the way in which Cantrill uses this strategy to 'question her own physical image using self-portraiture'. Seaman finds these mirror self-portraits are places in which to 'unravel some of the cultural and personal meaning invested in these moments'.

The film has also been discussed in terms of its use of still photographic images. In this vein Lesley Stern compares *In This Life's Body* with *A Song of Ceylon* (1934). Stern discusses the way in which the still photographic image, or what she described as 'the enacted photographic moment', is central to the form and the investigations of both of these films. Stern is concerned with the relationship between the still and the moving image, photography and death, presence and absence, time and duration. Stern singles out for particular attention the film's incorporation of family portraits taken in a mirror and Corinne Cantrill's more personal self-portraits, and finds in these images a tension between the tangible and the ephemeral, between something very real and a reminder of our own fragility. According to Stern, this tension is evident in the return of the opening negative image of Cantrill naked in the landscape into a film positive in the closing sequence. For Stern, 'these final still images incorporate a memory trace, the incorporation of the body here involves both a decomposition and a remaking'.

Certainly, following Stern's emphasis on the place of photographs in the film, with its simple combination of still photographic images and voice-over, *In This Life's Body* creates an intensely emotional effect. This effect comes in part from what the photographs show – the life that Corinne Cantrill has lived – as well as what they represent – the memory of a time that has past, a time to which it is impossible to return. The effect of looking at these images and listening to Cantrill's reflections is cumulative. As each image is shown, and then repeated, different meanings and emotions attach to them. An added poignancy comes from what the photographs do not show, from what they are unable to reveal, the spaces between Cantrill's memories, others memories and the material evidence of the photographs. Several sequences from the first part of the film reveal some of the ways in which our emotions are engaged as we are invited to think about the relationships between photography, memory and loss.

The first images in the film – which precede the title – are an abstract image of water followed by a negative image of a naked woman lying in the landscape that lingers on screen while Cantrill's voice-over begins to explain why she came to make this film. Doctors had told her she needed surgery and there was a possibility she might die and as a result she decided to review her life and prepare herself for death. To illuminate her medical problems she shows another negative image – an ultrasound scan of her uterus. She says that seeing her uterus, its beauty and eroticism, and the first home of her children, made her even more determined not to undergo surgery.

These opening images of her body and her uterus – the body that is the subject of the film and the source of her immediate concerns – establish both the context and reason for the story. Cantrill is lying in, and almost indistinguishable from, the natural world, reminding us that this is where our life begins and where it ends. The negative images are dark, abstract and mysterious. Their presence highlights problems of interpretation and reading. The photographic negative is an initial imprint of the world, before becoming a resolved reflection. This thoughtfully composed pre-title sequence not only establishes the film's biographical beginnings, but also its form and material reality.

Cantrill's life story continues with photographs from her childhood, including those taken on her second birthday on her first trip to the beach. They are delightful images, engaging mementos of a time long past, except she has no memory of these moments. The first image is a distant shot of a child on a sandy beach. It could be any child at the beach. The next image is a close-up of a beaming Corinne, smiling for the camera, unable to contain her joy. This image is followed by a two-shot of herself and her mother in shallow water. Cantrill observes that her mother seems proud of her and pleased with her. The camera moves to a closer view of her mother's face before returning to the two-shot. In voice-over Cantrill notes that her earliest memories are that her mother did not love her, and with these words the image that her mother entered in a competition for beautiful babies is repeated. As we linger on this image we understand Cantrill's questions and doubts. This repeated pattern of revealing images, questioning them, reframing them, puzzling over them, before abandoning them on the screen in silence, invites speculation. The final photographs in the sequence show Corinne with her father in the shallow water at the beach. She asks: 'Are the three of us faking happiness for the camera? Are these photos just posed illusion? Or are the feelings as genuine as they seem?' The apparent happiness in these holiday snap-shots is undercut by Cantrill's lack of happy memories. The effect is subtle, quiet, cumulative and relentless.

Following this sequence, Cantrill recalls: 'There is one transcendent memory from my very early years: I was in a large rock pool at Kilcare – ocean waves were breaking at its edge, the spray was like rainbows – every drop of water a tiny prism. It was as though I was standing in the midst of rainbows.' But in place of this image is a dark, mysterious, almost furtive photograph of Corinne as a child beneath a tree casting shadows across her face. It questions the distance between our memories and our photographs and our memories as photographed.

As with the endings of other chapters, Corinne lays out a collage of repeated images: photographs of her in her pram, and being held by her mother and her father. The beach images are also repeated. In multiple images she now appears to be looking directly at us, in a knowing and complicit way. Some images are cropped and reframed, and Corinne's narration switches to the third-person as if these images are no longer her own. At times the narration ceases. At the start of this project she believed that photographs provided an arbitrary record of a life. Yet now she surprises herself by finding a 'coherence of personality', as if looking at these photographs repeatedly and closely, comparing them with each other, they start to reveal things that were not immediately there. Together they have become the sum of more than their parts.

In 2003 Adrian Martin curated a programme for the Buenos Aires International Festival of Independent Films titled 'A Secret History of Australian Cinema (1970–2000)'. In this programme, which featured a very personal selection of lesser-known Australian films, he included *In This Life's Body*. In his catalogue essay Martin described the films as belonging to that 'other' Australian cinema, a cinema on the margins of the mainstream, a cinema that was largely hidden but one that was waiting to be discovered. When it came to talking about *In This Life's Body* he said that this film could be 'the greatest film in the entire history of Australian cinema'. Without doubt, *In This Life's Body* is a treasure that will reward and enchant those who go looking for it.

Anna Dzenis

REFERENCES

Cantrill, Corinne (1984) 'Notes on *In This Life's Body* by Corinne Cantrill', in *Cantrill's Film Notes*, 45–6, 54–71.

_____ (1987) 'Personal Statement', in Annette Blonski, Barbara Creed and Freda Freiberg (eds) *Don't Shoot Darling! Women's Independent Filmmaking in Australia*. Melbourne: Greenhouse.

Freiberg, Freda (1987) 'Time's Relentless Melt: Corinne Cantrill's *In This Life's Body*', in Annette Blonski, Barbara Creed and Freda Freiberg (eds) *Don't Shoot Darling! Women's Independent Filmmaking in Australia*. Richmond: Greenhouse.

Martin, Adrian (2003) 'A Secret History of Australian Cinema (1970–2000): Ode to a Feral Cinema', in Javier Porta Fouz & Hugo Salas (eds) Buenos Aires International Festival of Independent Films catalogue, Ciudad Autónoma de Buenos Aires.

Sands, Kate (1988) 'Women of the Wave', in Scott Murray (ed.) *Back of Beyond: Discovering Australian Film and Television*. Sydney: Australian Film Commission.

Seaman, Meredith (2003) 'The Self in the Mirror: Feminism and Australian Documentary Filmmaking', in Lisa French (ed.) *Womenvision: Women and the Moving Image in Australia*. Melbourne: Damned Publishing.

Stern, Lesley (1987) 'As Long As This Life Lasts', *Photofile*, Winter, 15–19.

THE PIANO

JANE CAMPION, AUSTRALIA/NEW ZEALAND, 1993

Jane Campion's film *The Piano* (1993) is one of the most high profile films to emerge from Australasia. It not only won an array of international prizes, including three Academy Awards, and was co-winner of the Palme d'Or at the Cannes Film Festival, of which Campion was the first female recipient, but it also attracted an unusual amount of discussion, both in academic circles and in the media. *The Piano* can be seen as representing nineteenth-century New Zealand in terms of a number of contradictions, which serve to stress both the freedoms and the constraints of settler culture. It is a film in which libidinal desires defy, yet remain curtailed by, contractual arrangements on the New Zealand 'frontier'. The film places equal emphasis upon the transcendent and the earthbound: the driving intensities of Michael Nyman's musical score, and the swooping camera movements which convey Ada's (Holly Hunter) exhilaration as she plays the piano, are offset by the grim realities of colonial life.

The Piano qualifies as an art film insofar as it displays authorial expressivity. Art cinema tends to emphasise psychological realism and character subjectivity, which results in characters that are more complex and less goal-orientated than their mainstream Hollywood counterparts. It also makes marked use of ambiguity, which is especially evident in the ending of *The Piano*, and often treats themes involving explicit sex and violence. Yet, unlike art cinema, with its traditional appeal to a relatively small audience, *The Piano* was a success at the box office (it was the tenth best-selling film in the US in 1993, and continues to sell strongly to television, and on video and DVD). It can therefore be viewed as a work which transcends the 'art cinema' label. The indeterminate status of the film is mirrored in the ambiguity of Campion's origins – she has been claimed by both New Zealand and Australia, since she was born in New Zealand, but has long been resident in Australia. Dana Polan has suggested that such a condition may be an asset in art cinema's new international market, in which indigenous references are seen as having an exotic appeal. That the film was set in New Zealand, produced by an Australian (Jan Chapman) and had French financing, complicates its nationality still further and makes it more obviously a product of global trends.

After studying anthropology in New Zealand and fine arts in Australia, Campion was accepted by the Australian Film, Television and Radio School (AFTRS), an organisation funded by the Australian Government in an effort to promote a national film industry. New Zealand did not establish a national film school and thus did not offer the tuition that Campion needed. Campion completed her short films *Peel* (1982), *Passionless Moments* (1983) and *A Girl's Own Story* (1983) while she was still at film school. She also made films for the Women's Film Unit of Film Australia and for television. *Sweetie* (1989) received a mixed reception at Cannes, but the film developed aspects of Campion's distinctive formal style, including angled camera work that graphically conveys a sense of mental disturbance and of domestic and social malaise. With the production, distribution and reception of *The Piano*, Campion moved from the periphery to the centre of world cinema, while still maintaining strong connections with New Zealand and Australia. The film employed well-known Hollywood stars, Holly Hunter and Harvey Keitel, it was distributed by Miramax, a Disney-owned company, and it received global recognition. Although Campion's subsequent works, *The Portrait of a Lady* (1996), *Holy Smoke* (1999) and *In the Cut* (2003), are very different from one another, they are all similarly situated in terms of their international production and distribution.

The Piano can be seen as both representative and atypical of Campion's work. On the one hand, the film reflects a number of concerns that are shared by her other films, including an interest in dysfunctional families, suburban satire, female subjectivity, female desire and sexuality and gender politics. On the other, the acclaim it received both locally and worldwide, which has not been given to any other of Campion's films, indicates that it is in a different league from her earlier (and later) works. Yet her films are often provocative in the sense that they transgress social and, in particular, sexual norms. Such an approach is exemplified in Campion's representation of sexuality, which is frequently treated in a confrontational or perverse manner, including incest, molestation and teenage pregnancy in *A Girl's Own Story*; sexual harassment in *After Hours* (1984); anarchic sexuality linked with madness and regression in *Sweetie*; sadism, masochism, voyeurism and rape in *The Piano*; anachronistic images of sexual fantasy in *The Portrait of a Lady*; sexual menace in *Holy Smoke*; and sexual violence in *In the Cut*.

Following the release of *In the Cut*, a film based on Susanna Moore's novel of the same name, Campion declared her intention to take a period of leave from filmmaking. In light of this decision, it is tempting to see this film as commenting on her previous work, since it reprises many earlier themes, from *The Piano* in particular. However, the differences between these films are arguably more striking than their similarities. Whereas *The Piano* deals with the articulation of women's desire, *In the Cut* represents violence against the female body. Just as Ada's finger is chopped off with an axe in *The Piano*, women's bodies are dismembered with a knife in *In the Cut*. If *The Piano* explores sexuality in a manner which emphasises female agency, *In the Cut* tends to represent women as more object than subject, more acted upon than acting. Both films treat nudity or sexuality in an unusually explicit way. Both works are centrally concerned with romance and sexual desire. But *In the Cut*'s interrogation of romantic love, in which engagement is inextricably linked with violence and death, is even more disturbing than Campion's previous works, *The Piano* included. What has remained consistent within Campion's filmmaking is her capacity to unsettle and provoke while employing a variety of subjects and methods.

The exploration and manipulation of gender roles is particularly marked in *The Piano*. The film locates the spectator within the subjective reality of Ada McGrath and establishes her strong will. The audience hears her 'mind's voice' state that she has not spoken since she was six. The narrational voice declares that her father has engaged her to a man she has not met and that she is to join him in his country – in keeping with the imperial practice of sending unmarried, impoverished and inconvenient women to the colonies. Gothic aspects of the scene link Ada with other strong-willed, nineteenth-century heroines, such as Charlotte Brontë's Jane Eyre. Subsequent shots inside a Scottish house introduce the spectator to Ada's ardent daughter, Flora (Anna Paquin), and to Ada's passionate piano playing, in which music expresses her often wild emotions.

Ada and Flora's arrival in New Zealand is turbulent and disorientating. They sleep on the sand beside the piano in a translucent tent made out of a hooped petticoat. The women are awoken by two Europeans – Ada's husband-to-be, the patriarchal Alisdair Stewart (Sam Neill), and George Baines (Harvey Keitel), whose *moko* (facial tattoo) indicates that he has 'gone native' – and a group of Maori men and women. The Maori, dressed in a mixture of native and European clothes, speak their language to Baines, who translates it into English for Stewart, just as Flora communicates in sign language with her mother and conveys Ada's wishes to the others. Ada's defiant attempt to take the piano with her into the hinterland is overruled by Stewart. Attracted by the abandon Ada displays when she plays music, Baines swaps the piano for land with Stewart and then arranges for Ada to give him lessons so she can earn it back, exchanging the ivory keys from the piano for sexual favours. Baines also appears to have a sexual relationship with Hira (Tungia Baker), one of the Maori women, and he participates in what the film portrays as the Maori's uninhibited sexuality, which contrasts with Stewart's Victorian prudishness and repression.

Although the initial relationship between Flora and Ada is uncannily close, Flora becomes distanced from her mother when she observes a growing intimacy between Ada and Baines. Flora alerts Stewart to the nature of their relationship and Baines elects to stop taking lessons and to give Ada back the piano. Stewart observes Ada making love to Baines and makes Ada promise not to see Baines again, but she carves a love message on a piano key and asks Flora to deliver it to Baines. Flora instead delivers the key to Stewart. Stewart confronts Ada and demands that she deny her love for Baines. When Ada refuses to do so, he chops off her index finger with an axe. Stewart carries Ada inside his hut and attempts to rape her. Once he realises that Ada does not love him, Stewart declares that he wishes her and Baines gone. As a group of Maori in canoes transport Ada, Baines, Flora and the piano to another location, Ada demands that the piano be heaved overboard.

Seized by a 'fatal curiosity', Ada slips her foot inside a coil of rope and is pulled deep underwater by the weight of the sinking piano. Yet the narrational voice-over states that Ada does not die, because her will chooses life: she manages to free herself and re-surface. The notion of an apparent rebirth is lent force by the subsequent sequence, which reveals that Ada is living in Nelson. Ada appears with Baines outside a white weatherboard house and is then shown giving piano lessons inside while Flora turns somersaults. To demonstrate the extent to which Ada has reformed, the voice-over announces that she is learning to speak.

Critical interpretations of the film have been remarkably varied. Generally, however, criticism of the film has tended to fall into two main categories: that which focuses on sexual politics, and that which emphasises postcolonial issues, particularly the vexed issues of nation and nationality. Indeed, there is a marked divergence between international and national views of the film, with overseas critics tending to analyse *The Piano* in feminist, art film and literary contexts, while New Zealand critics have dominantly examined the film's portrayal of New Zealand as a settler colony and its representation of Maori and Pakeha identities.

Interest in the film's sexual politics centres around the nature and extent of Ada's agency. Ada's response to her material circumstances has encouraged feminist readings of the film. Ada is an unmarried mother who is forced into an arranged marriage, who does not own property, and who is treated like a commodity, since she belongs to her father, her husband

and her lover, in turn. The parallels between the sexual contract between Ada and Baines and economic contract between Stewart and Baines emphasises Ada's status as her husband's chattel. Yet, although she is dependent and is literally without a voice, Ada exhibits various forms of wilful behaviour. Her muteness can be seen as an exercise of will, and, hence, as a form of resistance to social constraints. She openly rejects patriarchal norms, by disdaining her arranged marriage and by flouting her husband's authority. She is also motivated by her own libidinal desires, and she pursues sexual freedom in the face of fierce opposition, by choosing her lover over her husband. In these ways, Ada's rebellious behaviour can be taken as a model of female self-empowerment.

The Piano demonstrates Ada's agency in yet another way, since she becomes the subject and not the object of the gaze. Her astonishingly pale, delicate appearance accords with Victorian codes of femininity. It could be argued that her body is frequently displayed for the spectator's delectation, albeit clothed rather than unclothed. But, if Stewart can be seen as the archetypal voyeuristic male and Baines as the feminised male, then by making Baines the recipient of the female gaze, *The Piano* creates an alternative mode of female sexual desire. The episode in which Baines is most obviously the object of the spectatorial gaze occurs when we glimpse him naked and fondling the piano, which is a clear substitute for Ada. In this scene, Campion broke with the mainstream cinematic convention of not revealing male genitals, which anticipates her similarly unconventional (and even franker) depictions of oral sex in *In the Cut*. Other aspects of the film's depiction of sexuality are worth noting; for instance, Baines' seduction of Ada is remarkably sensual. Indeed, *The Piano* places great emphasis upon the senses, the sense of touch, in particular, as is suggested by Baines fingering a hole in Ada's stocking. Yet, despite its preoccupation with the erotic, the film has been praised for focusing on a woman without objectifying her, and for its exploration of female as well as male desire.

Campion's approach to gender involves more than just her depiction of Ada, since the film portrays memorable male as well as female characters. Stewart and Baines can be seen as embodying contrasting notions of masculinity: although they are both settlers, Stewart is a colonising Victorian patriarch, whose benighted attitudes exhibit the shortcomings of his peers, and Baines is a new man, who, in his enlightened behaviour towards women and Maori, can be viewed as an indigenised New Zealander. These figures are initially distinguished from one another by their class backgrounds, for whereas Stewart is a gentleman, Baines lacks social graces and is illiterate. Yet, these initial depictions are complicated by the characters' subsequent behaviour towards Ada: Baines is tender towards her, but Stewart shows himself to be capable of acting in a shockingly violent and brutal manner.

The film also invites the audience to draw some disturbing connections between Stewart's treatment of the land and his treatment of women. His compulsive desire to control his environment and to tame the wilderness is a correlative of his attempts to subdue Ada's will. When Stewart fences his land it is analogous to his imprisoning Ada in his cabin by hammering planks over the doors and windows. Similarly, Stewart cuts down trees on his land, an act which can be compared with his chopping off Ada's fingertip with an axe, leaving only a stump. However, Stewart's vulnerability when he first meets Ada suggests he is more than just a brute, just as Baines' coercion of Ada over the piano shows that he is not above using emotional force. Like Ada herself, both men can be seen as occupying the positions of tormentor and tormented. Thus, the notions of masculinity Stewart and Baines exemplify at the outset of the film are modified by their ability to confound gender expectations and to exchange roles.

In contrast to the focus by certain international critics on the film's representation of sexual politics, New Zealand critics have generally been concerned to analyse *The Piano*'s depiction of nation. In this way Leonie Pihama argues that this is not a New Zealand, so much as a Pakeha, film, one which is controlled by the colonial gaze and which provides a stereotypical view of Maori. Certainly, by including what purports to be a Maori perspective, constructed with the help of Maori advisors, Campion attempts to challenge dominant, Pakeha (European), views of nineteenth-century history in New Zealand. In practice, however, the Maori narrative tends to function merely as an exotic backdrop to the relationship between Ada and Stewart. For Lynda Dyson, Campion's film presents the colonisation of New Zealand as a narrative of Maori/Pakeha reconciliation, in which Ada jettisons her piano (a symbol of middle-class European culture), and thus her link to Britain, and begins life in a 'New Jerusalem' with Baines, who has already 'gone native'. Informing such perceptions, certain interpretations have emphasised postcolonial aspects evident in the film and in this way, for example, *The Piano* has been interpreted as reinscribing the dichotomy between European culture and Maori nature.

If, from a postcolonial standpoint, the ending of *The Piano* can be interpreted as a vision of nation that substitutes white New Zealand settlers for the Maori inhabitants of Aotearoa, those commentators preoccupied by sexual politics have not taken Ada's bourgeois respectability at face value either. Certain macabre and menacing features interrupt this domestic idyll. Ada has had her missing fingertip capped with a silver prosthesis, which taps ominously on the piano keys as she plays. She wears a bizarre-looking black hood when she practises her pronunciation, alone and after dark, because she does not want people to hear her 'bad speech'. Like the prosthesis, the hood hides that which is considered abnormal or socially unacceptable. As we watch Ada framed against this demure domestic backdrop it is not hard to take her mumblings for muffled complaints.

By portraying a seemingly submissive Ada, whose compliance is compromised by a few unsettling habits of dress and behaviour, Campion manages to both deliver a happy ending, and, simultaneously, to subvert it. To all intents and purposes, the film ends when Ada is pulled deep under water by her sinking piano, because only a melodramatic, deathly ending seems capable of accommodating the passions aroused in the characters. The coda in which the voice-over describes a happy fate for Ada has been variously interpreted as a parody of the happy ending; as the dream Ada has while she is drowning; and, on a formal level, as a way of achieving an emotional balance between death and life, to list but three readings of this ambiguous sequence in an ambiguous film. With its contentious and equivocal qualities, this ending functions as a microcosm for the film as a whole, in that it illustrates how *The Piano* raises sexual and national political issues that are far from settled.

Rochelle Simmons

REFERENCES

Dyson, Lynda (1995) 'The Return of the Repressed? Whiteness, Femininity and Colonialism in *The Piano*', *Screen*, 3, 3, 267–76.
Pihama, Leonie (2000) 'Ebony and Ivory: Constructions of Maori in *The Piano*', in Harriet Margolis (ed.) *Jane Campion's The Piano*. Cambridge: Cambridge University Press.
Polan, Dana (2001) *Jane Campion*. London: British Film Institute.

ONCE WERE WARRIORS

LEE TAMAHORI, NEW ZEALAND, 1994

In many ways, the story depicted in *Once Were Warriors* (1994) is perfect subject matter for a New Zealand film. It is distinctly local, yet deals with universal issues: the dispossession of an indigenous people through colonisation, crises in masculinity and the dilemmas and anguish of motherhood. The film's universality attracted New Zealand and international audiences, far beyond the white middle-class festival audience that director Lee Tamahori had targeted. Despite not being selected for competition at the Cannes Film Festival in 1994 it sold to every world territory in the first week of the open market there. Before the release of Niki Caro's *Whalerider* (2003), *Once Were Warriors* was the highest grossing film at the domestic box office.

The first shot of the film is suggestive. A billboard poster of a lake and mountains fills the screen. This stereotypical image of a pristine New Zealand is cynically juxtaposed against an urban wasteland of Maori slums crowding below the hoarding. As the camera pulls away the paper-thin myths of racial harmony, social equality and material plenitude generated by New Zealand's colonial past recede. *Once Were Warriors* is a confrontation, a melodrama and a tragedy; the depiction of a dispossessed Maori family caught at the edge of late twentieth-century urban capitalism. In the opening phrases the rhythm and the tone declare the narrative space as a vision of postcolonial Maori, figured within an eclectic mixture of the traditional beauty and the violence of the late twentieth century. Such eclecticism runs throughout a film invested with leather and animal- and snake-patterned fabrics, muscle and golden-toned tattooed skin, Maori language and a Maori-inflected English, and a soundtrack which mixes reggae and slow, heavy metal bass guitar chords with traditional Maori flute.

The story centres on Beth Heke (Rena Owen) and begins as she wheels a shopping trolley home through a working-class neighbourhood of Auckland. At the local market, Beth's husband Jake (Temuera Morrison) establishes his 'kingpin' status by simply glaring at a young pretender and emerging gang member. Beth's first born, Nig (Julian Arahanga), works out in a makeshift tin-shed gym, her second son Boogie (Taungaroa Emile), is arrested for burglary, while daughter Grace (Mamaengaroa Kerr-Bell) reads her versions of traditional Maori stories to her younger siblings, under a tree in the family's backyard.

The Heke family is in trouble. Jake 'the Muss' (muscles) is infamous for his vicious drunken brawling. Nig, lacking a father figure in Jake, is inducted into a local rival gang, and Boogie is heading for the remand home. Grace, surrogate mother and vestigial soul of the family observes, writes and finds some respite hiding away in a rusted car wreck, the shelter of her friend Toot (Shannon Williams). The drama begins when Jake arrives home with *kaimoana* (a seafood feast), an act of misguided conciliation after spending most of his severance pay from his latest job on drinks with his friends. Jake and Beth's passionate lovemaking is stemmed and the fissures in their marriage become apparent when Jake confesses to losing his job. Beth dreams of owning a home while Jake is happy to settle for welfare payments. Frustrated, Jake goes out for more alcohol, returning later that night with a group of drunken acquaintances. Beth parties along until, unable to contain her growing dissatisfaction with their life, she riles Jake, who thrashes and then rapes her. The children listen from their bedroom, fearful of how this savagery will end. In a desolate scene the following morning, Grace surveys the party's aftermath – a lounge-room littered with the wreckage of a marriage and smeared with Beth's blood. She begins to clean up the mess only to be goaded by Nig who warns her that as a Maori woman this is the future that awaits her. Beth, bearing the grotesque signs of her beating, is too ashamed to attend court for Boogie's hearing and Grace takes her place, watching helplessly as he is sentenced to a remand home.

Grace suggests a family trip to the country to visit Boogie. The journey coincides with a big win for Jake at the horse-track. The family shares a momentary accord as they set off on the road trip, though the sequence is uneasy. The framing, an interior shot of the family in the car, including mum and dad in the front and the kids in the back seat, suggests an advertisement for an ideal nuclear family. The car radio plays a Pacific reggae track, 'What's the Time Mr Wolf', and the family sings along in harmony. The choice of this song plays to the anti-colonial discourse that is embedded in the film. The words are taken from the children's game played across school playgrounds in New Zealand. The game was transformed into a hip hop/reggae song by a South Auckland band, Southside of Bombay, who reworked its lyrics within an urban Polynesian beat. The acculturation of Maori to Pakeha ways figures in the lyrics, 'Mamma, Pappa say you should go to school, I don't know what for. Now I've grown up and seen the world and all its lies.'

When the family stops at a lakeside close to Beth's *marae* (tribal home), Beth tells her children about Jake's wooing of her and her rejection of her tribal family in his favour. Jake has his own bitter version of the tribe's rejection of him because he was 'a slave' and of the wrong lineage for Beth. The *aroha* (love) of the drive seeps away. The placement of this nostalgic idyll is the midpoint of the film and the narrative pivots around the scene. Clouds build as the family leaves the lake and begins a relentless tread towards the tragic end. Jake sabotages the trip by taking a detour to stop for alcohol. When any chance of visiting Boogie disappears Beth takes the rest of the family home in a taxi in despair.

That night Jake brings another crowd of people home from yet another drinking spree. Beth lies upstairs in bed and refuses Jake's entreaties to join the party. Grace is upstairs too, sleeping, until her Uncle Bully (Clifford Curtis) slides into the bedroom and rapes her. It is with this act that the postcolonial racial disquiet, Western family dysfunction and the more universal question of gender disparity collide. The offence is exaggerated by Grace's innocence and purity, and the hope that she represents for the next generation of Maori fades as a result of the attack. The horror is intensified as Grace visits her old haunts, the city streets and Toot's burnt-out car, and finds no solace. When Toot innocently kisses her on the lips, any remaining faith she has in human nature is shattered. For the first time the city is cold and dark, its unrelenting surfaces indifferent to her pain. The *mise-en-scène*, predominantly low-angle, hand-held close-up shots, is invested with Grace's anguish as she wanders alone. A white-smocked Christian group sings, 'This is the day that the Lord has made,' with a guitar strum, as the camera tracks low-angle around the group to catch Grace walking behind the singers. An alcoholic beggar makes a Dickensian grab at Grace and the acoustic music flattens under the buzz of a tattooist's needle. The girl being tattooed stares at her from inside a wire fence and random people are side-lit in a harsh red. Grace looks into a makeshift gymnasium, this time lit so the men's shadows fill the wall, dancing in time with the percussion of their boxing gloves.

When Grace arrives home Jake is singing, 'Look what you've done, what you've done my baby', in the living room filled again with his drinking friends. Grace is framed in Jake's low-angle view of her as he rails at her for staying out. The returning shot is wide and low, of Grace standing facing the group of men. A moderating entreaty by one of the men is a straight two-shot with Bully in the foreground. These three shots play out as Uncle Bully asks Grace for a kiss goodnight. When she refuses, Jake's violence explodes into the frame. He grabs her and throws her at Bully's feet, ripping her storybook apart and blaming her insolence on her love of words. This unsteady view from the floor places the viewer below Jake and within easy reach of his raging fists. The recurring low-angle shot is a motif that is coupled with Jake's outbursts. It is used earlier when he rapes Beth in the couple's bedroom and later when he beats Bully in retribution for the violation of his daughter.

Reeling from her father's violence Grace returns to the backyard tree, in an abject version of the opening scene. Her desperation is established in the hand-held camera which frames her wildly in the dark. The next shot is from high in the tree, of Grace embracing the tree trunk as she contemplates suicide by hanging herself. The sequence ends with a shot of the branch with its twisted rope in the foreground. Beth discovers Grace too late to save her and in her grief knows that Grace's suicide will change their lives forever. Beth takes Grace back to her tribal *marae* for burial. Grace's spirit lives on in Boogie as he performs a *haka* (ceremonial dance) at the *tangi* (funeral) and Beth reconnects with her tribe. The reckoning for Grace's death happens in the hotel bar where Jake drinks. Beth reads of Bully's rape in Grace's storybook. She takes Nig with her to the bar and confronts Jake with the truth. In an act of extreme violence Jake beats Bully and smashes his face with a broken bottle. Avenged, Beth banishes Jake from the family, taking her place at the head. She leaves Jake sitting in the gutter outside the hotel to the sound of police sirens approaching.

Once Were Warriors is more than a cinematic rendering of urban Maori life. Don Selwyn – Maori actor, filmmaker and commentator – said that the film functions in an open-ended way as a forum, a point at which discussion begins, rather than a place of narrative closure, and that the life of the film beyond exhibition is as important as its screenings. For Maori, it initiated endless *hui* (forum) of topics relevant to Maori, including dispossession, discussion of screen presence and visual representation of Maori, and a search for solutions to the social problems that the film exposes. For Pakeha the film lifted the veil, demythologised the harsher aspects of Maori life, giving a view that had been previously apocryphal.

Such controversy was embedded in Alan Duff's source novel which had inserted itself into New Zealand's reading community and beyond with the same force and intensity as the film. The novel is a semi-autobiographical exploration of a Maori family's ghetto life, the story told through the voices of Jake, Beth and Grace. The stream-of-consciousness style is experiential and exaggerated, raw and visceral; the interior monologues crafted from Maori street dialects. This effect gives the novel a brutal authority, a view from inside a dispossessed, urbanised Maori family. The novel is a curiously successful combination of social realism based on personal experience and a larger-than-life rendering of the lives of an indigenous underclass. The figures of the novel, the thwarted warrior, beaten women and abused children, came to be used to describe existing social disorders in New Zealand/Maori life. In the process of adaptation the script had to move from the novel's series of interior monologues into a cohesive film narrative. The interiority posed problems. Speaking in 1994, Tamahori said he wanted to make 'a straight narrative drama' and 'a progressive realist text'. He thought the novel was too hard-hitting and that a realistic adaptation would alienate film audiences. Stylistically, Tamahori wanted to conform to Hollywood narrative paradigms and to marry his love of action/western films with social realism. He resolved these tensions by developing a 'polished' social realist style.

The film makes Beth the centre of the story – a 'South Seas Mother Courage'. Tamahori recognised that although Jake had a stronger voice in the novel, Beth's drive to protect her children was a more uplifting and universally identifiable theme. Her maternal drive to protect her offspring becomes stronger as each of her children is threatened and peaks when Grace kills herself. Interestingly, the film dispenses with almost all direct representations of Pakeha, instead limiting them to the nameless judge at Boogie's court appearance. This process necessitated locating the antagonist from within the film's represented community. Jake, initially an obstruction to Beth, becomes the antagonistic force. The question is whether Beth will take control of her situation by overcoming him. As Beth becomes stronger she is able to disarm Jake; he has less and less control and she finds redemption by finally denouncing him. Uncle Bully is a second rogue element that acts as a catalyst in this respect. The characterisation of these two violent men together takes the narrative focus away from the colonial dispossession of the Heke family and transfers it to an exposition of gender inequity. Jake's character has no journey or revelation and certainly no redemption. His salvation became the subject of the sequel to *Once Were Warriors*, *What Becomes of the Broken Hearted* (1999), based on Duff's sequel novel of the same name.

Finding a narrative resolution to Grace's story that was politically acceptable in feminist and racial terms proved difficult. The closure that Tamahori and scriptwriter Riwia Brown created is motivated by a class difference between Beth and Jake that is established during the picnic on the thwarted visit to Boogie. Beth's nostalgia for her roots alienates Jake as he remembers his lack of status in the eyes of Beth's family. In interview for the journal *Cineaste*, Tamahori argues that Jake's subjective inferiority with regards to his 'slave' status is apolitical in that it is not a result of colonisation but rather a psychological condition. Jake uses his unease as an excuse to sabotage the car trip and it is later that night that Grace is raped.

In Duff's novel, Jake's involvement in the incestuous rape of Grace is implied through the stream-of-consciousness style and retribution occurs when Beth takes the rest of the family away from him. The film takes the weight of the incest from Jake's character and makes Bully the guilty perpetrator. Grace's suicide then precipitates Beth's crisis and the climax is her realisation that their domestic situation does not afford her children the protection they need. Retribution for Bully's brutality had to be expected. In a complex turn, Jake metes out justice on Bully for Grace's death by beating him with a broken bottle, but this action is not enough to redeem Jake. There is a contradiction here in that the same violence that drives Beth to find a new life also resolves the tragedy of Grace's death. Tamahori was aware that this resolution might both exonerate Jake's previous behaviour and weaken Beth's position. Speaking in 1995 Tamahori said that he wanted to create a restorative end to the story where the audience felt vindicated without making Jake look heroic: 'Generally the audience doesn't think about it because the cathartic thing just washes over them and they buy into it. I was very pleased to see that the scene doesn't weaken Beth's position.'

Despite the avoidance of direct reference to colonisation, the root causes of the Heke family's dysfunction were not lost on international reviewers. In terms of genre, the film was aligned with other indigenous minority films that dealt with similar themes: family communities disaffected through economics and race, codes of male behaviour and social emasculation and, at the heart, spiritual loss. It is in the marrying of social realism with action narrative that some reconciliation of postcolonial issues occurs. The archetypes of the impoverished family with abusive emasculated man, battered woman, badly fathered sons, graceful daughter forced into a maternal role and the occurrence of incest are not Maori-specific aspects. They are archetypes of not just indigenous peoples, but other dispossessed groups. They are found in films from different cultures – Ang Lee's *The Ice Storm* (1997) and Atom Eyogan's *The Sweet Hereafter* (1997) are comparable tragedies. What identifies *Once Were Warriors* as Maori, and as a postcolonial response to the specific situation depicted, is the style of the film and some of the narrative solutions posed within it. The overarching narrative solution is Beth's return to her home *marae* for Grace's funeral through which she rediscovers her tribal affiliations. The future of Maori is rested in Boogie whose salvation is mastered by the Maori social worker/elder, Bennet (George Henare), teaching him the traditional pathway of the true warrior. Beth's redemption is culturally motivated. She is a prodigal daughter as far as her tribe is concerned, though, out of youthful pride, she has never taken her rightful place in Maori community. Even though she speaks Maori when talking to her aunt, her own children have had little exposure to traditional Maori culture. Beth's pathway from victim to leadership reflects the passage of women in taking leadership roles in the Maori renaissance of the 1980s.

Further, much of what identifies *Once Were Warriors* as a postcolonial text is in its cinematic treatment of its content. Warrior-hood is positively identified by decoration, uniform, weapons, physique and the grimacing or tattooed face, and portrayed as powerful. Tamahori glamorises Nig's gang by investing its members with a futuristic warrior-look that is elaborated with traditionally inspired *moko* (tattoo) and by using a Maori/Pacific Island music score that also invokes ''hood' films. Tamahori was aware that he was exploiting and refiguring the colonial tropes of the exotic native. He sensualises the *mise-en-scène* with eroticism and violence shot close and rendered unavoidable. When Beth and Jake are not warring their passion fills the screen.

Once Were Warriors was Tamahori's feature-film directing debut. It was unusual for a first-time director to have not made several short films before being entrusted by the New Zealand Film Commission with state funding for a feature film. Tamahori's career was established as a first assistant director on a number of New Zealand's better-known features and as a director of television commercials. His advertisements could be defined as 30-second short films, narratively driven vignettes populated with strong characters. Tamahori's more memorable advertisements included a serialised campaign produced for a dairy company. Fashioned after a daytime soap, the series was broadcast in New Zealand for nearly ten years. Tamahori was able to build on his experience in television in his direction of *Once Were Warriors* and beyond.

The critical and box office success of *Once Were Warriors* should have come as no surprise. There had been several films prior to this dealing with Pakeha/Maori relations in a colonial relation context. The earliest films in New Zealand were ethnographic depictions of Maori life or romanticised visions of the 'South Seas'. The only films of the 1940–70s period, made by John O'Shea and Rudall and Ramai Hayward, were either re-enactments of wars between Maori and Pakeha, or explorations of modern interracial relations from a personal point of view. Maori filmmaking and involvement in the film industry since the formation of the New Zealand Film Commission in 1978 has tended to reflect the ebbs and flows of both Maori resistance and renaissance occurring on a wider societal level. Even so, Maori control of their own filmmaking has been sporadic and *Once Were Warriors* is a rare example of a film being predominately Maori in terms of crew and cast. Of the films that have been motivated by Maori, two strands have emerged: hard-hitting urban stories of dispossession and the rural, though not always nostalgic, films of tribal life. *Kingpin* (1985) by Mark Walker and *Mark II* (1986) by John Anderson are two films that deal with the troubled lives of city-bound Maori and Pacific Island youths and are close to *Once Were Warriors* in intention. Merata Mita's *Mauri* (1988) and Barry Barclay's films *Ngati* (1987) and *Te Rua* are made by Maori filmmakers interested in representing their own concerns. *Whalerider* follows in this tradition, although it was adapted and directed by a Pakeha.

Once Were Warriors is an essay in indigene/settler relations in the late twentieth century. Often criticised simultaneously for the violence and romanticism of its depictions, *Once Were Warriors* stands as a tragedy. The crimes against Grace can be read as a symptom of a dispossessed nuclear family or as the inevitable outcome of the colonisation of an indigenous people, but her death at the centre is that of a noble warrior. She is the hope of a generation, of a people, and she is lost so that a people might recover themselves.

Hester Joyce

REFERENCES

Selwyn, Don (2003) unpublished interview with the author.

Sklar, Robert (1995) 'Social Realism with Style: An Interview with Lee Tamahori', *Cineaste*, Summer, 25–8.

Tamahori, Lee (1994) 'Directing *Warriors*', *Midwest*, 6, 14–16.

OSCAR AND LUCINDA

17

GILLIAN ARMSTRONG, AUSTRALIA, 1998

Gillian Armstrong's 1998 film version of Peter Carey's 1988 Booker Prize-winning novel, *Oscar and Lucinda*, borrows strongly from the literary text's eccentricities of character and narration. While set in the colonial period, in which New South Wales operates as a sign of both new opportunities and a wasteland of exile, *Oscar and Lucinda* is far from a conventional epic tale of romance. Instead, it focuses upon alternately tragi-comic intensities of faith and misunderstanding, and of the disparate powers of what is unsaid and what is passed on, forging new traditions of narrative and storytelling.

It is a story which deals with paradox, with individuals and ideas that do not necessarily fit neatly into any dominant picture. Told retrospectively through a convolution of generations (via the voice-over of Geoffrey Rush), the narrative is driven more by a series of striking images and abstract ideas than it is by the conventions of realism or cause-and-effect linear sequencing. Although *Oscar and Lucinda* might certainly be described in part as the tortured and luminous story of an eccentric English man of faith and a colonial feminist – a 'square peg in a round hole' as her mother describes her – who together take a gamble on the future, it is also a study of great passion, mistaken and displaced; of the beauty and the treachery of water, and of glass, its arrested counterpart; of faith itself, as a wager on the impossible; and of the iconic beauty of a glass-and-iron church floating down-river, resplendent and fracturing in the Australian sun.

The opening third of the film involves the alternation of the growing-up of the two central characters, Oscar Hopkins (Ralph Fiennes) and Lucinda Leplastrier (Cate Blanchett), with the increasing anticipation of their meeting and overlapping passions. Oscar is the son of a fundamentalist Plymouth Brethren Preacher (Clive Russell), living on the rugged coast of Devon. In a crucial early scene, the young Oscar follows his father down to the sea where, distraught at the death of his wife, he attempts to fling away her clothes. However, the heavy Victorian garments wash back to the shore, entangling themselves around Oscar's bare legs, and ensuring that forever after the 'sea smelt of death' and water was the cause of phobic anxiety for him. As a young man, struggling to differentiate between his father's implacable love and doctrinal rigidity, Oscar undertakes his first 'gamble', attempting to read in the signs of a human game the designs of the Almighty – which, he interprets, guide him into the dubious care of the Anglicans, and an Anglican ministry. However, he is introduced to the pleasures of the extended gambling 'flutter' at college, and it is guilt at this increasingly obsessive behaviour which finally leads him, cowering below decks, aboard the *Leviathan* and on his way to the Colonies.

Adrift on the terrifying ocean between two worlds of being and possibility, Oscar meets Lucinda, a wealthy young Australian woman who, orphaned and lonely despite her independence of character, has sought solace in two activities: gambling, in any form, and the production of glass, whose paradoxical 'fluid stasis' might be read as corresponding to her own state of potential and uncertainty. Linked, perhaps yoked, together by their passion for gambling, for the rush of displaced sexual intensity that comes from the high-risk activity of the wager, they are increasingly thrown together, as they shock and alienate a Sydney society attempting to be genteel, and the Anglican Church's requirement for propriety. However, despite the depth of their growing love and sexual passion, these feelings go largely unexpressed between them, as Oscar believes that Lucinda's heart is already given to the reserved Reverend Dennis Hasset (Ciaran Hinds), whose own friendship with the reckless Lucinda has led to his banishment from Sydney to a remote, church-less parish in Bellingen, northern New South Wales. Catching her passion for glass, Oscar proposes a wager to Lucinda, on the strength of both their inheritances: that he deliver to Hasset a church of glass, made by Lucinda's own Prince Rupert's Glassworks. The wild and impractical heights of this idea lead ironically to the nadir of Oscar's overland journey through uncharted territory – in order to avoid a far easier journey by water – in which he is abused and humiliated by the expedition leader Jeffris (Richard Roxburgh), who uses the opportunity to exercise violence and murder non-hostile Aborigines along the way. Profoundly traumatised by this experience, Oscar eventually murders Jeffris. With the assistance of the faithful Percy (Billie Brown) Oscar finally makes it to Bellingen, pathetically triumphant in the now-constructed glass church, to offer it to the newly-married Reverend Hasset. Beautiful and foolish, the church creaks and panes crack, the falling shards of glass only heightening the magnificent folly of the scheme.

Wishing to avoid more embarrassment from Lucinda, Hasset bundles the sunburnt, slightly hysterical Oscar off with a local widow, and potential husband 'nabber', Miriam Chadwick (Josephine Byrnes), who, as well as ministering to his wounds, sees an opportunity to take sexual advantage of the naïve and distressed Oscar. Feeling only further traumatised and dislocated from what he truly loves – his father in Devon and Lucinda in Sydney – Oscar retreats to the church, clutching the caul his father gave him to protect him from drowning, and falls into an anguished sleep. When he wakes, the church is adrift and capsizing, the iron frame locks him in, and the water of Bellingen's Bellinger River rushes in upon him from all sides. Frantic, Oscar sees the images of his father and then the face of Lucinda as he drowns.

Gillian Armstrong had long harboured the idea of adapting Carey's novel to the screen. By 1998, the year of the film's release, Armstrong was already a senior and respected figure in the Australian film industry. A graduate in the 1970s of the recently established Australian Film, Television and Radio School, Armstrong was a contemporary of other important Australian directors who, together, contributed to the rich output of 'New Australian Wave' cinema – figures such as Philip Noyce, Jan Chapman, Bruce Beresford, Fred Schepisi and Peter Weir. Armstrong made a number of short films (in the 1960s and 1970s) and a series of influential documentaries, from *Smoke and Lollies* (1976) to *Not Fourteen Again* (1996). Her work consistently reflects issues of aesthetics, often involving a focus on the ambiguous beauty of the landscape and the visual image, together with a fascination with the intersections of cinema-making, creativity and storytelling; and issues of social politics, the nuances and intricacies of how people function both as individuals and within the constraints of the social.

Her first feature film, *My Brilliant Career* (1979), which launched the acting careers of Judy Davis and Sam Neill, made evident Armstrong's interest in strong, independent-minded female protagonists, women who struggled with the seemingly competing demands of romance and creativity, of what might be expected from them and what they might want for and of themselves. For the character of Sybylla, the compromise involved the rejection of the complications of romance and becoming the teller of her own story – initiating a career, which is, like Lucinda's, both brilliant and the haphazard product of chance and confusion. Armstrong continued her interest in strong, struggling female characters in *Starstruck* (1982), *Mrs Soffel* (1984), *High Tide* (1987), *The Last Days of Chez Nous* (1992), *Little Women* (1994) and *Charlotte Gray* (2001) (the latter again using Cate Blanchett). Awarded the Women in Hollywood Icon in 1998, Armstrong makes films that can be said to reflect wider feminist concerns, challenging conventional notions of womanhood and femininity that have flourished from the 1960s and 1970s. Armstrong's women characters can all, in various ways, be seen to be in engaging, dramatised struggle with expectations from the past, and with determined, if often inevitably flawed, efforts to recast themselves and their lives in new and different ways. Like feminist issues in general, Armstrong's films track the historical movement of women's struggles for self-definition from the margins to the centre of Western culture, from the art house to the mainstream of cinema.

There are, of course, a number of frameworks available for interpreting the film *Oscar and Lucinda*. It might, for example, be read in the above context, as part of Armstrong's stable of feminist films. This is particularly relevant if Lucinda is seen as the key character who survives, literally and metaphorically, in the harsh new world of New South Wales; the one who is able to care for Oscar's orphaned child, introducing him, without fear, to the fluid pleasures of water, and all that water comes to symbolise in the narrative. In the character of Oscar however, played with such sensitivity and compassion by Ralph Fiennes, Armstrong is also able to call various conventional notions of masculinity into question. Oscar's intensity, his soul-searching and eccentricities are, through Lucinda's and Armstrong's eyes, seen to be far more worthy and attractive than any conventional machismo, certainly more than the brute violence of Jeffris. In this sense, the film is concerned with challenging broader notions of gender – masculinity as well as femininity – an equability that is reflected in the nature of the relationship between Oscar and Lucinda, in their parallel stories and the images of them side by side; this follows the even-handedness of the source novel's title.

Oscar and Lucinda might thus be read as a particularly *auteurist* film – that is, a film which derives its central and defining characteristics from the influence of its director. In the case of Armstrong's feature films, as Felicity Collins discusses, this suggestion might be evidenced by the films' persistent interest in women's lives and roles, with the primacy and the nuances of human emotional relationships, with the struggle between individual desires and social expectations, and with the focus upon key, vivid images. As Mary Colbert comments, Armstrong is, like the anthropologist she once longed to be, concerned with a close-up study of human nature which is prompted by a fascination with the misfit and the non-conformist. If that is the defining feature of Armstrong as *auteur* then it is clear that *Oscar and Lucinda* fits into this model, as a study of different, headstrong individuals in sometimes heroic, sometimes foolish collision with the demands of their time and place.

However, while the *auteurist* model does provide a useful frame of reference for reading this film, it is also important to remember the more diverse influences and individuals who might shape or 'author' a film, creating a context of intertextuality in which the complex meanings of the film are made and interpreted. These wider influences include Peter Carey, as the author of the novel (*Oscar and Lucinda* could equally be read in comparison to Carey's other texts, such as the eccentric storyteller of *Illywacker*); the actors who play the key roles and whose screen *personae* are themselves informed by previous work they have done (for example, Fiennes' characters in *Schindler's List* (1993) and *The English Patient* (1996) inform the way in which we receive his rendition of Oscar); the interpretations/adaptations of scriptwriter Laura Jones; the exceptional work of Geoffrey Simpson as director of photography, or Luciana Arrighi as production designer. Indeed, other Australian films that deal with either the colonial period and/or are literary adaptations have some resonance here (*My Brilliant Career*, *Picnic at Hanging Rock* (1975) or *The Getting of Wisdom* (1977)). The synergy of such a wide group of creative individuals, in addition to the specificities of location, inevitably complicates any hierarchical *auteurist* approach. While this film certainly bears many of the hallmarks of a 'Gillian Armstrong product' – a connection that also certainly helps in its marketing and distribution – it ultimately needs to be seen within this wider context of intertextuality and influence.

Being taken from such a well-known and successful novel, any reading of Armstrong's film must also grapple with the complex questions of adaptation. Certainly many reviewers of the film foreground the question of its 'fidelity' to the original – and thus, by problematic assumption, superior – text. To what extent can the film operate as an independent work of art, as a transformation rather than a slavish reproduction of a prior literary text into another media, albeit one which inevitably exists in intertextual reference to Carey's novel as well as to other historical novels, colonial texts of the period, other Carey novels, or other Armstrong films? And even if the literary text remains a dominant and unavoidable influence, and all the narrative details remain intact, in what ways is the film actually *able* to adapt the novel's techniques of literary narration to those of film narration – and what might be the effects for the viewer of the inevitable differences? Even cinema's use of the auditory and the visual, as well as the specificities of the *mise-en-scène* – costuming, sets, lighting, camera angles – ensure that the literary narrative is inevitably altered in the process of translation and reception. To *see* the church on the river, to *hear* the voice of the narrator reflecting on his family's history, is to draw the viewer into an inevitably different, more immediate, more visceral relationship with those narrative details than is available through the literary text.

There are also several revealing narrative differences between novel and film. For example, in the film, Miriam Chadwick dies in childbirth and Reverend Hasset gives the child – hers and Oscar's – to Lucinda to raise. Thus, although not biologically involved, Lucinda becomes part of the social family whose descendent becomes the voice-over narrator, and who, in the very final scene, is shown to be telling Oscar and Lucinda's story to his own daughter, while motor-boating on very similar waters to those in which Oscar drowned. In the novel, Lucinda loses not only Oscar himself and his unborn child, but her entire inheritance to his 'widow,' Mrs Chadwick – an experience of destitution that finally leads her into a politically active career. Saved from such a fate in the film by Hasset's clandestine destruction of the wager, a softer, perhaps happier ending is achieved: rather than activism and poverty, Lucinda has wealth, an ongoing connection with Oscar through his son, and a career that she has been able to inherit from the past, rather than one she must make from scratch for herself. These narrative shifts reflect the intervention of Armstrong as director, perhaps with an eye for translating the novel's raw and bleak sense of loss into something more positive, more comforting for audiences. In spite of Oscar's tragic death, these narrative changes to the film's conclusion might also be seen to link it more strongly to patterns of romance, of a great love story which is all the more poignant for the lovers' misunderstandings, misplaced reservations and bad timing – and thus swinging its emphasis from a more philosophical consideration of life and faith as our great and uncertain wagers, or from a particular study of the ambivalences of the colonial experience.

The image of the glass-and-iron church floating down the Bellinger River with Oscar inside it remains a pivotal one for any reading of the film. The sequence is shot through with beauty, contradiction and paradox, making it a microcosm of the film's themes and issues. Already devastated by the violence of white man to black man, and of white man to white man – and by his own complicity in that violence – Oscar struggles to regain the exuberance of this gift from Lucinda to Hasset. Indeed, as he approaches the embarrassed and horror-struck Hasset, as the church teeters on the brink of its own violent shattering, the misunderstandings and follies upon which it was constructed become more apparent. Forged from passion, the church is an externalisation, a displacement of the love between Oscar and Lucinda, *not* Lucinda and Hasset, and thus cannot last, cannot ever soar to the ecstatic heights imagined for it. As Aboriginal figures look up to see this church, afloat in their already-violated territory, its transportation, like the entire colonial exercise, is tacitly exposed as an arrogant imposition of European customs and beliefs onto a landscape of incredulous difference. Just as Oscar could not live with the imposition of Jeffris' style of power over the Aborigines, neither will he be able to live with the imposition of the church, the ultimate icon of colonial power, over the people and the landscape of this up-river country. Indeed, he is a man who, perhaps true to the beliefs of his father, cannot thrive within the institution, let alone the physical building of the church. Like Lucinda's, Oscar's faith is more nebulous, more doctrinally 'unhoused' than this. Even as a structure conceived of in the industrial city, Oscar and Lucinda's church is exposed as a grand mistake because it cannot withstand its own transportation and is shown to be useless and impractical in the heat of the northern bush. Even Lucinda must eventually ask that Hasset somehow make the broken church 'useful': 'Weatherboards attached or somesuch.'

The floating, doomed church is very much indicative of the postcolonial moment in which the film and the novel were produced, one which exposes the creaking, irresolvable dichotomies of Europe and Australia (home and exile, constraint and possibility, white and indigenous), city and bush, uncertainties and dogmatic certainty, society and the individual. On the one hand, the church suggests a beauty, a passion that is articulated, given form – even if it is a passion barely understood and its shape unsustainable and dangerous. However, the very image which Oscar hopes will bring triumphant release is the image which finally entraps him, drawing him forcibly into the watery spheres associated with his father and Lucinda – water as an image of death and mortality yet also of creativity, sexuality and a future characterised by adaptability. The point of Oscar's drowning, then, embodies the film's central paradox. As Oscar scrambles desperately to escape the sinking cage of the church, it is a moment of tragedy and loss, for Oscar himself, for Lucinda, soon to arrive in Bellingen, and for the viewer; and yet, despite being an image of death and entrapment, it also facilitates an almost baptismal movement into a re-envisaged future, the possibility of an escape from the shackled, colonial visions of the past.

The film's final sequence, as distinct from the novel's, reinforces this notion of transition into a future which is symbolically marked by water. Frolicking carefree in the waves with Oscar's child, Lucinda is at last able to bring Oscar into the sphere of her passionate and antipodean ways, even after his death. By the time we see Oscar's grandson (played by Fiennes with Rush's voice-over), narrating the story to his daughter in the gathering shadows on the river, we know that the acceptance of water, with all its potential to give and to take away life, is what has finally overcome the anxieties which Oscar brought with him from England about the maintenance of boundaries and control over the various impulses, appetites and limitations of the body. This series of images places the film's emphasis firmly upon lineage and continuity, sketching Oscar and Lucinda's family line as a genealogy both of physical bodies and of the stories which swirl about them, making them as beautiful and as fragile as a Prince Rupert's drop. In this sense, it is the combined production of children and of stories which *Oscar and Lucinda* offers as evidence of an ultimate faith in, or wager on, the unpredictable possibilities of the future.

This conclusion is reached within a film which brazenly situates Lucinda within the natural and social environments of Australia. In this way the film openly revises dominant literary and cinematic traditions in which males feature as central protagonists within generic representations of the Australian landscape. The intersections of gender and genre – and their revisions within that meeting – construct *Oscar and Lucinda* as a subtle and innovative film. Gillian Armstrong's filmmaking – from her debut feature *My Brilliant Career* to her recent docudrama *Unfolding Florence* (2006) – constitutes a significant body of work within Australian and international contexts. Within this trajectory, *Oscar and Lucinda* stands not only as a major film of Armstrong's career, but also marks an important work of an expanding Australian national film industry.

Rose Lucas

REFERENCES

Carey, Peter (1988) *Oscar and Lucinda*. Brisbane: University of Queensland Press.

Colbert, Mary (1998) 'Gillian of the Human Jungle', *The Age*, 23 January, 3.

Collins, Felicity (1999) *The Films of Gillian Armstrong*. Melbourne: ATOM.

AFTER MABO

JOHN HUGHES, AUSTRALIA, 1997

Despite the historical importance of the events it deals with, *After Mabo* (1997) has received scant critical attention. It was awarded an Open Craft Award at the Australian Film Institute Awards in 1998, and Highly Commended Best Television Documentary in the Human Rights Commission Awards, 1998, but there are few published reviews of the documentary. Perhaps the explanation for this absence derives from the formal complexity of the work. This chapter hopes to go some way to rectifying this situation, and to point to ways in which the significance of this work extends beyond the immediate events in Australia, to produce an evocative and multi-layered essay on indigenous rights, history, power and the processes of media representation.

After Mabo is directed and written by John Hughes from an idea by Richard Frankland. Stylistically the film draws on a mixture of observational modes and archival images (including television news images). Narratively it traverses the period from June 1992 to September 1997, an era of significant events concerning Aboriginal land rights. On 3 June 1992 the High Court of Australia recognised native title as part of Australian land law, thereby laying to rest the myth of 'Terra Nullius', the 'bizarre conceit that this continent had no owners prior to the settlement of Europeans', as the then Prime Minister, Paul Keating, put it. The determination recognised that native title continues in cases where indigenous people have maintained continuous connection with their traditional lands through traditional laws and customs, and where these rights have not been extinguished by an act of the Crown. This case has become popularly known as the Mabo case, after Koiki (Eddie) Mabo, one of five plaintiffs in the case. Prime Minister Keating referred to it in his speech at the Australian Launch of the International Year for the World's Indigenous People as 'an historic decision … an historic turning point, the basis of a new relationship between indigenous and non-Aboriginal Australians'.

In December 1993 the Federal Parliament enacted the Native Title Act, which set out to address the consequences of the recognition of native title and to establish rules for future dealings in relation to native title. The legislation was received with hostility by some farm and mining lobby groups. This hostility increased in 1996 when the High Court, in the so-called Wik case, decided that native title is able to co-exist with other interests in land and is not necessarily extinguished by the grant of a pastoral lease. In May 1997, the government of then Prime Minister John Howard responded with a 'Ten-point plan' – the 'Wik Amendment' to the Native Title Act. Also in May 1997, the Australian Reconciliation Convention took place in Melbourne. When John Howard addressed the convention many in the audience stood and turned their backs on him in a silent protest at the policies of his government in relation to native title and his response to *Bringing them Home: The Report of the National Inquiry into the Separation of Aboriginal and Torres Strait Islander Children from Their Families* (1997). These make up the major events traversed by the documentary. However, the documentary is not centrally concerned with the 'events', but rather with their discursive construction: the way they have been portrayed in the media, both at the time and since.

In recent times, debates around documentary have turned on the degree to which documentary can be seen as a factual discourse. Concern with the nature of documentary has also been an abiding feature of the documentary practice of John Hughes. Talking of his film *All That Is Solid* (1986–88), Hughes stated that the film is 'about trying to develop a form, a style for a documentary which can draw attention to and transgress some of the conventions and expectations people have about this kind of film, while enlivening it, enriching it … Because, today, for many audiences you can no longer put "facts" or arguments about the state of things unproblematically.' In an interview conducted fifteen years later Hughes commented that each of his films 'is engaged in a critical collaboration with orthodoxy. And part of that is an exploration of the poetic dimension of image and story.' This 'critical collaboration' with both the claims of the documentary as a project of enlightenment and understanding, and with the formal elements of the documentary (image, editing, and narrative and rhetorical structures) is a key to *After Mabo*.

A number of sequences in the work use the observational mode of documentary, in particular sequences in the offices of various indigenous groups, or of meetings with ministers of government. The observational documentary, which has its origins in the 'direct cinema' of the 1960s, makes claims to present events as they happened, in a relatively unmediated way. Typically, observational documentaries seek to present an event or series of events in such a way as to construct a chronology, from some position of 'objectivity'. As Gillian Leahy has argued, the observational mode of documentary has made claims to a greater 'fidelity' to the real than other modes.

After Mabo, however, is not primarily concerned with such 'fidelity'. In fact it works to problematise the observational mode in a number ways. One of the obvious ways it does so is by presenting several instances of government ministerial staff instructing the documentary crew to stop shooting. On each occasion the crew is allowed to film the 'photo opportunity' or the 'media event' but is not allowed to record the real discussions between ministerial staff and indigenous negotiators. The use of this device is consistent with Hughes' interest in the limitations of media representation: the fact that the real story is too elusive and is not necessarily evident in the media story. This was an issue first taken up in *Traps* (1985) in which Hughes set out to examine the role of the media in the construction of politics. In *After Mabo,* these sequences potentially alert the audience to one of the major limitations of the observational mode – the necessity for 'access' to events – and suggest that the power to determine access is not distributed equally.

The more powerful the participant in events the greater the power they have to determine how the events will be recorded and portrayed. In contrast to those in positions of power, 'victims' of power structures have less opportunity to determine how they are portrayed in the media, including documentaries. In other words, social, political and economic power confers discursive power, a point forcefully made in a number of sequences in *After Mabo.* One such example occurs 53 minutes into the film within a sequence featuring a media advertisement produced by the National Farmers' Federation ('Can black and white Australians live in harmony, when the High Court's Wik decision on Native Title has created uncertainty, especially for farmers?'). The advertisement points to the ways in which wealthy political lobby groups shape public debate in contrast to indigenous people who, frequently, are not able to attain such discursive power.

The theme of access to power, and who has the right to speak for whom and on what basis, is evident in other sequences. Early in the documentary Aboriginal spokesperson Noel Pearson raises the theme when he says (in voice-over): 'When we say representative, we're not replacing the real decision makers, being the traditional owners, rather we're just taking instructions from people.' (Pearson's comment initiates something of a pun in the documentary around the multiple significations of 'representation' – media representation and political representation.)

Later, Galarrwuy Yunupingu argues that it is Aboriginal law which gives him the right to speak. Law as a form of discourse threads its way through the documentary. The Mabo case, which appears to assert the legal right to land of some Aborigines, is contested by farmers, miners and the government, and Prime Minister John Howard argues that that law will be determined by Parliament, not by the courts. Yunupingu comments that the Wik Amendments will allow white interests to 'steal the land by your law'.

A second device by which the observational mode is challenged is by regularly cutting away from events, or freezing the frame or adding visual layers to the frame. This device challenges the realism and transparency of the image, and thus its ability to unproblematically present events. The observational mode frequently works to efface the position of 'enunciation', or to draw attention away from the constructed nature of the documentary. The content of the documentary is usually seen as more important than the form, which, particularly in expository modes of documentary, is regarded as secondary. *After Mabo*, on the contrary, constantly works to foreground the enunciation. In this way it does not construct a singular unified narrative from a single position of 'truth'. Indeed, one of the central concerns of this work, as with many previous works by John Hughes, is a concern to challenge the distinction between 'content' and 'form'.

Although dealing with contemporary events, *After Mabo* uses a range of 'archival' resources to place events into a historical perspective, including footage from television news broadcasts and from three earlier Australian films, one fiction and two non-fiction. The use of archival footage has a long history in the documentary and can be traced back to the work of Esfir Shub. Shub reworked and recontextualised home-movie footage of the Tzars in pre-revolutionary Russia to produce a powerful pro-revolutionary work of compilation. The transformation of postmodern economies from industrial to post-industrial has been accompanied by an increasing recognition that information itself is a commodity with commercial potential. This process, along with the development of sophisticated databases, has fostered a renewed theoretical interest in the role of the archive in culture and commerce. Hughes has regularly used archival resources in his work, indeed sometimes using the same footage in a number of works.

In his use of archival resources Hughes is particularly influenced by the work of the cultural critic Walter Benjamin. *One Way Street* (1993) is the documentary which most develops this interest. In this film Benjamin's words are used to make the point that 'quotations in my works are like robbers by the roadside who make an armed attack and relieve the idler of his convictions'. In reviewing the film Anna Dzenis observed that 'meanings and significances multiply, reflect and act as counterpoint to each other', an observation which is equally true of *After Mabo*, which, it could be argued, is composed entirely of quotations.

These take a number of forms. A striking feature of the visual style is the use of on-screen quotations, a feature of such diverse documentaries by Hughes as *Changing Schools* (1985) and *One Way Street* itself. Hughes' on-screen quotations have something of the style of a PowerPoint presentation as they slide up from the bottom of the screen, or emerge from the image itself. While PowerPoint is proprietary software, it has also become the dominant presentational technology in the corporate world (and, increasingly, in education) with both a developing aesthetic and a mode of 'knowledge production' of its own. As Edward Tufte has pointed out, the PowerPoint mode and aesthetic is particularly suited to an instrumental, instructional mode of thinking, and it seems fitting that Hughes uses such a style of quotation in a manner which can be read as subversive of such an instrumental mode. At the same time the quotations are reminiscent of the captions and titles increasingly used in television news programmes.

Quotations in *After Mabo* are not, however, restricted to the verbal register. Much of the film consists of visual and musical quotations and fragments culled from documentaries, television news broadcasts, television coverage of Parliament and music recordings such as Richard Frankland's *Long Tall Ships* and Yothu Yindi's *Treaty*. Commenting on this process in 1993 Hughes emphasised his approach when he stated that 'it's almost as though the work is constructed from, explicitly, a whole series of quotations', a point which is true of *After Mabo* and *One Way Street*. In both films, as Hughes observed, the use of quotation 'creates an immanent critique of the politics of representation … and ideology'. Among these fragments images, sounds and words become objects to be reworked, and recontextualised. The most obvious form of this approach is in the digital composite images which frequently serve as transitions from one part of the work to another, while at the same time developing the 'poetic dimension of image': the visual arts practice evident in Hughes' work from documentary collaborations with visual artist Peter Kennedy, art historian and curator Betty Churcher and earlier work on the cultural practitioner George Seelaf.

An example serves to make a number of points about such composite images. However, it is important to resist the temptation to read the images reductively, reducing them to some single, simplistic meaning. Rather I point to a number of ways in which the image, in collage style, addresses central issues in the documentary. The image, originally in colour and reproduced as the frontispiece to this chapter, is of Prime Minister John Howard addressing a number of people who appear to be media. The apparatus of the media is evident in the microphones in front of the lectern behind which Howard is standing, in the movie light above his head, in the number of microphones visible, and in the amount of cabling associated with the microphones. The lectern, which provides a pulpit-like solidity for Howard, features a stylised image of Federal Parliament House. All of these elements suggest that this is one of several media events which appear in the documentary – many of the events featured (press conferences, door stops and so on) have been specially set up for the media. Howard is flanked by the Australian flag, one of several symbols of the state and of his discursive power. The compositional logic of the image is centred on Howard. It is significant that the camera taking the shot on which this image is based is positioned low to the floor, and between rows of seats, creating a marginalised spectator position. On one level, then, this image participates in the discourse about media representation being constructed by the documentary.

Also evident in the image, as another layer, and further directing the eye to Howard, is a sheet of Prime Ministerial headed paper titled 'Wik 10 point plan'. Balancing this, in the right foreground of the image is a shot of Mick Dodson, a significant indigenous leader, and one of the negotiators and representatives who features in a number of observational sequences in the documentary. The composition situates Dodson next to Howard and his ten-point plan. Dodson is in the foreground, not part of the proceedings, but not to be ignored.

This complex image is one of many in the film in which ideas are presented in the form of evocative, allusive images. The visual and discursive complexity of the image opens a space for viewers to speculate and to question events, situations and their interpretations, rather than closing down debate by providing answers and solutions to the issues being raised by the documentary. The fragmentary nature of the documentary problematises the claim to a single unmediated truth, and dissolves continuities of time and space which commonly provide for the audience a position of knowledge and certainty about the events being portrayed. This approach seems appropriate in a documentary dealing with debates about 'certainty' in relation to land rights; however, this is not to say that the documentary lacks a clear perspective. The sympathies of the documentary are quite properly with the indigenous peoples of Australia, those who have the lesser power in the situation. The justice of their claims is made poignantly apparent in the final sequence in which Mary (Gunid) Tarran, standing on the edge of the land overlooking the sea, says: 'I believe in reconciliation. I believe in justice too. We're not here because we want to be here. I mean I love to be here, but not looking at those things, but we're here for a purpose. For the truth.'

Peter Hughes

REFERENCES

Davis, Paul (2003) '"Between Fact and Fiction": Speculating on the Documentary with John Hughes', *Metro*, 136, 108–11.

Dzenis, Anna (1993) 'John Hughes', *One Way Street*, *Cinema Papers*, 95, 33–5.

Hughes, Peter (1993) '"A Way to be Engaged with the World": the Films of John Hughes', *Metro*, 93, 46–55.

Leahy, Gillian (1996) 'Fidelity, Faith and Openness: Rescuing Observational Documentary', in *Media International Australia*, 82, 40-47.

Sklan, Carole (1988) 'John Hughes: Interview', in John Hughes, Peter Kennedy, David Malouf and Nancy Underhill (eds) *The Stars Disordered: John Hughes' All That is Solid*. Brisbane: University Art Museum.

Tufte, Edward (2003) *The Cognitive Style of PowerPoint*. Cheshire, CT: Graphics Press.

CHOPPER

19

ANDREW DOMINIK, AUSTRALIA, 2000

The opening sequence of writer and director Andrew Dominik's award-winning first feature, *Chopper* (2000) introduces – with great economy – the film's primary concerns. Initially, a disclaimer appears noting that the film 'is a dramatisation in which narrative liberties have been taken'. Later in the sequence a credit acknowledges that the film is adapted from the books of Melbourne's infamous ex-criminal turned popular author and media raconteur, Mark Brandon Read. The books are rambling yet vivid accounts of Read's life story. The personal mythology that surrounds Read (or as he is more commonly known, Chopper), the disclaimer and the acknowledgement all signal that this film is less concerned with revealing the facts behind the fabrications than undertaking an examination of the complexities of this glib, violent and colourful character. As the sequence continues we are introduced to Chopper, vividly portrayed by Eric Bana. In the reflected blue glare of a small television set, a thin trail of cigarette smoke wafting through the air, we see Chopper sitting on a prison bunk in a dark, narrow cell. Along with two prison wardens, he watches himself on the television being interviewed by a female news reporter. He sits with his legs spread, arms akimbo, the bulk of his torso a decorative canvas of prison-yard tattoos. His posture exemplifies a bulldog machismo. He talks and jibes, revelling in his celebrity status. On the small television screen Chopper in close-up, all silver dentures and handlebar moustache, argues that there are no victims to his crimes – only drug dealers.

Read is a 'one man war on drugs'. He enacts moral outrage, arguing that an influx of drugs has ruined the criminal world and could ruin so-called 'normal society' too. When asked for his opinion of himself, he sardonically replies, 'I'm just a normal bloke, a normal bloke who likes a bit of torture.' He then laughs, the screen goes black and the title of the film appears. The credit sequence continues: the sped-up time-lapse footage of a blue sky studded with white, puffy clouds casts fleeting shadows on the barbed-wire crowned stone walls, buildings and watch towers of Melbourne's Pentridge prison. The sequence is now infused with the sound of Frankie Laine's dulcet tones crooning Cole Porter's 'Don't Fence Me In'. The ironic allusion to the freedom of the western and its violent anti-hero is here humorous and strong.

It is impossible to disengage the personal mythology of the media figure Mark 'Chopper' Read from his characterisation in this film and the film's initial popularity, at least in Australia. Produced on a low budget, the film became a box office success. Read has spent nearly half of his life incarcerated, much of it in the notorious H division of Melbourne's now closed Pentridge prison. Although Read had no direct involvement with the film, nor received payment for the sale of the film rights, he did suggest to Dominik that the comedian Eric Bana would be appropriate to play him. His suggestion proved uncannily perceptive and the film helped launch Bana's international acting career.

Born in Melbourne in 1954, Read was first arrested in 1971. His crimes include attempting to kidnap a County Court judge, murdering a fellow inmate, assault and arson. He survived a brutal stabbing and at one point, fearing for his life, forced another inmate to slice off his (Read's) ears in a drastic action to ensure he would be moved out of H Division. He was acquitted of the murder of minor criminal 'Sammy the Turk'. This is only one of the 19 murders he has claimed to have committed. As Read has spent close to half his life in prison it seems appropriate that the film is structured in two parts and functions as a series of interior set pieces. The first section begins in 1978 and is set in the bleak and constrictive cells of H Division, where much of the film was actually shot. It deals with pivotal moments, including Chopper's murder of a fellow inmate, his stabbing by Jimmy Loughnan (Simon Lyndon) and the ear-slicing episode. Bana as Chopper is fresh-faced, lean and strangely sweet. There is a kind of manic energy about him as his behaviour skitters from shocking violent action to hesitation and uncertainty.

The second section of the film begins with Chopper's release in 1986. It focuses on Melbourne's underworld and its patronage of the infamous 'Bojangles', a sleazy night club where deals were struck, and guns and drugs bought and sold. After nearly a decade of incarceration, Chopper's expression has settled into a scowl and his body is now bloated. This half of the film explores Chopper's attempts to find a place in the outside world, his increasing isolation and escalating paranoia. The section culminates in the court case for the murder of 'Sammy the Turk' (Serge Liistro). Although acquitted of the murder on the grounds of self-defence, Chopper is sentenced to five years for maliciously wounding (for the second time) drug dealer Neville Bartos (Vince Colosimo), not to mention other 'assorted scallywag behaviour'. The film then completes its cycle by returning to the opening sequence.

On his release from prison in 1991 Read published his first book, *From the Inside: The Confessions of Mark Brandon Read*. A chaotic embellishment of his life, the book became a bestseller. He continued to write and published another nine books to further success, as well as releasing two music and spoken word recordings. His portrait by Adam Cullen won the Archibald portraiture prize in 2000. To the chagrin of many, Read has also published a children's book, and has mounted an exhibition of his paintings. Although his celebrity status has outraged law enforcement agencies and 'victims against crime' groups, the success of his books and his sensationalist antics have garnered him much media attention. He has been a guest on most of Australia's top-rated television and radio shows. In fact, his drunken appearance on the Australian Broadcasting Corporation's chat show *McFeast Live* jeopardised the funding for Dominik's film, which took seven years to complete.

The *Sydney Morning Herald* in 2000 noted that 'in a country that once served as a massive jail, Australian filmmakers and audiences have long had a fascination with crooks and prison life'. Indeed, the point can be demonstrated in a number of films, beginning with Norman Dawn's *For the Term of His Natural Life* (1927), one of the earliest films in this genre. By having David Field play Keithy George, an inmate that Chopper kills in a power struggle, Dominik ensures a resonance with several other Australian prison dramas. Field played the deranged Wenzil in John Hillcoat's deeply disturbing prison drama *Ghosts ... of the Civil Dead* (1988) which was banned by the Queensland Government. *Everynight ... Everynight* (1994) by Alkinos Tsilimidos, based on Ray Mooney's play about his experiences in prison, focuses on Christopher Dale, again played by Field, a man on remand. Yet apart from a public fascination with the criminal world, Read's story exemplifies a national fascination with outlawed 'social' bandits. The kind of Robin Hood mythology embedded in the national preoccupation with figures such as Ned Kelly is present in a bastardised form in the case of Read. The celebration of this self-proclaimed murderer is activated through his anti-drug stance and his righteous appeal that he only terrorises drug dealers and armed robbers. Critics Felicity Holland and Jane O'Sullivan argue that, historically, literary and filmic representations of Australian criminal masculinity have 'validated law-breaking as mere larrikinism – the high spirits and anti-authoritarianism of Ned Kelly or Mick Dundee'. However, they note, films like *Blackrock* (1997) and *The Boys* (1998) have reconsidered iconic assumptions about violence and Australian masculine culture. Holland and O'Sullivan argue that the films' critique of criminal masculinity represented in these films disturbs and offers a counterpoint to the myth of masculinity. These representations focus on the 'demonic rather than the heroic, and the interrogatory rather than the celebratory'. Such insights are astute, but Chopper seems more truly a 'lethal larrikin' than the humourless male protagonists of *Blackrock* or *The Boys*. There is no rejoicing in those characters' anti-authoritarianism, whereas with Bana's portrayal of Chopper we slide between celebration and condemnation, between attraction and repulsion.

Although having worked in advertising and made music clips, with *Chopper* Dominik focused on performance rather than design. Subordinated to performance, production design here works through the development of a strong but simple mood driven by colour and constricted space. This focus on performance distinguishes the film from many other Australian films that are more concerned with narrative clarity. What Bana as Chopper captures so brilliantly is the performative element of Read's gift for attracting attention. He is like some wheeling-and-dealing side-show alley spruiker flogging a range of endless interpretations of his actions. All the while, his performance is animated with familiar masculine, attention-grabbing gestures: the restless flicking and dusting of cigarette ash; the pursed lips and scowl; the rhythmic and definitive hand movements.

Initially, there is a boyish humour to Chopper's behaviour. When we first meet the young Chopper he is in a shared recreation yard in H Division. The whitewashed stone walls and the flourescent gloom of the prison feel repressive. The yard is divided by loyalties. At one end Chopper and his mates sit around a table, eyeing off their rivals. At the other end of the room, Keithy George and his gang mirror their behaviour. While Keithy marks his territory by pacing up and down, the garrulous Chopper whispers and jokes with his mates. He launches a verbal attack on Keithy and easily outsmarts the older criminal. Lips pursed, one hand in pocket, the other gesturing, Chopper performs, a sing-song tone to his speech. There is a rising inflection at the end of each line of his witty tirade. It is an inflection generally associated with a gendered reading of uncertainty and questioning in the speech of Australian working-class and suburban women. Here it is shown to be what it so often is, an obvious rhetorical device. It is a performative call to attention, which invites a form of response. He playfully jests with Keithy, saying that bashing him was 'good for a bit of giggle'. The embittered Keithy calls him insane, but Chopper just continues to relentlessly insult him: 'You've got a head that needs regular panel-beating.'

Speaking in 2002, Dominik commented that his initial interest in the project occurred after his second reading of Read's first book. What fascinated Dominik about Read was the chaotic and contradictory nature of his thought patterns and point of view. Dominik studied Read's police interviews and court transcripts, tracing the speech patterns and the recurrence of ideas. In the film, the rhythms of Chopper's idiosyncratic and colloquial language are pivotal and complex. For Chopper, meaning seems to be the consequence of action. Through storytelling, he constructs and reconstructs his behaviour. He is utterly confident when in physical action; it is the morality of his conduct that seems to baffle him. So he endlessly recreates narratives for his random actions as a means of justification and as a way to appease moments of intense guilt. The use of idiomatic language brings him and us alike to a sense of recognition and even intimacy. There is something in Chopper's language and humour that a local audience immediately recognises and shares. We sense that in his strange yet familiar world, there is nothing worse than been called a 'sook'.

Through tight framing and a relentless focus on the figure of Chopper, Dominik creates a sense of entrapment. In the first part of the film, we are constricted to the confined and bland interiors of prison cells, with an occasional cut-away to a shot of an empty, ominous prison corridor lined with the doors of cells and suffused with artificial light. In this world, the young Chopper is a beacon of brightness, energy and life. But his warmth and charm can swiftly turn to shocking menace, before reverting to a kind of ambiguous regret. In the sequence after Chopper's verbal attack on Keithy, we see him flanked by wardens being led back into the prison yard. Chopper stands by the barred cell door, head hung low, breath laboured; he looks to both sides and then determinately crosses the line into Keithy's end of the yard. Chopper grabs Keithy and, in slow motion, repeatedly and ferociously stabs him, all the while voicing a primeval scream. He then swiftly heads back to his side of the yard. In shallow focus, shadowy figures pace while blood spurts from Keithy's wounds, as he drops to his knees and, in unison with the blaring climax of a race call, collapses to the floor.

We return to Chopper panting, almost crying. He rocks back and forth, his face contorted, chest heaving. He quietly curses to himself. It is as if he is shocked by his own action; it is as if he could not help himself. The other prisoners huddle at either end of the room as Chopper begins to edge his way along the wall to where Keithy lies in an ever-increasing, slippery pool of his own black-red blood. With concern evident in the gentle tone of his voice, Chopper asks, 'Are you alright, Keithy?' Apologising, he tells him not to worry, that the 'screws' are coming, and lights him a cigarette. Keithy, trying to stop the blood pumping from his wounds, yells, 'You bash people for no reason, just to make a name for yourself.' In an instant, Chopper's mood changes. He acknowledges that he now runs the division, and, joking, begins to make fun of Keithy. When we next see Chopper, he is being interviewed about the attack. He systematically voices well-rehearsed stories to cover all his mates' whereabouts, but seems shocked to hear that Keithy is dead.

Dominik has noted that with *Chopper* he 'wanted to explore the consequences of violence from the point of view of a perpetrator'. In the film, Chopper acknowledges that he dreams about his violent actions. Chopper is in every scene and the camera works to suggest his segregation and isolation through framing. Inside prison, he is lonely and fearful; outside prison he is paranoid that everyone is looking at him. In Chopper's world, anyone who is not your best mate is always a combatant. Even in peacetime, he says, 'nothing's ever forgotten', 'they're still your enemies'; 'it's just human bloody nature'. Yet when his two best mates turn on him, he seems incapable of retaliation. From a low angle, we see Chopper flanked by Jimmy and his other mate, Bluey (Dan Wyllie), talking and pacing in a cell. Suddenly Jimmy turns on Chopper and we hear the impact of a blow. Chopper's body registers the impact but his face does not acknowledge any pain. Jimmy stabs him again and in close-up we see an incredulous look on Chopper's face as disbelief and hurt illuminate his dark eyes. He slowly looks down, touches the blood seeping through his jacket and looks in wonder at the drops falling on his boots. He holds up his hand and, in a surreal moment, patiently asks Jimmy to 'hang on a minute' as he places his half-rolled cigarette in his pocket.

With bafflement evident in the tone of his voice, he asks Jimmy what he thinks he is doing. Jimmy stabs him repeatedly. Chopper's body shudders from the thrusts; he turns, moves away and then back to Jimmy. But instead of attacking, he hugs him to his chest. In the middle of the room in the midst of the embrace, Jimmy says he is sorry. Again we have an apology after a violent action. There is a sense in which these men's actions seem predestined. It is as if they are hard-wired to perform violence, without thought of consequence. Chopper, with a soothing lilt to his voice, pats Jimmy on the back and, like a father, tells him that 'it's all right'. In the corner of the cell Bluey looks on and writhes in agitation. But then Jimmy breaks the embrace. He viciously stabs him again and this time we see the pain register on Chopper's face. Chopper gingerly takes a few paces up and down, as if trying to ascertain the damage, as if trying to make sense of what is happening. He looks Jimmy in the eye and says, 'If you keep stabbing me you're going to kill me.' Jimmy lunges again, but this time Chopper grabs him close and in a lover's gesture gently rests his forehead against Jimmy's, tousling his hair. But Jimmy lunges again.

Finally, Chopper retaliates and slams him against the wall. Eventually, Jimmy drops the knife and Chopper releases him. He says to Jimmy, 'Full marks for treachery' as he begins to disrobe. Taking off his singlet, some blood smears his forehead. He touches the blood leaking from the numerous wounds on his torso. With muscle-bound, tattooed arms, thick shoulders, smeared forehead and bloodied torso, he resembles some primitive warrior. Adrenalin glistens in his eyes, but instead of pride we sense bewilderment. He chews on his gum and tells Jimmy that it doesn't hurt. Jimmy is now scared that Chopper is going to bleed to death, so he tries to help him. He lies him down on the prison cell floor and cradles his head in his lap. We hear a deep and repetitive ominous chime like the sound of a heartbeat, as Chopper slips into a dream-like state.

Although in the media Chopper takes an anti-drug stance, in the second part of the film his antics are often amphetamine-fuelled. When we first see him on the 'outside', he is walking in a crowd. The camera captures him in close-up slow motion; eight years on and all traces of his youthfulness and vibrancy are gone. He seems huge, his body is ballooned and menacing and he wears a permanent grimace on his face. It is harder to like the older Chopper. The scenes at the 'Bojangles' club are drenched in red, broken up by the insistent throb of a white strobe light. The outside world seems to cause Chopper high anxiety. The consistent use of hot, orange-red lit environments creates a mood and reflects Chopper's inner turmoil and rage.

When Chopper takes his girlfriend Tanya (Kate Beahan) to 'Bojangles', he is greeted like a minor celebrity. Yet he is consistently on the defensive and Tanya acts like a pacifier. Inside the club he is confronted by the drug dealer Neville Bartos (hilariously played by Colosimo). Although Neville limps from a gun wound that Chopper inflicted, with bare chest strung with numerous gold chains, permed hair and tattoos, he tells Chopper he is doing just fine and buys him a drink. Initially, Chopper accepts the drink; his mood then begins to fracture oscillating from a sense of guilt which compels him to apologise to Neville, to making jokes at his expense about 'cripples'. (Throughout most of this half of the film we continually see this escalating, unpredictable behaviour.) Chopper ends up dragging Tanya out of the nightclub, firing into the air with one of his many guns. Sitting in his car outside Tanya's house he apologises, saying that he gets 'a bit schizoid'. But he then accuses her of having an affair with Neville; they fight, and she refuses to let him into her house. Splay-footed, fleshy, dog-faced and sour, Chopper stomps back to his car and starts kicking it; he then marches back up to Tanya's and breaks down her door.

We are repelled when he viciously beats her, head-butts her mother and blames her for his actions. The cheekiness and innocence has gone. Chopper's world is now permanently infused with a kind of numbing sense of rage. However, his hair-trigger temper is as humorous as it is unpredictable. He goes to Neville's suburban house and demands money. When it is not forthcoming, he shoots Neville, but then, in a hilarious move, agrees to take him to the hospital. He becomes a police informer and learns that Neville and the other 'fairy godfathers' have put a contract out on him. His old mate Jimmy Loughnan is supposedly also involved, so Chopper pays him a visit. Jimmy, now hopelessly addicted to heroin, is living with his pregnant partner and children in a run-down flat. The door to Jimmy's flat becomes a screen divide. A dark-clad Chopper stands in the corridor outside Jimmy's door – the corridor is drenched in the dull red we have come to associate with his character. The dishevelled and scrawny Jimmy stands on the inside of the door, his flat infused with a sickly, green gloom. The use of primary and intermediate colours is powerfully suggestive of environment and mood.

Jimmy demands Chopper hand over his weapons. They seem to just keep coming – three guns and a stick of gelignite. Disgusted with the state of Jimmy's flat, Chopper – friendly yet full of veiled threats – queries Jimmy about the contract. He pulls out another hidden gun and holds it to Jimmy's head, demanding information. When he does not get it, he apologises. Jimmy and he then discuss his need to relax. Outside the door of the flat, Chopper gives Jimmy a generous wad of cash so he can look after his family and fix up his flat. As soon as Chopper leaves, Jimmy betrays him, making a call to Neville about his whereabouts – and we begin to understand some of Chopper's paranoia.

Although we cannot easily extricate the personal mythology circulating around Read from Dominik's film, there is much more to *Chopper* than just colloquial appeal. The film's international success suggests as much. Along with an Australian Film Critics Circle Award and several Australian Film Institute awards, *Chopper* also won at the Stockholm Film Festival. Its enthusiastic reception at the Toronto Film Festival convinced US distributors to sign a deal for the film rights. Dominik claims that he initially conceived of *Chopper* as an 'exploitation' or genre film but it ultimately came to life as a study of a pathological and violent character. It is the focus on Bana's performance, actions and environment that warrants the film's broader appeal, and its place in the history of cinema. Some writers have commented on the way in which Bana's enormous weight gain to play the second half of the film reprises Robert De Niro's weight gain in *Raging Bull* (1980). However, Chopper seems to have a closer kin in Scorsese's *Taxi Driver*'s (1976) in which Travis (De Niro again) wipes all the scum off the street. In contrast to Travis, however, Chopper's vigilantism is performed with a great deal more bravado.

As noted, there is a resonance here of another kind of anti-hero, that of the western hero. The snatches of 'Don't Fence Me In' which play in ironic counterpoint over images of prison yards, walls and watchtowers at the beginning of the film have, by its conclusion, come to suggest something significant about violence and institutions. The western hero longs for the freedom of the wide-open plains but his existence has always also embodied a sense of loneliness. Freedom is gained but incurs a loss of social engagement. Having lived the rigid routines of prison existence for half his life, Chopper seems ill-equipped to deal with freedom. In prison, life is containable and friendships enforced by necessity.

On the outside, Chopper is avoided and feared, and the social environment (seems) chaotic and random. Unlike this 'lethal larrikin', the classic western hero is always reluctant to take up violence. However, his obligation to protect society ensures that he must do so, with the result that he is then tainted by his actions. He must leave town or undertake a form of social recuperation. Chopper explodes in spontaneous violent action but is then wracked with guilt. His erratic and violent behaviour puts him outside of 'normal society'. The pathology of his actions ensures that he is ostracised by the criminal world. Dominik has commented that the consequences of violent actions 'come down to one thing: loneliness'. At the end of the film we return to the opening sequence. After they finish watching his television interview, the wardens lock Chopper up. The camera lingers on his bulk, sitting on his narrow bunk in the cramped, cold blue interior of his cell.

Gabrielle Murray

REFERENCES

Dent, Jackie (2000) 'Inside Job', *Sydney Morning Herald (Metro section),* 28 July, 112–13.

Dominik, Andrew (2002) 'Pass on the Hatchet-Chopper', in Raffaele Caputo and Geoff Burton (eds) *Third Take: Australian Film-Makers Talk.* Sydney: Allen and Unwin.

Holland, Felicity and Jane O'Sullivan (1999) '"Lethal Larrikins": Cinematic Subversions of Mythic Masculinities in *Black Rock* and *The Boys', Antipodes,* 13, 2, 79–84.

THE GODDESS OF 1967

CLARA LAW, AUSTRALIA, 2000

The Goddess of 1967 (2000) was released at the turn of the millennium, amid *fin-de-siècle* paranoia and global anxiety. It is a film that explores issues surrounding emergent identities, transforming cultures and changing definitions of home and nation. It is also a film that reflects the late modernist fascination with perception, by prioritising senses beyond the visual and by defamiliarising landscapes. The film pivots on an emerging connection between its Australian and Japanese characters, investigating the vicissitudes of their relationship as they travel from an unidentified outer suburb to an unmapped underground opal mine. It contrasts the 'radar' of the Australian with the wide-eyed, naïve gaze of the tourist. In prioritising form to defamiliarise the landscape, Clara Law's film could be envisaged as Australian/Asian art cinema. In its representation of the landscape as alluring and dangerous it can be compared with Peter Weir's *Picnic at Hanging Rock*. *The Goddess of 1967* and the bigger-budget film *Japanese Story* (2003) provide evidence of the increasing fascination with a connection between Australia and (south-east) Asia. Both films address issues relating to shifts in personal and national identities, multiculturalism and globalisation, home, landscape, gender, spiritualism, materialism and alienation.

The Goddess of 1967 begins with the text: 'I want to buy God.' With this opening message Law highlights the desire for the spiritual within the material world that is represented in the pre-credit sequence, which features dramatically stylised images of Odaiba, the island built on reclaimed land in Tokyo Bay in 1851. Originally Odaiba functioned as a series of fortresses providing a defence against Commodore Perry's Black Ships. The impetus for redesigning Odaiba emerged from the fascination with prototypes for future cities displayed at Expo 1985. With its expanse of empty space and eccentric ultra-modern architecture, Odaiba was rebuilt as a leisure and commercial zone, a space that offered an alternative to the densely populated Tokyo, visible across the bay. The steely blue-grey toned abstracted images of the opening montage are shot from a driverless monorail as it rushes through Odaiba. This pre-credit sequence features the inverted pyramids of the 'Tokyo Big Sight' building and contains glimpses of the polished, reflective surfaces of Kenzo Tange's landmark Fuji Television building. Elliptical shapes and the floating text of the credit sequence allude to the *Alien* series, highlighting the film's science fiction design and dystopian aesthetic. Law's film begins within a highly-stylised commercial space, one that is eerily devoid of humans, introducing the themes of disconnection and alienation. In the first sign of life, JM (Rikiya Kurokawa), or Japanese Man as he identifies himself, is shown travelling through Odaiba on a train holding a mysterious blue box.

For JM a Citroën, the goddess of the film's title, offers the possibility of escape through the fantasy of space travel. The car promises to take him beyond 'Mars', which is how JM describes Tokyo. JM needs the Goddess to complete his identification with Alain Delon's character Jef Costello, in *Le Samouraï* (1967). Jef Costello is an existentialist hit man with a huge collection of keys who steals Citroëns and uses them as getaway cars. Law describes JM's alienation:

> I think he's the product of excessive materialism and the taking over of our life by science and technology and big corporate [organisations] ... He's this guy who's very angry inside, who's very disconnected, who cannot find his connection with the world and people. He spent his life trying to be connected to something, he connects himself to a snake and he's tried to connect himself with this car ... [he is] clinging to an obsolete dream of technological perfection.

The final member of the cast is introduced when JM arrives on the doorstep of a house in outer suburban Australia, asking to see the Goddess. BG (Rose Byrne) answers the door and closes it again, introducing the motif of interruption, something that becomes characteristic of their relationship. *The Goddess of 1967* is a film built on schematic detail with information implied rather than revealed explicitly; it is a film intent on raising more questions than it answers. The narrative avoids the use of dialogue whenever possible. Law says, 'We don't like using dialogue to give information. As much as possible we try to use what is specific to cinema and that is the images.' The film relies on alternative methods of communication, like music, the imposition of text onto the screen, character expression, gesture, framing and an experimentation with cinematography. When BG finally lets JM into her house she reveals that her cousins have been involved in a murder/suicide. Her rawness and detachment is revealed when she leads JM through the house asking: 'Did you see the blood, the brains on the ceiling? He blew her head off with a shotgun, then shot himself. Right between the eyes.' Whilst the effect is explicit, the exact cause is uncertain.

BG stands for Blind Girl, a young woman with a traumatic past. The death of her cousins has left her with their infant daughter and the Citroën, a family heirloom. JM's test drive turns into a five-day trip across Australia, a journey navigated by BG without a map or clear directions. BG is also a sharp shooter. She fires blanks at mysterious men in a Volvo in a road rage incident. BG is both responsible and reckless. She gives the child clear details about the death of her parents and who to call in an emergency before abandoning her at a service station. Whilst this abandonment might seem harsh, it pales in comparison to the depiction of BG's childhood.

The Australian home is represented as a site of danger throughout *The Goddess of 1967*. Initially it is depicted as a murder site, but in a series of flashbacks BG's childhood home becomes tainted with menace and incest, a place where parents cannot be trusted. A flashback, identified by the text 'Ten Years Ago', reveals that BG's grandmother Esther left home amid mysterious circumstances, her blood-stained scarf was found in the abandoned Citroën. BG's mother Marie (Elise McCredie) slips into the role of wife/lover and becomes tormented by her guilty, incestuous love for her father. Marie is unable to protect BG from a lecherous grandfather/father (Nicholas Hope), a character who believes that their isolation sanctions his incestuous behaviour. Marie becomes crazed and attempts to purify herself and BG in an immolation ritual whilst ranting about being unclean and sinful. BG escapes. When BG finally returns to her grandfather/father's home, she finds him living in a subterranean mine, waiting hopelessly for Esther to come home.

Placing the sightless, traumatised heroine and the neophyte traveller hero within dangerous domestic spaces and unfamiliar, stylised landscapes, *The Goddess of 1967* provides a counterpoint to Australian film tradition. Conventionally, Australian cinema portrays its characters as asserting their dominance over an unforgiving landscape. As Ross Gibson argues, 'because it has been presented as so tantalising and so essentially unknowable-yet-loveable, the land has become the structural centre of the nation's myths of belonging'. Rather than re-circulating myths of belonging, *The Goddess of 1967* contests conventional notions of ownership and possession by depicting a landscape that can be alluring, but is also often precarious and alienating. By emphasising the defamiliarisation of location, Law draws parallels between representation of the ancient Australian landscape and the futuristic images of Odaiba.

One mark of Law's 'auteurship' is her engagement with contemporary shifts in the definitions of home and identity. Focusing on a visually impaired protagonist, *The Goddess of 1967* complicates the association between vision and understanding. Law represents the Australian landscape through a combination of JM's direct vision and BG's sensory experience. JM is seeing Australia for the first time and BG understands the landscape through her 'radar', a synaesthetic impression derived from the stimulation of other senses. One shot that is remarkable in expressing the native landscape as nurturing frames BG sleeping in the crevice of a log after having escaped the lascivious advances of the Drummer Boy (Tim Richards). BG is shot from an aerial point of view, surrounded by protective dingos.

As has also been noted by Dian Li, Law's cinema defamiliarises the landscape, producing an uncanny space, a landscape that is both familiar and strange. With the use of an expressive colour palette and abstracted landscapes, *The Goddess of 1967* presents a challenge to a perception that is in danger of becoming automatic and habitual. Law and her cinematographer Dion Beebe produce a location that appears hyper-real. Law and Beebe used a bleach bypass whilst processing the negative to obscure certain colours and to accentuate others. This technique has the effect of giving the scenery a strange, electrified appearance, one that could be interpreted as a displaced expression of the troubled psyches of JM and BG. Whilst the displacement of inner turmoil into the exterior is a sign of the influence of German Expressionism, experimentation with colour links the film to developments in later European art cinema such as Michelangelo Antonioni's *Il Deserto rosso* (*The Red Desert*, 1964) and particularly *Il Mistero di Oberwald* (*The Mystery of Oberwald*, 1981).

Law describes *The Goddess of 1967* as 'a journey of colours'. The first impression of JM's apartment in Tokyo is of a place that is cold and wet. The design is minimalist and the décor features cool, watery blues. Replete with a snorkel and flippers, JM swims through the rooms as if in the ocean. The blue box that he was carrying when we first met him is opened to reveal snap-frozen mice, food for his cold-blooded snakes. Shiny glass surfaces offer the impression of a science laboratory, rather than a home, Odaiba on a domestic scale. In contrast, images of the public spaces of Tokyo, filtered through JM's memory, become saturated in neon colours. Law acknowledges the contrasts central to Japanese culture by placing JM in a plastic tent-like structure challenging a friend to a noodle-eating competition. This make-shift structure sits beneath a train track, producing a contrast between temporary prefabrication and seamless innovation. When JM's friend is hit and killed by a truck on his way home, the shot expands to reveal the train silently snaking along its track, a poignant image of progress unhindered by the tragedy. Law remarks that, 'just showing Tokyo in a film … can make a very succinct point about post-modernism: the wealth and materialism, the sense of isolation, the coolness and the beauty of surfaces.'

The Goddess of 1967 further dislocates its characters from their surroundings with the deployment of back projection, as in scenes where JM first drives the Goddess. In an allusion to Jean-Luc Godard's *Alphaville* (1965), exterior landscapes are superimposed onto the Citroën's bubble windows, effectively producing parallel 'realities' within one shot. The insertion of abstracted external fantasy landscapes extends the futuristic design of the car into outer space. This doubled landscape links the Australian landscape to Mars. Driving the Citroën for the first time, JM remarks that 'it's not like driving, it's like flying'.

With its hallucinatory landscapes, mosaic narrative structure and its complication of a definition of 'home', *The Goddess of 1967* is a film that evades simple generic classification. Whilst it establishes the primary concerns of the family melodrama it repeatedly and violently destroys any conventional family structure. By emphasising mobility, Law's film extends the conventions of the road movie as described by Meaghan Morris, who writes that 'cars promise a rabid freedom, a manic subjectivity: they offer danger *and* safety, violence *and* protection, sociability *and* privacy, liberation *and* confinement, power *and* imprisonment, mobility *and* stasis'. Negotiating each of these binaries and more, *The Goddess of 1967* becomes a hybridised road movie and 'journey film' with the Citroën as the central conductor. Considering the film in terms of the journey broadens its scope and affords the film a mythic edge. Primarily this is a rite-of-passage narrative, a film that is not restrained by roads, nation, space or chronology: a tragic family melodrama with a perverse Oedipal undercurrent that challenges the limitations of genre classification.

As well as evading generic classification, *The Goddess of 1967* also resists industrial categorisation as 'diasporic multicultural cinema', a category outlined by Tom O'Regan. He writes that 'filmmakers like Pauline Chan, Monica Pellizari and Clara Law (*Floating Life* [1996]) are also creating a *diasporic multicultural cinema,* but they suffer the same problems as the mainstream – they can only ever be another instance or a significant variant of a larger international whole'. Rochelle Siemienowicz approaches Law's cinema with a more fluid notion of classification. She argues that this 'allows films to be read and reread not only as individual texts produced by authorial vision and generic conventions, but also sites for intertextual, cross-cultural and transnational struggles over meanings or identities'. Siemienowicz articulates the previously unspoken issue central to the representation of home in Australian cinema: 'The history of Australian national cinema is one of visually claiming the nation as our own, of depicting history, the landscape and the people in such a way as to take possession of them; of allowing a sense of being at home in a place where there is ambivalence about our right to feel at home.' Writing before the release of *The Goddess of 1967*, she argues that persistent and recurring themes in contemporary Australian cinema include displacement, alienation and homelessness, themes that are expressed with sensitivity in Law's cinema.

Law's cinema has been described by Li as 'a poetry of the Chinese diaspora ... Diaspora, for Law, is the ultimate paradox of modern life, a metaphor for all our ambiguities and contradictions in viewing the Self through the prism of the Other'. In *Floating Life* the Chinese-Australian characters are given the dominant vision and voice. Like many of her earlier films, *Floating Life* reflects the fears and anxieties associated with a changing culture and the consequences of this for individual and national identities. The release of *Floating Life* coincided with a marked split in the socio-political approach to immigration in the mid-1990s. This was a moment in Australian history that saw the rise of the One Nation Party with Pauline Hanson delivering her maiden speech in Federal Parliament calling for a restriction on immigration. Hanson argued that the Australian population was in danger of becoming 'saturated' in Asian culture. Hanson's xenophobic remarks emerged as a part of a backlash against the previous Labour Party led by Paul Keating who emphasised the importance and value of perceiving Australia as part of an Asian network.

Law's investigation of evolving definitions of identity and home reflects her interest in the impact of evolution and change. Law grew up in Macau and Hong Kong. She studied film at the National Film and Television School in the UK, graduating with *They Say the Moon is Fuller Here* in 1985. Law returned to Hong Kong to work in radio, television and film. In the early stages of her film career Law became caught up in the demanding pace of the Hong Kong film industry at a time when it valued a high turnover of sensational, kinetic generic hybrids. Law's early films enabled her to transcend constraints imposed by an industry that was geared towards an economic imperative by producing innovative cinema. She quickly became recognised as an important filmmaker within the Hong Kong film industry's 'second wave' and was linked to directors as influential and eccentric as Wong Kar-Wai and Stanley Kwan. Films produced by second wave directors display an interest in cinematic art as a poetic way to capture transformations in cultures and identities.

In Hong Kong Law directed *Wo Ai Tai Kong Ren* (*The Other Half of the Other Half*, 1988) and *Pan Jin Lian Zhi Quian Shi Jin Sheng* (*The Reincarnation of Golden Lotus*, 1989), films that were produced by Teddy Robin Kwan for the Golden Harvest Company. But it was not until 1990 that her films began to attract international attention. In 1990, Law directed *Ai Zai Taxiang De Jijie* (*Farewell China*) starring Maggie Cheung and Tony Leung, a film that explores the desire for immigration to the West, specifically to New York City. She followed this with *Qiuyue* (*Autumn Moon*, 1992), which was written by Law's partner Eddie Ling-Ching Fong. *Autumn Moon* concerns a friendship between a young Japanese tourist in search of the 'taste' of China, and an expert cook, 'Granny'. This premise provides the central force through which Law and Fong examine immigration and the struggle for self-definition amid a turbulent background. With *You Seng* (*Temptation of a Monk*, 1993) Law and Fong produced a big-budget, epic film that focused on issues of loyalty and betrayal in seventh-century China. Its large-scale battle sequences provided an opportunity to travel to Australia to complete post-production. Law and Fong settled in Australia in the mid-1990s, producing both *Floating Life* and *The Goddess of 1967*, and most recently the poetic documentary *Letters To Ali* (2004), films that have enriched Australian filmmaking culture.

Wendy Haslem

REFERENCES

Gibson, Ross (1992) *South of the West: Postcolonialism and the Narrative Constitution of Australia*. Bloomington, IN: Indiana University Press.

Li, Dian (2003) 'Clara Law', *Senses of Cinema: Great Directors – A Critical Database*, http://www.sensesofcinema.com.

Morris, Meaghan (2002) 'Fate and the Family Sedan', *Senses of Cinema*, 19, http://www.sensesof cinema.com.

O'Regan, Tom (1996) *Australian National Cinema*. London: Routledge.

Siemienowicz, Rochelle (1999) 'Globalization and Home Values in New Australian Cinema', *Journal of Australian Studies*, 55.

MOULIN ROUGE!

BAZ LUHRMANN, AUSTRALIA, 2001

Moulin Rouge! (2001) was publicised in Australia as a local achievement, although it could hardly look less 'Australian': it shows no identifiable Australian landscapes, masculine stereotypes or social histories. It is devoid of the Australiana usually associated with Australian cinema. However, this cinematic musical fantasy was, literally, 'made in Australia', and directed by Baz Luhrmann as the third in what is known as his 'Red Curtain' trilogy, movies that present hyper-theatrical versions of idealised romantic worlds (*Strictly Ballroom* (1993) and *Romeo + Juliet* (1996) being the others in the set). The Bazmark production consolidated the turn-of-the-century development of local, big-budget, international 'postmodern' entertainments. Following *Babe* (1995) and *The Matrix* (1999), *Moulin Rouge!* is a similarly internationally-oriented commodity, one whose Australian origins only implicitly inform the realised movie.

The new millennium rendition of the world of the Moulin Rouge boasts an exclamation mark in its title. Perhaps this is to distinguish it from its many namesakes made in Hollywood, England or France (from at least the 1920s). In these films, the red mill and Montmartre are largely little more than the settings for stories of liberation and/or romance. None of the earlier movies so cheekily exploit Moulin Rouge iconography of the bohemian underworld to create hyperbolic fun as Baz Luhrmann's pastiche.

For a movie made in Australia, *Moulin Rouge!* is exceptionally ambitious. Indeed, many critics saw it as self-indulgent and excessive. Statistical superlatives litter the websites that proclaim the movie's status as the most elaborate local production ever. Over 750 crew worked on the film, and it also employed 650 extras and took more than 180 days to shoot on five sound stages at Fox Studios in Moore Park, Sydney. Total production costs exceeded $50 million. This figure is also celebrated in the fan-sites through reference to such book-of-records trivia as the fact that it took sixty crew members to handle make-up and hair styling (85 coloured wigs were made for the film).

Of more importance is the fact that *Moulin Rouge!* employed the sophisticated Fox Studio facilities and was shot almost entirely on the complex sets built there. In this respect, it echoes the studio musicals of the 1950s and 1960s that created theatrical sets in huge sound stages for their operetta-style productions. Like the Arthur Freed musicals made by MGM, *Moulin Rouge!* achieves very high production values in art direction, lighting, costumes and, of course, in dance and musical arrangement and performance. The technological revolution effected through digitisation, however, has meant that, in 1999, post-production options were emerging that MGM directors could not have imagined in the 1960s. For example, *Moulin Rouge!*'s post-production advanced the integration of optical and digital effects shots by virtue of Sydney-based Atlab's facilities and expertise. Rachel Turk has discussed these and other technical innovations:

> When Godfrey [Chris Godfrey, visual effects supervisor] and Bazmark approached Animal Logic Film, Catherine Martin and the design team had created 300–400 design stills and rough-cut sequences. Everything created by the effects house over the following eighteen months – previsualisation, 3D animation, art direction, digital composing, development of proprietary software – was designed to serve the vision. 'This was the main achievement of Animal Logic', says Godfrey, 'matching the visual effects beautifully with the overall theatrical style. This had to be as inspirational as the rest of the movie without consuming it.'

Meticulous attention to the subtleties of film grading before optical effects were produced was a signature of the sophisticated post-production team. Selecting frames from longer takes and matching effects to the original shots that surround them had to be seamlessly achieved to give the film its painterly, Hollywood-studio subtleties. Dominic Case points out that Luhrmann and designer Catherine Martin wanted lush and vivid Parisian colours, but set 'in the context of the grey industrial poverty that the patrons and the girls came from'. Post-production involved meticulous attention to detail: 'Atlab's optical department produced about 500 optical effects shots, delivering, among other effects, speed changes … dissolves and other transitions, and a number of very fast cutting or one-or-two-frame sequences, which are too short to splice together in the negative itself.'

The sophistication of cinematographers and of post-production laboratories has been lauded in relation to other Fox-studio productions such as *Babe* and *The Matrix* and their sequels. Each of these productions also involved elaborate, innovative digital effects. *Moulin Rouge!* consolidated Fox Studios' reputation for Australian technical sophistication and ingenuity. Designers, technical crews and facilities were predominantly local, and the hyper-real musical that looked like an extended music video was celebrated as an 'Australian' production, even though, culturally, it appeared as far from Uluru and Australiana as one can imagine. Of course, the nationality of the crews and location of the digital facilities is invisible on the screen, but, in the global entertainment industry, local success could be claimed for the significant artistic and technical achievements of the internationally-financed production. With Nicole Kidman's visibility as an Australian/international 'star', the movie was able to wear its 'made in Australia' badge with the pride usually reserved for international sporting success.

Moulin Rouge! clearly aims to arrest the attention of global audiences. It is a star-studded commodity that makes no apologies for its commercial intent, even as it seeks to transcend the art-or-commerce divide. Its production credits are part of its authenticity as local-yet-global. Don McAlpine's elegant photography, Jill Bilcock's dizzying editing, Animal Logic and others' visual effects – none needs to represent anything 'real', let alone 'Australian', to demonstrate the quality of this really Australian production.

Moulin Rouge! is more than a 'movie'. As a commodity it is integrated with other commercial merchandising: a DVD, a worldwide web-based 'club'. Consumers (what used to be called 'audiences') can do more than just go to see *Moulin Rouge!* at the cinema. They can re-play selected sequences, numbers, effects or images, and participate in on-line discussions about the movie and its stars. As a cultural product, *Moulin Rouge!* is the key element in a larger range of sophisticated digital merchandise. It can be owned and enjoyed in various modalities, domestically or on-line. While this is true of many movies, *Moulin Rouge!* seems to have been designed to be *the* postmodern musical experience or, more accurately, audiovisual experience, ideally suited for DVD which was emerging as the new medium of domestic entertainment when the film was made. Having no plot to speak of (though it presents a skeleton story) the film is a hybrid form – simultaneously both cinematic whole and music-video parts. *Moulin Rouge!* is a new kind of movie, one that fully exploits the technologies of production *and* of distribution afforded by the digital age.

At the close of the twentieth century, Australian export earnings were increasingly derived from tourism, education, wine and entertainment, and less from raw materials, wool and meat, the staples of the early postwar years. Being an Anglophone, European (though self-proclaimed 'multicultural') culture meant that Australia had natural advantages in the globalising technological and cultural economies of a world where nationalistic frontiers as well as culture borders between 'high' and 'low' or 'elite' and 'popular' culture were breaking down. In an important sense, as the new century dawns, it is no longer possible to categorise a great many commodities as 'Australian' other than in the limited sense that indicates some features of their production or likely consumption. This is increasingly true of entertainment, especially *post*modern films, whose identities and origins are as hybrid and provisional as their audiences are ethnically and culturally diverse.

Even the film's reviews called it 'postmodern'. So what might this term mean and why is it so apt for *Moulin Rouge!*? Such a utopian fantasy might seem to be a quintessentially *modern* homage to the cultural world that grew out of the industrial revolution and was powered by electricity and Western capital. Set at the cusp of the nineteenth and twentieth centuries, but made at the end of the twentieth, *Moulin Rouge!* does, however, *reflect on* rather than merely *reflect* modernity and its cultures. It does this in aesthetic terms that are usually defined as *post*modern. Jim McGuigan offers a concise definition of the utopian postmodern aesthetic as 'a pervasive pick-n-mix and commodified culture in which modern boundaries between forms, media and spheres of social activity are crossed … and dissolved'.

'Post' implies an aesthetic that celebrates anachronism, 'depthlessness' (superficiality, or at least surfaces), playful irony or parody, and an audience already 'in the know'. Other than *Moulin Rouge!*, the most flamboyantly postmodern Australian cultural example of this century is the Opening Ceremony of the Sydney 2000 Olympic Games. Here, historical clichés, pop musical styles (even for the singing of the national anthem!) and postcard clichés of geography and culture were used to celebrate a vibrant multicultural community that appeared modern but not historically very specific. Australia became an imagined and imaginary place, recognised, but not necessarily understood, by many millions of viewers worldwide. *Moulin Rouge!* adopts a similar aesthetic of overstatement, spectacle, pastiche, sentimentality and anachronism. History is just another set of images to play with in what Baz Luhrmann calls his 'comic, tragic, operatic cinema' in which his signature is patent, or maybe blatant: artifice as art, energetic, feelgood stories, colour, movement and animation-style caricature.

Moulin Rouge! glorifies the postcard nostalgia of place and period, proclaiming what Roland Barthes might have called their 'French-ness' – the connotative complexities of an idealised, un-real and self-contained social world where passion is more passionate, art more artistic, life more lively (and fun is more fun), than in any real nineteenth-century city. Though the city is shown as an underworld, it is the antithesis of, say, the grimy London, etched by

Dickens' prose or the alienating early modern metropolises that replaced Montmartre in the early twentieth-century Modernist imagination.

Montmartre is, literally, a utopia – a 'no-place' of immaterial delights, though also an actual place haunted by the doomed stories of Continental Romanticism. It is an imaginary and imagined place, where men write and paint using their minds and women dance and entertain with their bodies; a virtual world where virtue can only be discerned below the layers of taffeta and lipstick by the true Romantic hero – predictably a writer, an 'enchanted, nature boy', an innocent seer, who wanders into this heavenly Hades from 'very far, very far, over land and sea'. The innocent author from afar, mesmerised but also seduced by the dark enticements and glittering sensuality of the modern underworld suggests the stereotypical Australia abroad – is it too far-fetched to see *Moulin Rouge!* as a peculiarly *Australian* re-vision (as in seeing again) of the myth of Orpheus or of the Hindi equivalent echoed in the Bollywood parody that climaxes the movie.

Moulin Rouge! can be seen as a film that enthusiastically celebrates what the modern Bohemian cultures of Europe have become in the popular imaginings of postmodern Western world at the turn of the millennium. It is possible to see the innocent abroad, the 'nature boy' of the refrain, as a figure that Australian audiences in particular will recognise – a sentimental bloke, perhaps? After all, the object of his naïve affections, the cancan dancer with a heart of gold, is none other than a movie-made-perfect image of 'our Nicole', Satine. Kidman is the very image of the movie star, and self-consciously performs and parodies herself, singing and dancing beyond her assumed abilities – 'I didn't know Nicole could sing!'

Moulin Rouge! is not a conventional movie in the sense that allows for discussion of plot, characters or themes. Rather, it offers novel kinds of audiovisual, theatrical and cinematic *experiences*. If audiences enjoy its particular rhythms, references, refrains and quotations, it will speak of their participatory involvement, of 'humming along'. They will admire the glamorous way Kidman is shot, or marvel at her surprising voice. To enjoy *Moulin Rouge!* is to go to a party, a fancy dress party, in costumes and masks, in a dance hall of postcard icons from *la belle epoch* and Hollywood movies, and to immerse oneself in a soundscape of musical bric-à-brac, from Offenbach to Elton John.

It is important to remember that *post* does not just mean 'after', though perhaps it means 'beyond', and therefore it connotes the self-conscious quotation of the clichés of modernism. Thus, it may celebrate not criticise, and enjoy not reject, the originals it refers to or recycles. As Marsha Kinder notes in *Film Quarterly*:

Moulin Rouge demonstrates the international scope of the musical, tracing the ... genre to its roots in European vaudeville, cabaret culture, stage musicals and operas ... Bombay-Masala films ... *The Umbrellas of Cherbourg* ... *Yellow Submarine* ... and – from outback and down under – its Aussie director's ... *Strictly Ballroom*.

Postmodern culture often deals with the remnants of modernist representations, emptying their clichés of their original meanings and, instead, playing with their semiotic husks: surface and signs, not depth and significance. Yet the originals need to be recognised if the audience is to have fun. So the postmodern consumer at least knows there once was a song, a city, a star 'like that'. *Moulin Rouge!* is obviously a pastiche, having fun with 'cult' icons as recent as Madonna (whose sexual bravado is 'camply' parodied in 'Like a Virgin'). Yet it also indulges in the sentimentality of other popular songs ('Nature Boy', 'One Day I'll Fly Away'). The moods and degrees of parodic inflection of the various songs vary widely. 'Diamonds are a Girl's Best Friend' (from *Gentlemen Prefer Blondes* (1953), starring Marilyn Monroe) is presented in 'straight' cabaret style. The young lovers' story would become maudlin unless distanced by the parodic styles Luhrmann invokes. Anyway, *Moulin Rouge!* gives its audience too little time to cry!

Theatricality itself is ironised affectionately throughout: the proscenium arch, the curtains opening to reveal a joke at the expense of Twentieth Century-Fox. Christian (Ewan McGregor) is both parodied and presented as truly 'Romantic', despite being such a cliché: 'There was a boy, a very sad, enchanted boy...' fades up over a refrain from *The Sound of Music* ('The hills are alive...' though, mercifully, without the lyrics). And the story itself is also pure cliché – the secret lovers; the dying courtesan; the innocent writer; the jealous Duke; the story-in-the-story. Only within the movie's camp aesthetic could the narrator get away with lines like: 'a force darker than jealousy and stronger than love had begun to take hold of Satine'; or 'no lie, however brilliant, would save Satine'. Despite this, many of the musical numbers that move the story along are presented without irony. Duets involving the sentimental bloke (Christian) and Satine, for instance, 'Come what may ... till my dying day' and 'Roxanne', arranged as a dark tango, are both presented without any obvious parodic intent.

The use of stylised (especially blue-tinted) close-ups increases as Satine's tragic fate looms. Again, the self-conscious ramifications of pathos sit quite comfortably with the theatrically-clichéd comic antics of the murderous Duke (Richard Roxburgh) and the chorus that seeks to protect Satine. Bollywood climax notwithstanding, the film closes with the pathos of Satine's death and the immortality of romantic love, or at least, the recyclability of romantic pop songs that proclaim love until death, 'come what may', because 'The greatest thing you will ever learn is just to love and be loved in return.'

By any criterion of musical originality, *Moulin Rouge!* sounds undistinguished. But 'originality' is not the point: instead it re-cycles and frequently parodies (albeit, lovingly) popular songs from the last century. Ensemble dancing, choruses and musical duets rather than solo performances (dance or vocal) predominate. This contrasts with, say, Fred Astaire or Gene Kelly musicals, or even *Oklahoma!* (1955) or *The Sound of Music* (1965), in which individual virtuosity as well as ensemble celebration are highlighted. Romantic solos by Satine or Christian quickly merge into duets symbolising their love, and these tend, in turn, to lead into orchestrally rich or vocally up-tempo chorus-based songs. Musicologist Theo van Leeuwen notes that these latter arrangements connote 'solidarity, consensus, a positive sense of joint experience and belonging to a group'. The individual lovers' elevated emotions (the higher pitch and extended notes of their signature melodies and lyrics) blend with and are supported (literally) by the community that is the Moulin Rouge. While this musical structure seems unexceptional, it is more seamless than the classic MGM musicals of the 1950s and the earlier Astaire/Rogers showcases.

The success of the film lies in its ability to segue from one mood to another, to hold the emotional movement like an extended violin note, yet to bounce softly into increasingly energetic crescendos and then retreat to the plangent single voice or the pathetic refrain. In this respect *Moulin Rouge!* resembles a conventional musical. The whole film is constructed musically, rather than as a drama with musically intense interludes. The editing and camera mobility are both orchestrated and choreographed as one with the musical refrains and spectacular set pieces. However, these showstoppers do not stop the show. Instead they flow into the continuous flood of image and sound that immerses the audience in the riches of twentieth-century popular culture.

The sound in *Moulin Rouge!* is full, loud, generous. It quite literally *does things* to the audience. As Theo van Leeuwen points out, music (independently of lyrics) has a 'dynamic and interactive character'. Melodies, for instance, may not only 'express tenderness' they may also at the same time caress their listeners, just as a song caresses the lovers in the movie. Musical sounds literally move the listeners who, in turn, respond by moving their body, tapping their feet, singing along, weeping or laughing. The audience in the cinema is incorporated into the film's world by means of the plenitude of its sound – sound literally fills up the space between screen and audience. Solos (interior monologues or voice-over narration) offer only brief breathing spaces in the boisterous sonic world visited by Christian.

The originality and appeal of the energetic vocal arrangements lies in their recognisability and difference – 'Like a Virgin', for instance. The chorus creates, or accentuates the sense that the cabaret is a lively community – an eccentric, motley community where pleasure reigns and everyone participates regardless of status, body shape, gender or talent. The musical plenitude of the many chorus-based renditions enact an egalitarian playground, threatened only by the jealousy and possessiveness of the comically degraded aristocrat (who cannot sing, cannot dance; and so is an interloper!). Energy and sensuality drive the musical set pieces, which create the enclosed social universe that was Romantic Bohemia, a place the various and varied movie's audiences can only visit in their twenty-first-century dreams.

Quadraphonic sound fills the theatre and fills out the visual *mise-en-scène*. *Moulin Rouge!* is 'big' – the fullness of its music is its exclamation mark. Audiences are invited to join this party that celebrates and echoes the popular musical cultures of the century on whose cusp it dances. The kinetic showstoppers transform the original songs and music video performances that they reprise: nostalgia at 100 decibels! Yet the wall of sound will not be broken by these set piece performances, and each is integrated, if not seamlessly, then at least smoothly, into the continuous background musical refrains (often of slow, romantic tempo) that link the action of the chorus-and-dance numbers.

As Rick Altman points out, most (classical Hollywood) musicals 'are designed to move from a preponderance of sexually unmarked novelty or comic numbers in the opening reels, to a heavy concentration of paired or antiphonal songs toward the end'. He suggests that 'quite apart from plot, the tendency of the musical is towards … sexual definition of the film's … principles'. The musical coding of the couple in *Moulin Rouge!* also reflects what Altman sees as a genre rule in American musicals in which a thematic dichotomy is recognised and rehearsed, one side of which 'is closely associated with the work ethic and its values' (literally Christian), 'while the other is devoted to those activities and qualities traditionally associated with entertainment' (Satine, the singer/courtesan, mocking traditional virtue, as in 'Diamonds are a Girl's Best Friend').

In musicals, audience emotions are 'managed', as Heather Laing comments: 'It's kinda nice when a character breaks into song and dance because [this] excuses the greatest euphoria or deepest despair … The excessive emotion can … be shared … the musical forms, especially if familiar to the audience, ensure that emotions never get out of control, that they return to equilibrium.' Through recognition and irony, the emotions provoked by *Moulin Rouge!* are 'controlled'. The tone is therefore self-conscious and playful, and this is, perhaps, appropriately 'Australian': linguistic and intellectual complexity is avoided; innocent sentimentality and a comical, ironic attitude to sex and death prevail. Don't take it all too seriously! It's only a movie!

If, at the turn of the millennium, there can be no 'Australian' film in the sense defined in the 1970s, the local industry can at least offer a gift to the cinema, popular music and their devotees. It is a fun-filled affirmation that Australians understand they are part of European/ American postmodern cultures that now circulate through the digital mediasphere. *Moulin Rouge!* may be seen as a local response to the cosmopolitanism that Paris once signified and that today lives a virtual life via television and cinema. Australia is part of this cultural conversation. The *Moulin Rouge!* carnival asserts Australia's special place in the postmodern cacophony (where, if you listen carefully, you may just hear traces of the ironic Aussie accent, one legitimate inflection among many). So the final 'Red Curtain' trilogy film may be thought of as 'Australian' in the same sense as the Opening Ceremony of the Sydney 2000 Olympic Games. Both proclaimed Australia's right to celebrate its enjoyment of, and participation in, contemporary Western culture. Both the film and the TV spectacle are a kind of 'showing off' (to use an Australianism). They are displays of technological sophistication and of innocent maturity, proclaiming that Australia knows it is part of the postmodern world.

Philip Bell

REFERENCES

Altman, Rick (1987) *The American Film Musical*. Bloomington: Indiana University Press.

Case, Dominic (2001) '*Moulin Rouge!* at the Lab', *Metro*, 129/30, 18–24.

Kinder, Marsha (2002) Review of '*Moulin Rouge*', *Film Quarterly*, 55, 3, 52–9.

Laing, Heather (2000) 'Music and Structure, Emotion by Numbers: Music, Song and the Musical', in Bill Marshall and Robynn Stilwell (eds) *Musicals: Hollywood and Beyond*. Exeter: Intellect.

McGuigan, Jim (1999) *Modernity and Postmodern Culture*. Philadelphia: Open University Press.

Turk, Rachel (2001) 'Children of the Digital Revolution', *Metro*, 129/30, 6–15.

Van Leeuwen, Theo (1999) *Speech, Music, Sound*. Basingstoke: Macmillan.

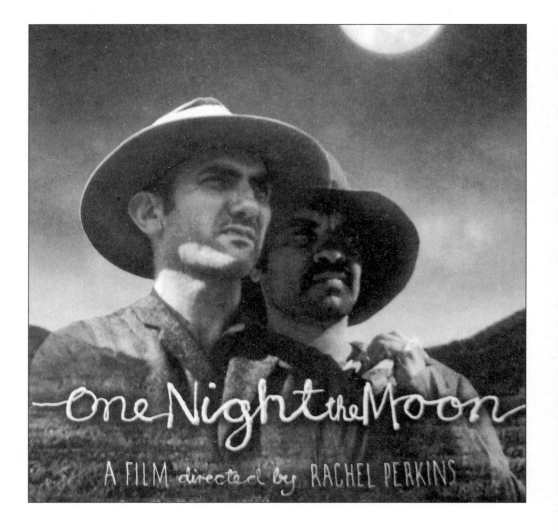

ONE NIGHT THE MOON

RACHEL PERKINS, AUSTRALIA, 2001

It seems curious that one of the most cinematically impressive Australian films ever produced began as a project intended only for television. A small screen, relatively subdued sound reproduction and a domestic viewing area subject to daily life's sporadic distractions comprise a set of conditions that deplete the richness of any film. But *One Night the Moon* (2001), with its mesmerising vistas of outback landscape complemented by arresting music that propels the story and conveys its deepest implications, is particularly enhanced by the cinema's large darkened theatrical space illuminated only by a wide screen. On television it is engaging and provocative, a good watch; in a theatre it is utterly absorbing, a 57-minute immersion into a set of events and their surrounding world that seem more vividly realised than reality itself. There can have been few other instances of 'made for television' movies that have garnered so many screen awards and such lavish praise from film critics as this unorthodox Australian creation.

The originating idea for *One Night the Moon* came from composer Mairead Hannan in response to a public call by ABC Television Arts and Entertainment, Oz Opera, and MusicArtsDance Films for submissions envisaging film projects that would utilise music in ways that made it integral to the narrative. Having viewed with admiration Michael Riley's 1997 documentary *Black Tracker*, which told of the life of his grandfather, the renowned Aboriginal tracker Alex Riley, Hannan conceived of an unorthodox musical narrative that would be based upon an actual 1932 incident in which a white child went astray in the bush and Riley was banned from participating in the search party. A creative team was subsequently assembled to work on the project. The group included, most prominently, Aboriginal activist and singer-songwriter Kevin Carmody; Carmody's friend and sometime collaborator Paul Kelly, one of Australia's internationally famous composer-performers; and the acclaimed playwright, screenwriter and novelist John Romeril. The initial choice for director was Michael Riley, but illness prevented him from participating. Eventually the director's chair was occupied by Rachel Perkins who was at that time already regarded as one of Australia's most brilliant young filmmakers, having previously impressed moviegoers and critics with her luminous and energetic *Radiance* (1998) as well as a number of shorter pieces for television.

One reason why *One Night the Moon* is a remarkable film may be that its production phase was, to a greater extent than is the case with most film projects, a team effort. Hannan has spoken of an elaborate and protracted workshopping process in which the major artists had 'input and ownership all along the way.' Moreover, it appears that there was from the start a sense that all aspects of the project would be susceptible to revision and innovatory departures from narrative and cinematic norms. Thus, for example, Perkins was brought in as director at a relatively late stage – the film was already in production – and her script alterations shifted the emphasis of the narrative more in the direction of the mother's relationship with the child than had been the case in the original conception. Moreover, it was at her instigation that dialogue was pared away from the screenplay to such a degree that the narrative progression became overwhelmingly cinematic and musical. Similarly, the film's distinctively pallid look derives from a suggestion by cinematographer Kim Batterham that the unusual 'bleach bypassing process' be employed to make the colouration subtly less true to what the human eye would normally render. As a result of constant group consultations, even teleconferencing at times, significant alterations and revisions continued right up to the start of shooting. As Perkins has observed, the project 'was challenging in a lot of ways because it was sort of coming up with a new genre.'

Superficially, the story is a simple one that invokes a narrative that has recurred so frequently in Australian cultural history that it must be regarded as a deeply-rooted national nightmare – that of the child lost in the great outback wilderness. A married couple, Jim and Rose Ryan (played Paul Kelly and Kaarin Fairfax), and their 8-year-old daughter Emily (Memphis Kelly) live on a farm in the Flinders Ranges of South Australia in 1936. The little girl, inspired by a favourite bedtime song that gives the film its title, wanders off from home while her parents are asleep on a dreamy full moon night, and does not return. Upon discovering Emily's absence the following morning, Jim appeals to neighbours in the local community to organise a search party. The group is formed quickly, and enlists the aid of Albert (Kelton Pell), the finest 'blacktrakka' in the area. At the critical moment when the party is about to begin its task in earnest, however, the father objects loudly to the presence of an Aboriginal on his property, and in consequence the tracker is banned from participation. Days, then weeks, of attempts to locate the girl are unsuccessful. Eventually Rose seeks out the tracker and asks for his expert assistance. The two trace the girl's route, which proves to have been in the opposite direction from the areas that the search party explored, until her lifeless body is found. She is carried back to the house and placed in the arms of her father.

Afterwards, the two emotionally bereft parents clearly feel alienated from one another, and the father is driven to commit suicide.

Such a retelling of the rudiments of the story belies, however, the richness and complexity of *One Night the Moon*, qualities that are apparent from the very beginning. For although otherwise the film adheres closely to the chronological progression outlined above, its opening is situated just prior to the climactic suicide in the period following the death of the child. At the start of the film the parents are in the throes of grief and despair, but the reason why they are thus stricken is not apparent. While the presence of a daughter is intimated by a brief glimpse of the child's bedroom, she herself is unsighted. And in another respect as well the film challenges the viewer from the outset: it uses music and song to establish characterisations and set the plot in motion before a word of dialogue is spoken. The employment of a format commonly associated with light-hearted musicals in such a context is daring, almost intimidating. Early interior shots reveal a domestic site that seems only barely and tenuously removed from poverty, an impression corroborated by the haggard expressions and weary demeanours of the two actors. When the desperate-looking male character opens his mouth as though to speak for the first time, we have been cued by these and other indications of a cheerless reality to expect naturalistic dialogue, or perhaps even a cry of anguish – anything but a song. Yet startlingly, a song is what we get, and its lyrics, laconically intoned in a beautifully understated performance by Kelly, deliver the anticipated sense of despair with an eloquence that naturalistic dialogue could never achieve.

The effect of the puzzling, unconventional opening sequence is to initiate the story with a question powerfully put to the viewer: why are these two people so emotionally aggrieved? The question is made all the more pressing by the sequence that follows, instantly recognisable as a flashback, in which the family members are seen travelling on a horse-drawn wagon to their property, engaging in the mundane work of running a farm and a household. During this sequence the little girl plays, and at night in the child's bedroom her parents sing her to sleep with the fanciful lullaby of the film's title. The brief sequence is so inveigling in its presentation of the deep contentment experienced by the family that the anguish of the film's opening becomes, retrospectively, dire as well as wrenching. We know that the rest of the story that has now 'begun' so tenderly will be haunted by the sombreness of the mood established at the start. And that sense that something tragic is imminent is heightened by the next portion of the film in which the child, entranced by the song's fantasy of a heavenly lunar body that benignly summons 'all the sleepers' to come for a ride, leaves her bedroom and her home and sets off across the great outback expanse in the direction of the luminous moon. The scene, visually rendered so as to make distance and space almost soft and tangible like a child's toy, is further lulled into the slumberous alertness of a vividly felt dream by the soundtrack's choral backing. A wordless murmuring seems to enfold the little girl and her vast surroundings as she walks off toward the moon's milky radiance, and the outdoor setting seems only a storybook emanation of the warmly protective bedroom.

It is a spellbinding experience – almost. For the child, who disappears into the farther reaches of the cinematic field, the spell is complete; the viewer, however, retaining impressions of a harsh actuality in which pain and desolation of spirit are predominant, experiences the moonlit magic more distantly and forebodingly. It is foreknown that there is to be no fairytale ending to this moonlit idyll. That premonition is enforced in the film's ensuing sections, which trace the parents' and the local community's efforts in the following days to locate the child by tracking her path into the countryside, as well as the Aboriginal tracker's reaction to the community's exclusion of him. Relying on only occasional smatterings of dialogue to dramatise important plot developments, the film constructs its story by advancing through a series of musically articulated scenarios in a pattern that has more in common with opera than with conventional naturalistic drama of the stage and screen. The attempts of the white search party to find the girl, for example, are accompanied by a three-part Mairead Hannan composition that conveys, in music reflective of European Australia's Anglo-Celtic heritage, the initial solemn determination of the trackers and their subsequent frustration and despondency: 'The Gathering' begins as a march and is transformed into a dirge. Similarly, the inner pain felt by the mother and the tracker as a result of the father's ideologically-charged decision to act in accord with racist dogma even to the detriment of his own child's welfare, is conveyed by a Kelly and Carmody song, 'Unfinished Business'. At the start of the duet, performed by Fairfax and Pell, the white mother and the black tracker are shown on separate screens, each singing of his or her respective emotional loss; by the last chorus, however, the two voices are joined in a harmony that represents the commonality of their respective concerns.

Several commentators have noted that 'Unfinished Business' is a phrase that has considerable resonance in the Australia of the early twenty-first century. From the earliest days of the white occupation of the Australian continent, the indigenous peoples were subjected to the ill treatment meted out to native populations in every area of the world invaded and settled by Europeans: genocidal warfare, economic and sexual exploitation, racism, deracination, legal discrimination and, of course, the usurpation of the lands that had been theirs for millennia. Not until the 1960s were indigenous Australians legally entitled to vote. And although the decades since that period have marked many advances in their social and economic fortunes, many legal, cultural and economic problems and injustices remain unresolved, especially with regard to land rights. Thus, as Fiona Probyn and Catherine Simpson have pointed out, 'it seems particularly pertinent that a contemporary Australian film about "unfinished business" between black and white returns to the past and the (ongoing) issues of landscape and land ownership'. Yet it is another duet, and cinematic tableau, that captures those concerns more fully. In what is perhaps the film's most memorable sequence, the farmer and the tracker express through song the very different impressions each holds of his relationship with the land. Whereas the Euro Australian property holder declares aggressively 'this land is mine', the indigenous tracker sings 'this land owns me'. It is clear that Albert's prowess at tracking is due in large part to his cultural heritage, and that Jim's racist mentality inhibits him from admitting that an Aborigine can be his superior in any way with regard to a portion of the land that is 'his'. But the expressions and intonations of the white farmer tell us that his bigoted response has even deeper roots than cultural or racial pride, and several lines in his portion of the song indicate what they are.

This land is mine, Yeah I signed on the dotted line
Camp fires on the creek bank, Bank breathing down my neck
They won't take it away

His hold upon the farmland is tenacious but tenuous, subject to the fluctuations of agricultural commodity prices and the bank's mortgage rates – but what has that to do with his missing daughter, or the question of whether to allow an Aboriginal to participate in the communal effort to locate her? The implication is that his treasured property is an extension of his identity, an embodiment of who he is and aspires to be. The prospect of losing it to the bank in the event of a financial crisis is a constant anxiety, so much so that it is exacerbated by a crisis of a different and unrelated kind. When an Aboriginal Australian is nearly incorporated into the crisis, that figure so demonised by European Australia becomes, through the irrational logic of racism, representative of the external forces that threaten the farmer's hold upon the land he sees as a reflection of his very self. In no literal sense is the tracker identifiable with a 'they' who are empowered to 'take it away'. But psychologically his presence within the space that embodies the white man's identity constitutes a spectre of reappropriation that cannot be tolerated.

And as the film progresses it becomes ever clearer that the difference between the Euro-Australian and the Aboriginal conceptions of the land is not just a matter of contrasting conceptions of ownership. The white farmer, it is implied, believes that land can be tamed into real estate because he fails to apprehend fully the awesome underlying spirituality of the natural world, and humanity's subordinate place within it. The indigenous Australian, by contrast, knows that the land is not mere inert matter lying supine before the efforts of humans to dominate it for their own purposes. Batterham's cinematography renders an Australian earth and sky that seem mystically natural – lucidly immediate and 'real', yet somehow otherworldly. The 'bleach bypass processing' applied to the celluloid has something to do with this. It is a technique, Batterham has explained, that has the effect of draining film images of the vividness of their colouration. The result is not the bleak pallor that one might be led to expect, however, but a material world that seems subtly suffused with luminescence. This striking visual embodiment of the Aboriginal conception of a world that incorporates an awesome if ineffable presence is perceived only vaguely by the white Australians. To them the Australian land can seem enchanting, but in a restrictive make-believe fashion. Their limited apprehension of its allure had been conveyed early on by the nursery rhyme bedtime song. For all the charm of the scene in which it features, the joyous lullaby 'One Night the Moon' makes the moon a jolly imaginary playmate, and the natural world a site of transcendent power only in childish fantasy.

And that, the film implies, may be why the death of Emily is experienced by the parents as an absence almost beyond the power of spiritual wisdom to assuage. Upon discovering her daughter's body, the mother sings a song of mourning in which she laments not just the loss of her child, but the natural processes of decomposition that have in her view made the corpse only vacant matter.

These little bones, Washed by the rain,
Worn by the wind, Whitened by the sun
These tiny bones, they'll never grow
I'll never know what you could have become.

The sense that the child's very being has been utterly erased from the world is conveyed strongly also by the image that climaxes this portion of the narrative: the swathed body, looking doll-like in its inertness, is placed by the tracker in the arms of the stricken, uncomprehending father. At this point the sequence with which the film began is resumed, and the verses of the song sung by the father resonate with tragic import, for it becomes clear that his (and his society's) notion of life's meaning has always been grounded in a belief that the world is divisible into clearly delineated categories.

Once I knew how the world worked
You earned your bread, Said your prayers well
You loved your own, you helped your neighbour
I don't know anything any more.

Once I knew what was wrong and right
God was good, black was never white
Once I knew what I was living for
I don't know anything any more.

The lament is for an even greater loss than that of his daughter; it is for his apprehension of how the world is structured meaningfully into rigidly exclusive zones of wrong and right, black and white, having and not having. Not to 'have anything any more' is 'not to know anything any more'. Obscurely he realises that there was some fundamental flaw in his understanding of what is right, and that the principled behaviour that followed from it caused him to drive away from his private domain the one neighbour who could have aided the rescue effort effectively. But the belated awareness of the inadequacy of his culturally-induced vision of the world and his place in it is too faint and has come too late. The sequence climaxes with Jim, carrying his rifle over his shoulder, walking away from the camera into the distance of the landscape until, when he is almost incorporated within it, the screen turns completely dark for a few seconds and the report of the gun is heard.

For Rose it is at least slightly different. The unlocking of her culturally-instilled assumptions had begun earlier, when she first considered seeking the assistance of the black tracker. In yet another of the film's stunning dramatic duets, she sings of her perplexity, desperation, and hope:

There's a story hidden in your eyes, I wish I could see
Clouds of sorrow shadowed in your eyes, Calling to me.
What do you know? What can you see?

Clearly the words are not meant to be regarded as an actual address to the tracker. They represent, rather, the eloquent non-verbal communication that can take place even between two people who do not know or understand each other very well. His response, also a worded expression of thoughts and feelings that we sense emanate from him in mostly in non-verbal ways, offers more than the literal tracking skills he is renowned for.

I can track the shadows of the moon, Across the winds of time
From the heart to the limits of the land, The path is well defined
Beyond the known, we're not alone

Tracking, in other words, is a metaphor for the Aboriginal apprehension of the natural and material universe. The shadows of the moon, like all natural phenomena, are trails and patterns that if rightly read can put us on a pathway of awareness that offers solace to the otherwise despairing, isolated heart.

In all cultures it is religion, traditionally, that offers such solace. In the burial scene that follows the death of Jim, the father and daughter have been laid in adjoining graves, with members of the community – significantly, black as well as white – gathered in mourning. The Christian understanding of the communal connection between the living and those who have passed beyond the limits of the land to the unknown realm of the dead is conveyed through the singing of the traditional spiritual 'Breathe on Me' by Albert's wife (Ruby Hunter). It is a song of acceptance of what must be, and a plea for the soul-saving breath of spirituality that might enable those who grieve to maintain faith in eternal life. Hunter's inspired rendition, delivered with her characteristic low, throaty fluidity, seems to wrest life-giving music from despair even as the screen has extracted bleach-bypassed light from the complete darkness that marked Jim's self-inflicted death. The words of the song, and the cinematic bleakness of the setting, suggest that the Christian response to death's power over the imaginations of the living is as tenuous as the European conception of power over the land. But although Christianity's vision of an eternal life beyond the grave, beyond the land, is contrasted with an Aboriginal belief that the dead have not departed the earth but merged with it, the profundity of Christian spirituality is communicated respectfully and powerfully. As the Christian spiritual is performed by an Aboriginal person, there is a strongly conveyed implication that Christianity's desire for an unearthly eternal life emanates from an experience of despair that is common to both cultures.

The film advances to its conclusion with an aerial shot of the grieving Rose on her knees by the grave site. Her emotional pain is apparent as she looks upward, at which point the camera, as though following her gaze, pans to a last lyrical montage of the surrounding countryside. The land and sky still look sombre yet ruggedly beautiful, as they have throughout the film, and the voice of Kevin Carmody singing his composition 'Moonstruck' is heard and continues into the closing credits. The lyrics offer a response to the 'One Night the Moon' lullaby's storybook natural world, as well as to the otherworldly spirituality of 'Breathe on Me'. In moonlight's pervasive radiance, they hint, is the key to an understanding of the domestic interrelatedness of all that is.

> No-one's lost who finds the moon, Or the sweetness of the wattle's bloom
> Rebirth with the rain in spring, Dingos howl on the autumn wind
> Spirit of the moon he calls me home, Spirit of the moon he guides me home.

It is left to the viewer to imagine whether or not the song expresses Rose's newly awakened awareness of the indigenous Australian understanding of life, death and the spirituality of the land. The last image of her face conveys with certainty only grief. Nonetheless, it seems significant that her train of vision has lifted from the grave site, and that that of the viewer is directed upwards and outwards. Although the tenor of the film as a whole is unmistakably tragic, the ending implies that Australia's unfinished business, the divide between the two cultures, may yet be negotiated to the benefit of all – if the country will only draw upon the knowledge of those who have learned the land, felt it and imagined it for many centuries before the Europeans arrived to take control.

Richard Pascal

REFERENCE

Probyn, Fiona and Catherine Simpson (2001) '"This Land is Mine/This Land is Me": Reconciling Harmonies in *One Night the Moon*', *Senses of Cinema*, 17. http://www.sensesofcinema.com.

THE LORD OF THE RINGS: THE FELLOWSHIP OF THE RING

PETER JACKSON, NEW ZEALAND, 2001

The Fellowship of the Ring (2001), by New Zealand director Peter Jackson, is the first in a three-part adaptation of the British author J. R. R. Tolkien's fantasy novel, *The Lord of the Rings*. It was filmed in New Zealand in a marathon 15-month shooting schedule, requiring a cast and crew of 2,500, and as many as seven units shooting simultaneously. Tolkien's epic trilogy has sold over 100 million copies worldwide to generations of fans. However, until now, filmmakers – from Disney to Stanley Kubrick – have been frustrated in their efforts to translate it to the screen. Ralph Bakshi's 1978 animated version remained incomplete because it ran over budget and is generally considered a failure. The story gaps, inconsistencies and poor quality of animation in these adaptations have always rankled Tolkien fans but, by general consensus, Peter Jackson has accurately captured the mythopoetic quality of the original, the elusive sense of something Tolkien called 'faerie' ('the power of making immediately effective visions of fantasy') that many readers feel has been lost when his work is imaginatively transposed into other media.

The story begins in a land called Middle-earth, in a quiet rural backwater known as the Shire, inhabited by simple comfort-loving creatures known as hobbits. A hobbit named Frodo Baggins (Elijah Wood) learns from the wizard Gandalf (Ian McKellen) that an heirloom inherited from Frodo's uncle Bilbo (Ian Holm) is in fact an awesome instrument of evil: the great One Ring, forged centuries ago by Sauron, the Dark Lord of Mordor, who is even now seeking to reclaim it and harness its power to enslave the world. Pursued by terrifying servants of Sauron, the nine Black Riders, Frodo and his loyal gardener Samwise Gamgee (Sean Astin) flee the Shire bearing the Ring. Aided by a human named Aragorn or 'Strider' (Viggo Mortensen) and Arwen, an Elvish woman (Liv Tyler), they make their way to the comparative safety of the Elven stronghold at Rivendell. There, reunited with Bilbo and Gandalf, the hobbits take part in a great council, which determines that the ring must be carried into the land of Mordor and thrown into the Cracks of Doom, the subterranean fires beneath Mount Doom in Sauron's dark land where it was first made. Frodo volunteers for this task and he is sent on his way with a fellowship of eight others: the hobbits Sam,

Merry (Dominic Monaghan) and Pippin (Billy Boyd); Legolas the Elf (Orlando Bloom); Gimli the Dwarf (John Rhys-Davies); the humans Aragorn and Boromir (Sean Bean); and Gandalf the Wizard. Together, these nine individuals must face ring wraiths, orcs and worse; travel through strange lands, including the dreaded mines of Moria and the Elven tree-world of Lothóriel presided over by Galadriel (Cate Blanchett); and face mistrust within their fellowship.

Peter Jackson, arguably New Zealand's most important filmmaker, was born in the capital Wellington, in 1961. At the age of eight, Jackson was given a Super-8 camera by his parents and began making his own versions of the stop-animation movies that had impressed him as a child, including *King Kong* (1933) and *The Seventh Voyage of Sinbad* (1958). Self-taught in film production, Jackson left school at 17 and tried to obtain employment unsuccessfully with the New Zealand National Film Unit. Working as a photo-engraver for a local newspaper, with the help of friends he began shooting his first feature *Bad Taste*, in 1982, on a newly acquired 16mm Bolex camera. This film took Jackson and his friends four years to complete and was cut on Jackson's parents' dining room table, although it received some finance from the New Zealand Film Commission towards the production of the soundtrack. *Bad Taste* (1987) combines the staple iconography of horror and science fiction with slapstick comedy, and is peppered with side-glances to such New Zealand icons and institutions as sheep, chainsaws, charity collectors and 'mateship'. Since its release, *Bad Taste*, which was awarded the Prix de Gore at the Paris Horror Festival, has become a cult classic and recouped its costs many times over.

Jackson's next completed film was *Meet the Feebles* (1989), based on the backstage lives of a puppet performance troupe. In this bawdy, and at times gory, Muppet parody Jackson identified the lineaments of a subgenre that critics were soon referring to as the 'sluppet movie'. *Braindead* (American title *Dead Alive*, 1992), a satire of the repressed suburban middle-class world of New Zealand in the 1950s, and a psychodrama of a boy's relationship to his mother, was to take the splatter subgenre of horror to a point of implosion with gory birthing scenes ('just treacle and red dye' Jackson assures us) and multiple homage to the zombie movie tradition.

In 1995 *Heavenly Creatures* won a Silver Lion at the Venice Film Festival and its shift away from the excesses of the horror genre reflects the influence of Jackson's personal and professional partner, Fran Walsh. This successful art-house film was based on a murder in the conservative city of Christchurch that shocked New Zealand in 1954. This involved a *folie à deux* relationship of two teenage girls, and the beating to death of the mother of one of the girls. *Heavenly Creatures*, which represents Jackson's first foray into digital effects, is an odd but effective combination of meticulous attention to local historical details and a sophisticated computer-aided realisation of the girls' shared imaginary medieval kingdom of Borovnia.

Forgotten Silver (1995), a mockumentary that purports to be a biographical account of a hapless pioneer of early cinema, Colin McKenzie, deliberately plays with the codes and conventions of documentary. Viewer response to its screening on national New Zealand television ranged from those highly indignant at being duped (it caused one viewer to resign his Film Society membership 'after a lifetime of interest in film') to ecstatic praise for the film's entertainment values. *The Frighteners* (1996), produced for Universal Pictures by Robert Zemeckis with a budget of US$30 million, was at the time the most expensive film to be filmed and produced in New Zealand and signalled Jackson's shift from art-house and cult status to the mainstream of (Hollywood) blockbuster cinema. It is generally accepted that the film's confused plot and uncertainty regarding its genre affiliations (comedy or horror?) were the reasons for its lacklustre performance at the box office.

In the late 1990s, Jackson had two projects on his drawing board – a remake of *King Kong* and an ambitious, two-film adaptation of Tolkien's *The Lord of the Rings*. For a while, it looked like *King Kong* would be given the green light, but the project was shelved in the wake of the failure of Sony's *Godzilla* (1998) and Disney's *Mighty Joe Young* (1998). As a result Jackson turned his attention to *The Lord of the Rings* and, after early interest from Miramax Films, found a backer in New Line Cinema, which added a third film to his project. The Time-Warner company invested nearly US$300 million for the package deal of all three movies which were to be filmed back-to-back-to-back. Including publicity and marketing, the overall price tag approached around US$500 million. The three films went on to win 17 Academy Awards.

Jackson has created a secure niche for himself both in cult film and in mainstream practice and he is one of the few New Zealand filmmakers to gain international recognition and critical acclaim who has not been lured away by Hollywood (Geoff Murphy, Roger Donaldson, Vincent Ward and Lee Tamahori could be cited as examples of New Zealand's 'director drain'). Jackson has also met the challenge and attractive pull of the Hollywood studio by trying to better it in Miramar, a suburb of Wellington now affectionately dubbed 'Wellywood', where he has built an extensive studio and special effects facility (WETA, overseen by Richard Taylor) that houses his production company, WingNut Films. By demonstrating that sophisticated computer-based digital effects – a form he melds with a rigorous mode of generic mixing – can be produced cheaper in New Zealand, Jackson hopes that his example will reverse the trend of emigration of filmmaking talent to Hollywood.

Genre application and genre mixing have long been a potent creative catalyst for New Zealand filmmakers. Pioneer filmmaker John O'Shea adapted the European art movie to the road movie in his 1964 film *Runaway* and Geoff Murphy's *Utu* (1983) mixed the western with a political critique of colonialism. These 'local concoctions' have not always been understood by critics and audiences elsewhere (Murphy's movie, for example, had to be re-cut for American audiences). Jackson's *Lord of the Rings* film trilogy might be read as a (local) adaptation of the genre of the fantastic. When Tolkien began writing *The Hobbit* in the 1930s, he was not the first author to write what would eventually be labelled fantasy, but his synthesis of elements – mythology, stories of larger-than-life heroism, the supernatural, and fairytales – was unique. Nothing on the scale or scope of *The Hobbit* and *The Lord of the Rings* had previously been seen. During the past three decades fantasy has entered mainstream literary and screen culture and Tolkien's work has been essential in defining the genre and securing its audience.

Certain questions beg to be asked here. Specifically, is Jackson an auteur? Is *The Fellowship of the Ring* an auteur film? Does it emerge from the single creative influence of its director and reflect the thematics and direction of his corpus of work? Graham Fuller thinks not, for he feels 'nothing in the movie reveals a shaping personality' and it lacks a 'subtextual and psychological complexity' which might provide a space for more than 'pictorially splendid pop culture'. In contrast, Jo Morris believes that what distinguishes Jackson's films is their quality of 'excess', found in a literal excess of special effects, overblown soundtracks and costume wizardry and also in the 'excess' of intertextuality, its pastiche of forms and ironic use of (New Zealand) icons and referents. While it needs to be seen in the context of its source text, its special effects advisors and the agendas of its studio producers, it is clear that the film carries with it a 'Peter Jackson brand'. Indeed, given its commercial success, it could be argued that Jackson's work is crucially important for understanding what factors might shape the 'author' of a film and national cinema in general.

Another question we might ask, and have perhaps pre-empted by including this film in the present volume, would be is *The Fellowship of the Ring* a New Zealand film? Andrew O'Hehir opens his *Sight and Sound* review by suggesting that 'perhaps the secret ingredient in Jackson's extraordinary film interpretation of the first volume of Tolkien's *The Lord of the Rings* is New Zealand itself'. Months after the release of the third film in the trilogy an Air New Zealand advertising campaign in major international magazines exhorts us to 'Visit Middle-earth. They have not taken the set down.' New Zealand's national airline has also decorated several of its jumbo jets with images of scenes from the *Lord of the Rings* trilogy, and postage stamps of characters and scenes from the film have been issued by New Zealand Post. It is clear that New Zealand offered the filmmakers enormous geographical diversity, from rural pastoral farmland, dramatic volcanic topography, to exotic native 'bush'. Jackson himself recognised the special affinities of the New Zealand landscape with Tolkien's fantasy world: 'Even though we are right down here at the bottom of the world, we have mountains, forests and fields, rivers, lakes and waterfalls that have a familiar yet slightly fantastical appearance.' In his exploitation of the New Zealand landscape as backdrop Jackson is not unique, New Zealand has already functioned as a global commodity in the international film market: as Korea in *The Rescue* (1988); the hills of Lyttleton Harbour stand in for the American Northwest in Jackson's *The Frighteners*; in *Vertical Limit* (2000) Mt Aspiring becomes the Himalayas; in *The Last Samurai* (2003) Mt Taranaki becomes Mt Fuji; in *Sylvia* (2003) Dunedin becomes the US state of New England.

Descriptions of landscape in Tolkien's writing are powerful; readers and fans attest to the importance of maps and their absorption into the imaginary topography of Middle-earth as an important part of the pleasure of reading Tolkien's book. This is a landscape that offers itself as both material and knowable, yet one that requires the imaginative investment of a reader to interpret and 'invent'. The story of *The Lord of the Rings* is not plot-driven and linear, but spatial and told as the extension outwards of space. Such a non-chronological narrative easily produces the sense of bewilderment of 'being lost in a wood' that is evoked so effectively in Jackson's film. If New Zealand is Middle-earth, and the special DVD edition of the film contains a section 'New Zealand as Middle-earth' which is also supported by a bestselling, separately-published location guidebook, this does not preclude the fact that the film also contains, as Thierry Jutel insists, 'virtual cartographies'. Jackson's digitalisation of the landscape image makes it difficult to distinguish natural landscapes (mountains, forests, fields) from artificial landscapes (mines, caverns, exotic cities). As Louis Menand observes: 'One senses in almost every frame of the movie a lot of digital fine-tuning of the image. The meadows are too manicured, the streams too sparkling, the skies too dazzling or too lurid. Your eye never relaxes because the image is both life-like and too life-like. You find yourself unconsciously looking for the seams in a seamless picture.' For Jutel, this mix illustrates the film's Playstation 2 game aesthetic where 'the intrinsic link between Tolkien's mythic continent and Aotearoa New Zealand is not so much an erasure of colonial history but an assertion of the transformative powers of the virtualisation of the landscape'. In this sense, as a 'production', Jackson's vision of Middle-earth is simply the latest in a long line of attempts to 'virtualise' the geography of the landscape of Aotearoa New Zealand, from attitudes to the land in Maori mythology through nineteenth-century colonial practices of land clearing, to twentieth-century industrial agrarianism.

In working with Tolkien's book Jackson and his fellow screenwriters Fran Walsh and Philippa Boyens had to grapple with the complex issues of adaptation. As already noted, many reviewers and internet fans had questioned the fidelity of earlier screen adaptations to the originating novels. In the pre-production stage of filmmaking Jackson regularly interacted with fans on the internet to get feedback on the decisions he proposed. According to one of the film's lead actors, Sir Ian McKellen, *The Fellowship of the Ring* is 'perhaps the most faithful screenplay ever adapted from a long novel'. Certain scenes (in particular those with the character Tom Bombadil and other hobbits) have been cut or condensed in the name of pacing, and the role of one character, the elf warrior Arwen Undómiel, who carries the injured Frodo on her magnificent white stallion to the city of Rivendell (instead of the male elf Glorfindel as the book has it), has been expanded to enhance a romantic angle, something that was largely absent from Tolkien's work. Galadriel, Queen of the Elven kingdom of Lothlórien, is similarly given a more extended profile. Despite the apparent fidelity, Graham Fuller also asks if Jackson's film is 'simply a populist interpretation or does it reflect at least a modicum of Tolkien's literary ambition?'

J. R. R. Tolkien (1892–1973) spent his working life as a philologist. He was Reader then Professor of English Language at Leeds, then Professor of Anglo-Saxon at Oxford from 1925 until 1945, then Professor of English Language at Oxford until his retirement in 1959. Tom Shippey, the most formidable figure of contemporary Tolkien criticism, a philologist who has himself held Tolkien's Chair at Leeds, has analysed how the philology produced the epic work of fantasy and not vice versa, how Tolkien devised the languages, the legends, the songs and all the detail that appears in his appendices first to give his story body. Shippey is full of praise for Peter Jackson's fidelity to this visual, linguistic and narrative detail.

For Shippey, Tolkien is also a writer of the twentieth century, his imaginings are a reflection of the century's turbulent history, in particular industrialised warfare. Tolkien himself lost most of his close friends in World War One and served in the Lancashire Fusiliers at the front from which he was hospitalised with 'trench fever'. As a veteran of the Somme, he transformed the experience of being traumatised in battle in his writing. The young Frodo is, like Tolkien, a young man being sent over the top of the trench from which he suspects he may never return. 'I think [Tolkien] was very preoccupied with the nature of evil, the nature of technology, the way in which things could be abused, the way good intentions are subverted,' writes Shippey. The politics of *The Lord of the Rings* thus comprises a mixture of infatuation with power (dramatised in the film's cataclysmic battles) and awareness of one's own helplessness beside it. Themes of death and resurrection, or the magical evasion of death (by Frodo who is mortally wounded twice), permeate Jackson's film.

Given the complexities of Tolkien's book, Jackson's adaptation resulted in a work which, by its nature, is not an actor's film. Its characters are lacking in psychological complexity and moral ambivalence, and many of them appear for only isolated intervals in the storyline. It is difficult to feel little more than detached bemusement at Jackson's rendition of a hobbit – a small, sturdy, rather conventional species of humanoid with furry feet and a fondness for pipe smoking. For Tolkien, it would seem, the hobbits were a compromise between the desired state of childhood and the miserableness of the adult condition. Hobbiton in the Shire with its round painted doors and well-kept holes in the ground where cheerfully unassuming inhabitants puff pipe-weed, eat six meals a day, and frown on anything that smacks of adventure is almost a parody of rural England in the 1930s. However, such intimations and complexities of character are glossed over in Jackson's representation. The book and the film contain moments which might be described as 'male bonding', with underlying tones of possible homoeroticism, that reflect Tolkien's (and Jackson's) interest throughout his life in male camaraderie and heroic friendship. In contrast to the paucity of 'character roundness', the palpable images a viewer takes away are the film's harbingers of evil: the crowd scenes of hundred of orcs swarming in underground caverns; enormous armies fighting battles on endless plains; the Black Riders, the Nazgûl, reminders of the dreaded hooded phantom of Jackson's earlier film *The Frighteners*.

Perhaps the real secret ingredient of *The Fellowship of the Ring* – what stirs the blood – is its dizzying digital effects. Peter Jackson observes how 'technology has caught up with the incredible imagination that Tolkien injected into [the] story' and 'the way in which Tolkien's imagination converges with our notions of virtual reality'. Let us follow these techniques of screen adventure through one pivotal sequence, if at warp speed. At the gate to the Mines of

Moria, the fellowship is attacked by a squid-like Watcher with twelve tentacles, one of several computer-generated creatures in the film. The thrashing Watcher was developed from a larger detailed clay maquette scanned by 3D scanners and then computer enhanced. The fellowship survives the Watcher and enters the Mines of Moria, the abandoned realm of the dwarves. For the wide views within the mines of Moria, 'little people' – scale doubles, often in masks or applied make-up, resembling the principal characters – stood in for the hobbit characters. In other cases, 'hobbit scale' was achieved by placing actors next to oversized props. Deep within the cavernous mines, the fellowship discovers the long-abandoned city of Dwarrowdelf. Its repeating rows of columns extending into infinity were constructed digitally. The performers were shot separately against a bluescreen and then composited into the computer-generated set or, if the virtual camera was filming from some distance, digital replicas of the characters were inserted into the image. Similarly, foreground, 'life-size' interior sets of the mine were extended into the distant background through the use of miniatures. In a chamber deep within the caverns of Moria the fellowship is set upon by dozens of orcs and a giant cave troll. The fight with the computer-generated troll, like the Watcher, which was developed from a (five-feet high) clay maquette, was first worked out in previsualisation (a crude 3D animation was used to prove a shot would be technically feasible).

Having slain the hulking troll, the fellowship flees through a forest of stone columns as thousands of digitally-produced orcs emerge streaming over the cavern walls and floors. The group of friends makes their way to an enormous stone stairway leading to the bridge of Khazad-dûm, which leads over a fiery chasm. The WETA Workshop built a large-scale (21-feet tall) miniature (dubbed a 'bigature' by the crew) for this pivotal sequence. The dizzying stairs, atop huge stone arches, begin to collapse as the fellowship descends and its members jump from teetering column to teetering column. For many shots in this sequence the fellowship actors were filmed against a bluescreen and composited into the miniature photography. In the final frames of this sequence, the monstrous Balrog steps into view, and Gandalf the wizard turns to face it. Described by Tolkien as a creature of 'shadow and flame', the 'look' of the Balrog was created using 'sprites' – digital particles onto which film images are texture-mapped. To create the fiery form, elements of flame and smoke were mapped onto the particles and laid over a computer-generated model that incorporated characteristics of animal movement. Distraught over the loss of Gandalf who, together with the Balrog, has fallen into the fiery pit below, the fellowship emerges to the surface of Middle-earth and proceeds to the Elven tree-top city of Lothlórien.

For medieval scholar Jane Chance, Peter Jackson has produced 'a flashy, high-tech adventure film', simply 'an action film in which the important complex thematic meanings and characterisations are discarded or subordinated to the sentimental'. This, she argues, is because Jackson strips Tolkien's text of the episodes where the hobbits play key roles and diminishes the character of Frodo to a two-dimensional child-like figure whose decision to lead the fellowship of nine against the dark forces of Mordor hardly rings true. For Tom Shippey, Tolkien's late twentieth-century champion, Jackson has handled the problems of Tolkien's non-continuous narrative structure effectively (in the book the reason for the hobbit's journey is never revealed until the Council of Elrond), and he believes that Tolkien's message 'gets through in a different genre, a different culture, a much-changed world'. Jackson's three films thus become part of the machinery that has kept 'Tolkien's appeal so unpredictably alive'. Whichever point of view one accepts, the filmed version of *The Lord of the Rings* will remain one of the biggest box office phenomena of the early twenty-first century. It manifests the complexities and scale of globally-released megamovies, all the detailed craft that goes into them, and the franchises, fans and merchandise that accompanies their release, and as such it is a remarkable global media production, nudging well over US$1 billion in earnings, from a small country of four and a half million inhabitants with only a nascent film industry.

Laurence Simmons

REFERENCES

Chance, Jane (2002) 'Is There a Text in This Hobbit?: Peter Jackson's *Fellowship of the Ring*', *Literature/Film Quarterly*, 30, 2, 79–86.

Fuller, Graham (2002) 'Trimming Tolkien', *Sight and Sound*, 12, 2, 18–20.

Jutel, Thierry (2004) '*Lord of the Rings*: Landscape, Transformation, and the Geography of the Virtual', in Claudia Bell and Steve Matthewman (eds) *Cultural Studies in Aotearoa New Zealand: Identity, Space and Place*. Melbourne: Oxford University Press.

Menand, Louis (2002) 'Goblin Market', *The New York Review of Books*, 17 January, 8–9.

Morris, Jo (2000) 'Peter Jackson as Auteur', *New Zealand Journal of Media Studies*, 7, 20, 45–52.

O'Hehir, Andrew (2002) '*The Fellowship of the Ring*', *Sight and Sound*, 12, 2, 49–52.

Shippey, Tom (2000) *J. J. R. Tolkien: Author of the Century*. London: HarperCollins.

_____ (2003) 'From Page to Screen: J. R. R. Tolkien and Peter Jackson', *World Literature Today*, 10, 69–72.

RABBIT-PROOF FENCE

PHILLIP NOYCE, AUSTRALIA, 2002

From 1931 to 1971, Australia's Aboriginal children were routinely taken from their families and placed with white foster families or held within the care of the State or churches. Phillip Noyce's *Rabbit-Proof Fence* (2002) details one aspect of this narrative of the so-called stolen generations. The film deals with three Aboriginal children – Molly Craig (Everlyn Sampi), Daisy Kadibil (Tianna Sansbury) and Gracie Fields (Laura Monaghan) – who escape a fate which befell many other black children and travel 1,500 miles across Australia to return to their home of Jigalong in northwestern Australia. The story is based on the book *Follow the Rabbit-Proof Fence* (1996) written by Doris Pilkington/Nugi Garimara, the daughter of Molly Craig.

Introduced to the story by receiving a phone call at 3 am in Los Angeles, Noyce eventually read the script and loved it immediately. During this time, he was working on the script of *The Sum of All Fears*, the third of his adaptations of Tom Clancy novels starring Harrison Ford, but the actor refused to commit to the film. Tired of waiting, Noyce just woke up one day and thought 'I've had enough of this. I'm gonna go back to Australia and see if I can get Rabbit-Proof Fence going'. This project was the antithesis of the type of film he had been making in Hollywood for the past decade.

Once in Australia, Noyce embarked on his usual intensive research. In Perth, he met up with Pilkington and travelled the footsteps of his heroines as he drove along the rabbit-proof fence to Jigalong. There he met the real Molly Craig and her sister Daisy Craig Kadibil, who were in their eighties at the time and who told Noyce their stories and answered many pressing questions. In the official press release announcing his return to Australia, Noyce gave his reasons for this film project: 'This is a marvellous adventure story and thriller, celebrating courage and the resilience of the human spirit ... But I knew the hardest hurdle would be to find kids to play the three children. So began a three-month search across Australia, aided by casting director Christine King – who had done *Moulin Rouge!* and *Two Hands* [1999] – but also helped by community leaders, schoolteachers and parents deputised to interview children in the four corners of the continent. Of about 2,000 kids interviewed I probably saw 800 personally … We were looking for very specific children, who had to be of mixed parentage – not full blood – and possess the charisma of movie stars. Seventeen kids were chosen from all over the country and flown to Broome in northwestern Australia for two days of intensive casting workshops.'

Having cast the children Noyce noted that 'the greatest challenge during shooting was working with the eldest of the children, 12-year-old Everlyn Sampi, whose mother was a part of the stolen generations, having grown up in a church-run institution. Everlyn was a very highly-strung young girl – proud and seemingly confident, but underneath extremely unsure of herself and overwhelmed by all sorts of fears. She was perfect for the part of Molly because of her natural rebellious personality and healthy disrespect for authority, coupled with remarkable determination.' Noyce felt it important to secure a recognisable star to accompany the unknown leads and to assist sales. Kenneth Branagh was chosen for the part of Mr Neville. The role of the tracker went to David Gulpilil, an Aboriginal actor who first appeared in 1970 by the name of 'Gumpilil' in Nicolas Roeg's *Walkabout*. Thirty years on, he has become the quintessential Aboriginal character actor in Australian cinema.

As with the casting, Noyce had definite ideas concerning the way the landscape should be represented in the film. 'Over the years a very predictable style for shooting the Australian landscape has developed, with pretty pictures and classical composition, but I wanted this film to evoke a different feeling of Australia. The audience shouldn't think that once the kids have escaped from Moore River Native Settlement they are safe. There's still a hell of a long journey ahead of them and for the major part of that trek you should fear for them, because it's not just the authorities they have to battle, but also their own personal limitations and unfamiliarity with the land. That's why I didn't want the landscape to look welcoming. And I wanted Chris [Doyle, director of photography] to give the film a quasi-documentary look with his hand-held camera and off-centre framing. As he himself isn't at ease with nature, the viewer feels Chris's own alienation from the outback.' Doyle remembers that 'I was looking for something that suggested the torment, the cruelty of the journey, the loneliness, the isolation and the expanse. We've gone for a washed-out look … There's a lot of extremity, of whiteness to the landscape. There's a bleakness to what lies before them and we achieve that by desaturating the colours, by certain exposures, little tricks and by the way we process the film.'

In addition to the technical considerations, the film's production involved a process of interracial collaboration. As Noyce notes in the film's press kit, 'the three real children of the story came from Jigalong in Western Australia, so the elders from there sent representatives to the set whenever we were depicting their country and people, to advise us on cultural matters. Doris Pilkington-Garimara, the writer of the novel, was the script adviser, and she participated in the editing by looking at various cuts and giving her comments. At all stages and everywhere we filmed, local elders and representatives were also consulted.' In total, the shoot lasted seven weeks. Locations were spread around South Australia but mostly in the Flinders Ranges. The total production cost was A$10.5 million.

Peter Gabriel agreed to provide the music for the film. He was, as Noyce has noted, attracted to the project because it fitted into his 'world music' notions. 'The 9-month collaboration on the soundtrack was mainly done by the exchange of MP3 files of music and sound effects via email. My team of sound editors working at Soundfirm in Fox Studios, Sydney, emailed natural sounds of the Australian bush over to Bath in the UK where the crew at Real World would synthesize musical notes based on those sounds and incorporate them into the music, which they would then email back to us.'

The background of the film – the stolen generations – was inevitably bound to touch a raw nerve in Australian domestic politics. Noyce knew 'that the 1997 Royal Commission had recommended that an official apology be given to indigenous Australians, for the stolen generation policies. But I thought it was just the single-minded dick-headedness of Prime Minister John Howard that prevented him from acknowledging the findings of a Royal Commission that had been instigated by a previous Labour government. Once the film came out I became well aware that, in fact, there were certain commentators in the country – who enjoyed a strong following – who were determined to convince Australians that the policies of forced separation were for the good of Aborigines, and that basically there is no such thing as the stolen generations because no one was really stolen. And that it all had been an invention of manipulative Aborigines and their left-leaning, guilt-ridden white supporters.'

With a prime minister denying the Aboriginal community any gesture of reconciliation, it was hardly surprising to find Australian conservatives on the barricades even before the film was released. Orchestrated attacks appeared in the Murdoch press in early 2002. The attacks denounced perceived factual errors in the plot, throwing in some populist ingredients for good measure (like the receipt of $5.3 million taxpayers' money in production funds); dismissed the stolen generations as pure fabrication (the children were never taken but voluntarily sent off by their loving parents, away from the danger of camp life); and lashed out at Noyce ('Your film shames not us, Phillip Noyce, but you', went one headline).

Noyce noted that 'the commentators were trying to destroy the movie and its message, and their attacks had nothing to do with art, nothing to do with history, nothing to do with truth – but everything to do with ideology. And it was interesting to realise there was a minority – or maybe not – in Australia who were in massive denial, and who would go to any length to encourage others in that blinkered view of ourselves. Once the movie became a success, Andrew Bolt and Piers Ackerman, writing in the Murdoch press, tried to discredit me personally by attacking my credibility and motives, even suggesting that I was un-Australian for allowing the story to be exported. Publicist Emma Cooper tried to fuel the controversy to make up for our lack of advertising dollars. So whenever one of these attacks appeared, she would immediately demand equal space to rebut it.' Cooper's strategy worked. The newspapers that had initially published the attacks were flooded with letters to the editors, in most cases strongly in favour of the film. By the time it opened around the country in late February 2002, *Rabbit-Proof Fence* was a topic of general discussion.

The Australian was the first newspaper to write about the project, in a long piece in June 2001. Noyce gave unlimited access to different phases of pre-production and production to the Channel Nine network which produced a five-part series on the film for its *Today Show*. Another outcome was the 20-minute 'The Making of Rabbit-Proof Fence', broadcast on television just eleven days prior to the premiere. By that time Noyce was busy travelling up and down the country, conducting previews of the film, often accompanied by a member of the crew or cast. When the film eventually opened on ninety screens throughout the country on 21 February, it had in fact become a *cause célèbre*.

Serious film critics reacted enthusiastically to the picture, typically lauding the performances of the girls as well as the cinematography depicting the barren Australian landscape. Noyce's directorial skills were praised and the political overtones of the story received wide comment. Exemplifying the positive reviews, David Stratton in *Variety* stated that *Rabbit-Proof Fence* is

> bold in concept and inspirational in intent, [the film] tells its tale of dogged courage and fortitude with a straightforward directness, and benefits immensely from the luminous presences of the children involved … Noyce is an accomplished storyteller, and while *Rabbit-Proof Fence* lacks the poetic vision of a film like *Walkabout*, it succeeds emotionally in the cause of what seems to be its primary aim, to advance an attitudinal change in Australians not normally sympathetic to the Aboriginal cause.

Papers that had attacked the film on their opinion pages now published some of the most enthusiastic critical reviews. One was from Leigh Paatsch in the *Herald Sun*:

This is a landmark Australian film ... marking a triumphant return to form for director Phillip Noyce after far too long on the schlockier end of the Hollywood assembly line ... Without taking a tub-thumping stance, *Rabbit-Proof Fence* subtly shifts the Stolen Generation debate to where it should have been all along: as a tragic humanitarian riddle that still eludes fathomable answer.

The *Courier Mail* conceded that 'Noyce hasn't come home to make a "message" movie. He has preferred to let history speak volumes ... [His] meticulous casting and commitment to drawing genuine "acting" from the young trio has paid dividends.' Furthermore, 'it is one of the most finely crafted, most emotionally satisfying films ever made in this, or any other country', raved the Nine Network.

Undoubtedly the original criticisms of *Rabbit-Proof Fence* resulted in some way from the fact that Noyce's film constructs a positive image that unsettles conservatives: Aboriginal heroines in a feat of endurance, heading back to the roots of their culture – being one with the country, with nature, and surviving. Noyce's approach to the topic possibly made more people aware of this dark chapter in Australia's history than any scholarly text had. By taking the story from an abstract political domain to a concrete personal level, each member of the audience was likely to ask themselves at some point: 'How would I feel if my child were taken away?'

The simple question is proposed in a film that draws on sophisticated approaches to production and marketing. Noyce commented: 'I have tried to take some of the lessons I learned in Hollywood, particularly about marketing films, and apply them to selling an extremely independent-minded production like this. We used some of the Hollywood information saturation techniques to try and sell the picture, so that when it opened almost everyone knew about the movie – even though it had a tiny budget and is in theory what normally might be considered art-house fare.'

The film made A$7.2 million in 2001, making it the second-biggest grossing Australian film of the year after the comedy *Cracker Jack* (2001). The last time a film with indigenous characters worked at the Australian box office was back in the 1950s with Charles Chauvel's *Jedda*. Noyce stated that 'it was gratifying to come back to Australia to make a project of historical and social relevance that would enter the nation's popular culture. I was attracted by a great and emotionally compelling story. But also by the idea of overturning conventions. The character portrayed on the film's poster is a strong, determined, loving, sensitive, attractive and intelligent Australian who is also black. Where have you seen that before? Probably only once: Olympic 400 metres track champion Cathy Freeman ... When I grew up we knew nothing about Aborigines, we didn't talk about them even though every large country town in my state of New South Wales had a reserve outside of town where indigenous people were forced to live. Aborigines weren't counted in the census until 1967 or given the vote until then. They weren't citizens. They were a second category of human beings. The idea of making a story where the heroine is the Aboriginal girl and you are presenting that as a normal, everyday part of popular culture, and selling it aggressively in cinema multiplexes in the suburbs, made the whole project worthwhile.'

In fact, the role Aborigines usually play in Australian feature films largely reflects their standing in society in general: largely invisible. With a notable exception like *Jedda*, their roles were generally confined to strange, almost exotic extras in the background – fun-loving and easily deluded or treacherous and savage. Ken G. Hall famously quipped that Aborigines were 'death at the box office'. Since the renaissance of the Australian feature film a number of directors have tried different approaches. *The Last Wave*, *The Chant of Jimmie Blacksmith*, *Manganinnie* (1980), *The Fringe Dwellers* (1986) and *Black Fellas* (1993) all put Aborigines or Aboriginality in the spotlight. But their characters are deeply tragic and for different reasons these films were deemed failures by the critics. Interestingly, in the same year as *Rabbit-Proof Fence*, both *Beneath Clouds* by Ivan Sen and *The Tracker* by Rolf de Heer – films involving Aboriginal characters – won major critical acclaim and were even moderate financial successes. In both films, the main characters achieve self-confidence and set about to successfully break away from the strict confinement of white society. There is hope at last that Australians might finally develop a rapprochement with Aborigines, at least on the silver screen.

Noyce does not simply paint political issues black and white. For example, the character of Neville is depicted as neither good nor totally bad. The Chief Protector of Aborigines is not just a racist caricature. Noyce continued this pattern of complex villains in *The Quiet American* (2002) and his 2006 film, *Catch a Fire*. It would be misleading, however, to only emphasise the political implications when trying to come to terms with the film. As Noyce points out: '*Rabbit-Proof Fence* is ... a story of any outsider who exceeds their own expectations of themselves and the limitations other people place on them. It's about any underdog who overcomes the odds. And essentially it's not about the uniqueness of Aboriginal culture, but the ways in which we're all the same. It's about communality and the ties that bind, about love and interdependence between all parents and their children. Plus, it's about freedom. These are all elements that anybody can relate to.'

The underdog, the so-called 'little Aussie battler', is a powerful Australian icon. He may eventually lose, but the triumph lies in the attempt, in the enduring. Australian history is littered with examples of the type – from the Eureka Stockade to Gallipoli, from Burke and Wills to Ned Kelly. Only two of the girls in *Rabbit-Proof Fence* make it back to Jigalong. Nevertheless, the 2,000-kilometre trek along the fence erected to keep rabbits from entering cattle country is a feat of epic proportions, no matter what the eventual outcome. Being on the road – without a determinate destination – is also deeply enshrined in the Australian psyche and is evident in the nation's unofficial anthem, 'Waltzing Matilda', and in the popularity of the *Mad Max* films. In this respect, *Rabbit-Proof Fence* is a genuine Australian film.

In 1978, Noyce started his directorial career with *Backroads*, a road movie dealing with (black and white) drifters on a car trip. They head to the Eastern seaboard where all traces of Aboriginal culture have long since vanished, and one by one the protagonists perish. It is a deeply pessimistic film. In 2001, Noyce returned to his homeland and embarked on another road movie which inverts the narrative of *Backroads*. In *Rabbit-Proof Fence* the three girls head inland from the west coast to the deserts of Western Australia, where Aboriginal identity can still be found. They have a clear destination and they undertake the journey in the traditional black man's way, by walking. They are helped and betrayed by both blacks and whites, and they finally make it home. It is a truly inspiring, optimistic film.

Ingo Petzke

REFERENCES

Noyce, Phillip (2002–04) Interviews with the author: 24 March 2002; 11 December 2002; 27 May 2003; 2 June 2003; 24 January 2004.

Paatsch, Leigh (2002) 'Full Proof', *Herald Sun*, 14 February.

Partridge, Des (2002) 'Australian Story', *Courier Mail*, 23 February.

Petzke, Ingo (2004) *Phillip Noyce: Backroads to Hollywood*. Sydney: Pan Macmillan.

Stratton, David (2002) 'Rabbit-Proof Fence', *Variety*, 18 February.

FILMOGRAPHY

THE STORY OF THE KELLY GANG 1906
Director: Charles Tait
Production: John Tait, Nevin Tait, Millard Johnson, William A. Gibson
Screenplay: Charles Tait
Photography: Millard Johnson, Orrie Perry, Reg Perry, William Gibson
Editing: Milliard Johnson, William Gibson
Cast: Elizabeth Tait (Kate Kelly), John Tait (schoolmaster)
Running length: 4,000 (?) ft

THE WOMAN SUFFERS 1918
Director: Raymond Longford
Production: Southern Cross Feature Film Company
Screenplay: Raymond Longford
Photography: Arthur Higgins
Cast: Lottie Lyell (Marjory Manton), Boyd Irwin (Philip Masters), Roland Conway (Ralph Manton), Paul Baxter (Little Phillip), C. R. Stanford (John Stockdale), Ida Gresham (Mrs Stockdale)
Running length: 8,000 ft

DAD AND DAVE COME TO TOWN 1938
Director: Ken G. Hall
Production: Ken G. Hall for Cinesound
Screenplay: Frank Harvey, Bert Bailey
Photography: George Heath
Editing: William Shepherd
Composer: Hamilton Webber
Art Direction: Eric Thompson
Sound: Clive Cross
Cast: Bert Bailey (Dad Rudd), Shirley Ann Richards (Jill), Fred MacDonald (Dave), Billy Rayes (Jim Bradley), Alec Kellaway (Entwistle), Sidney Wheeler (Pierre), Connie Martyn (Mum), Ossie Wenban (Joe), Valerie Scanlan (Sarah), Muriel Ford (Myrtle), Leila Steppe (Sonia), Marshall Crosby (Ryan Snr), Peter Finch (Bill Ryan), Cecil Perry (Rawlings), Billy Steward (Bob Thompson), Marie D'Alton (Miss Quince), Leslie Victor (Brown), George Lloyd, Jack Settle, Sid Doody, Cyril Northcote (bailiffs), Raymond Longford (policeman)
Running time: 97 mins

THE PHANTOM STOCKMAN 1953
Director: Lee Robinson
Production: Chips Rafferty, George Heath for Platypus Productions
Photography: George Heath
Editing: Gus Lowry
Music: William Lovelock
Sound: Hans Wetzel, John Heath

Cast: Chips Rafferty (the Sundowner), Jeanette Elphick (Kim Marsden), Max Osbiston (McLeod), Guy Doleman (Stapleton), Henry Murdoch (Dancer), Bob Darken (Roxey), Joe Scully (the Moth), Albert Namatjira (himself).
Running Time: 67 mins

THE BACK OF BEYOND 1954
Director: John Heyer
Production: John Heyer, Shell Film Unit
Screenplay: John Heyer, Janet Heyer, Roland Robinson
Photography: Ross Wood
Editing: John Heyer
Music: Sydney John Kay
Production Manager: John Heyer
Sound: Mervyn Murphy, John Heath
Running time: 66 mins

JEDDA 1955
Director: Charles Chauvel
Production: Charles Chauvel
Screenplay: Charles Chauvel, Elsa Chauvel
Photography: Carl Kayser
Editing: Alex Ezard, Jack Gardiner, Pam Bosworth
Music: Isadore Goodman
Art Direction: Ronald McDonald
Sound: Arthur Browne
Cast: Ngarla Kunoth (Jedda), Robert Tudawali (Marbuck), Betty Suttor (Sarah McMann), Paul Reynall (Joe), George Simpson-Lyttle (Douglas McMann), Tas Fitzer (Peter Wallis), Wason Byers (Felix Romeo), Willie Farrar (little Joe), Margaret Dingle (little Jedda)
Running time: 101 mins

FREE RADICALS 1958
Director: Len Lye
Production: Len Lye
Editor: Len Lye
Running time: 4 mins

RUNAWAY 1964
Director: John O'Shea
Production: John O'Shea
Screenplay: John Graham, John O'Shea
Photography: Anthony Williams
Editing: John O'Shea
Music: Robin MacOnie
Production Manager: Bob Ash
Sound: Lindsay Anderson, Ron Skelley, John McCormick
Cast: Colin Broadley (David Manning), Nadja Regin (Laura Kossovich), Deidre McCarron (Diana), Kiri Te Kanawa (Isobel Wharewera), Selwyn Maru (Joe Wharewera), Barry Clump (Clarrie), Gil Cornwall (Tom Morton), Sam Stevens (Tana), Tanya Binning (Dorothy)
Running time: 98 mins

THEY'RE A WEIRD MOB 1966

Director: Michael Powell

Production: Michael Powell for Williamson-Powell International Films

Screenplay: Richard Imrie (pseudonym for Emeric Pressburger) from a novel by Nino Culotta (John O'Grady)

Photography: Arthur Grant

Editing: G. Turney-Smith

Music: Laurence Leonard and Alan Boustead

Art Direction: Dennis Gentle

Sound: Alan Allen

Cast: Walter Chiari (Nino Culotta), Clare Dunne (Kay Kelly), Chips Rafferty (Harry Kelly), Ed Devereaux (Joe), John Meillon (Dennis), Slim de Grey (Pat), Alida Chelli (Giuliana), Anne Haddy (barmaid), Charles Little (Jimmy), Muriel Steinbeck (Mrs Kelly), Judith Arthy (Dixie), Doreen Warburton (Edie), Jeannie Drynan (Betty)

Running time: 112 mins

SLEEPING DOGS 1977

Director and producer: Roger Donaldson

Production company: Aardvark Films

Screenplay: Ian Mune, Arthur Baysting (from a novel by C.K. Stead)

Photography: Michael Seresin

Editing: Ian John

Music: Murray Grindlay

Art Direction: Roger Donaldson, Ian Mune

Sound: Craig McLeod, Peter Fenton

Cast: Sam Neill (Smith), Ian Mune (Bullen), Nevan Rowe (Gloria), Ian Watkin (Dudley), Clyde Scott (Jesperson), Donna Akersten (Mary), Bill Johnston (Cousins), Warren Oates (Colonel Willoughby), Don Selwyn (Taupiri), Davina Whitehouse (Elsie)

Running time: 107 mins

TWO LAWS 1981

Directors: The Borroloola Community with Alessandro Cavadini and Carolyn Strachan

Production: Alessandro Cavadini and Carolyn Strachan and the Australian Film Commission

Editing: Alessandro Cavadini and Carolyn Strachan

Photography: Alessandro Cavadini

Sound: Carolyn Strachan, Linda McDiny

Assistance: John Avery, Denne McLaughlin, Bob Domm, Jack Doolan, Joy Irvine, Ronda Macgregor, Ian Cohen

Running time: 130 mins

THE YEAR OF LIVING DANGEROUSLY 1982

Director: Peter Weir

Production: Jim McElroy

Screenplay: David Williamson, Peter Weir, C. J. Koch (from a novel by C. J. Koch)

Photography: Russell Boyd

Editor: William Anderson

Music: Maurice Jarre

Art Direction: Herbert Pinter, Wendy Weir

Sound: Gary Wilkins

Cast: Mel Gibson (Guy Hamilton), Sigourney Weaver (Jill Bryant), Linda Hunt (Billy Kwan), Bill Kerr (Colonel Henderson), Michael Murphy (Pete Curtis), Bembol Roco (Kumar), Kuh Ledesma (Tiger Lily), Domingo Landicho

(Hortono), Noel Ferrier (Wally Sullivan), Paul Sonkkila (Kevin Condon), Cecily Polson (Moira), Mike Emperio (Sukarno), Norma Uatuhan (Ibu)
Running time: 117 mins

VIGIL 1984
Director: Vincent Ward
Production: John Maynard, Gary Hannam, Piers Davies for John Maynard Productions in association with the New Zealand Film Commission, and The Film Investment Corporation of New Zealand for First Blood/Last Rites Partnerships, Wellington
Screenplay: Vincent Ward, Graeme Tetley, with assistance from Fiona Lindsay
Photography: Alun Bollinger
Editing: Simon Reece
Music: Jack Body
Art Direction: Kai Hawkins
Sound: Graham Morris, Ken Saville
Cast: Bill Kerr (Birdie), Fiona Kay (Lisa Peers, 'Toss'), Gordon Shields (Justin Peers), Penelope Stewart (Elizabeth Peers), Frank Whitten (Ethan Ruir), Arthur Sutton, Snow Turner, Bill Liddy, Maurice Trewern, Eric Griffin, Emily Haupapa, Debbie Newton, Bob Morrison, Lloyd Grundy, Joseph Ritai, Josie Herlihy, Sadie Marriner, Bill Brocklehurst, Rangitoheriri Teupokopakari
Running time: 91 mins

IN THIS LIFE'S BODY 1984
Director: Corinne Cantrill
Production: Arthur and Corinne Cantrill
Scriptwriter: Corinne Cantrill
Narration: Corinne Cantrill
Photography: Corinne and Arthur Cantrill
Photographers: Corinne Cantrill, Ponch Hawkes, Fred Harden, Phillip Noyce, Bernard Poinssot, Arthur Cantrill, Ivor Cantrill, among others
Editing: Corinne and Arthur Cantrill
Running time: 147 mins

THE PIANO 1993
Director: Jane Campion
Production: Jan Chapman
Screenplay: Jane Campion
Photography: Stuart Dryburgh
Editing: Veronika Jenet
Music: Michael Nyman
Art Direction: Andrew McAlpine
Sound: Gethin Creagh, Tony Johnson, Annabelle Sheehan, Lee Smith, Peter Townend
Cast: Holly Hunter (Ada McGrath), Harvey Keitel (George Baines), Sam Neill (Alisdair Stewart), Anna Paquin (Flora McGrath), Kerryu Walker (Aunt Morag), Genevieve Lemon (Nessie), Ian Mune (Reverend), Tungia Baker (Hira)
Running time: 120 mins

ONCE WERE WARRIORS 1994
Director: Lee Tamahori
Production: Robin Scholes

Screenplay: Riwia Brown (from a novel by Alan Duff)
Photography: Stuart Dryburgh
Editing: D. Michael Horton
Music: Murray McNab, Murray Grindlay
Art Direction: Shayne Bedford
Cast: Rena Owen (Beht Heke), Temuera Morrison (Jake Heke), Clifford Curtis (Uncle Bully), Mamaengaroa Kerr-Bell (Grace), Julian Arahanga (Nig), Taungaroa Emile (Boogie), Shannon Williams (Toot)
Running time: 102 mins

OSCAR AND LUCINDA 1997
Director: Gillian Armstrong
Production: Robin Dalton, Timothy White
Screenplay: Laura Jones (from a novel by Peter Carey)
Photography: Geoffrey Simpson
Editing: Nicholas Beauman
Music: Thomas Newman
Production Design: Luciana Arrighi
Sound: Andrew Plain, Ben Osmo, Gethin Creagh
Cast: Ralph Fiennes (Oscar Hopkins), Cate Blanchett (Lucinda Leplastrier), Ciaran Hinds (Reverend Dennis Hasset), Tom Wilkinson (Hugh Stratton), Richard Roxburgh (Mr Jeffries), Clive Russell (Theophilius), Billie Brown (Percy Smith), Jospehine Byrnes (Miriam Chadwick), Barnaby Kay (Wardley-Fish), Barry Otto (Jimmy D'Abbs), Linda Bassett (Betty Stratton), Geoffrey Rush (narrator), Polly Cheshire (Young Lucinda)
Running time: 132 mins

AFTER MABO 1997
Director: John Hughes
Production: Richard Frankland, Debra Annear and John Hughes
Screenplay: John Hughes, after an idea by Richard Frankland
Photography: Peter Zakharov, Andrew Blunt, Ralph Rigby
Editing: Uri Mizrahi
Sound: Mark Tarpey, Chris Izzard, Debra Annear, Ian Luta, Lauren Marsh
Running time: 85 mins

CHOPPER 2000
Director: Andrew Dominik
Production: Michele Bennett, Cherub Pictures
Screenplay: Andrew Dominik
Photography: Geoffrey Hall, Kevin Hayward
Editing: Ken Swallows
Art Direction: Paddy Reardon
Sound: Frank Lipson
Cast: Eric Bana (Chopper), Vince Colosimo (Neville Bartos), Simon Lyndon (Jimmy Loughnan), Kate Beahan (Tanya), Dan Wyllie (Bluey), Bill Young (Detective Downie), David Field (Keithy George), Kenny Graham (Keith Read)
Running time: 94 mins

THE GODDESS OF 1967 2000
Director: Clara Law
Production: Eddie Ling-Ching Fong, Wouter Barendrecht, Akiko Funatsu, Dennis Kiely, Helen Loveridge, Peter

Sainsbury, Michael J. Werner for NSW Film and Television Office
Screenplay: Eddie Ling-Ching Fong and Clara Law
Photography: Dion Beebe
Editing: Kate Williams
Music: Jen Anderson
Art Direction: Nicholas McCallum
Sound: Peter Grace
Cast: Rose Byrne (BG), Rikiya Kurokawa (JM), Nicholas Hope (Grandpa), Elise McCredie (Marie), Tim Richards (Drummer Boy), Bree Beadman (BG aged 9), Satya Gumbert (Marie aged 9), Tina Bursill (Esther)
Running time: 119 mins

MOULIN ROUGE! 2001
Director: Baz Luhrmann
Production: Martin Brown, Baz Luhrmann, Fred Baron
Screenplay: Baz Luhrmann, Craig Pearce
Photography: Don McAlpine
Editing: Jill Bilcock
Music: Craig Armstrong, Chris Elliott
Art Direction: Ann Marie Beauchamp, Ian Gracie
Sound: Roger Savage
Cast: Nicole Kidman (Satine), Ewan McGregor (Christian), John Leguizamo (Toulouse-Lautrec), Jim Broadbent (Zidler), Richard Roxburgh (Duke of Worcester)
Running time: 127 mins

ONE NIGHT THE MOON 2001
Director: Rachel Perkins
Production: Aanya Whitehead, Paul Humfress, Kevin Lucas
Screenplay: John Romeril
Photography: Kim Batterham
Editor: Karen Johnson
Art Direction: Rob Webb
Musical Director: Mairead Hannan
Cast: Paul Kelly (Jim Ryan), Kaarin Fairfax (Rose Ryan), Memphis Kelly (Emily Ryan), Kelton Pell (Albert Yang), Ruby Hunter (Albert's wife), Chris Haywood (The Sergeant), David Field (Allman)
Running time: 57 mins

THE LORD OF THE RINGS: THE FELLOWSHIP OF THE RING 2001
Director: Peter Jackson
Production: Barrie M. Osborne, Peter Jackson, Fran Walsh, Tim Sanders
Screenplay: Fran Walsh, Phillipa Boyens, Peter Jackson (from a novel by J. R. R. Tolkien)
Photography: Andrew Lesnie
Editing: John Gilbert
Music: Howard Shore
Art Direction: (Peter) Joe Bleakley, Rob Outerrside, Phil Ivey, Mark Robins
Sound: Christopher Boyes, Gethin Creagh, Hammond Peek, Michael Semanick
Cast: Elijah Wood (Frodo Baggins), Ian McKellen (Gandalf), Liv Tyler (Arwen), Viggo Mortensen (Aragorn 'Strider'), Sean Astin (Samwise Gamgee), Cate Blanchett (Galadriel), John Rhys-Davies (Gimili), Billy Boyd (Peregrin 'Pippin' Took), Dominic Monaghan (Meriadoc 'Merry' Brandybuck), Orlando Bloom (Legolas), Christopher Lee (Saruman), Hugo Weaving (Elrond), Sean Bean (Boromir), Ian Holm (Bilbo Baggins), Andy Serkis (Gollum),

Marton Csokas (Celeborn), Craig Parker (Haldir), Lawrence Makoare (Lurtz), Alan Howard (voice of the ring), Noel Appleby (Everard Proudfoot), Sala Baker (Sauron)
Running time: 178 mins

RABBIT-PROOF FENCE 2002
Director: Phillip Noyce
Production: Jabal Films, Phillip Noyce, Christine Olsen, John Winter
Screenplay: Christine Olsen
Photography: Chris Doyle
Editing: Veronica Jenet, John Scott
Music: Peter Gabriel
Art Direction: Laurie Faen
Sound: Craig Carter
Cast: Everlyn Sampi (Molly Craig), Tianna Sansbury (Daisy Craig), Laura Monaghan (Gracie Fields), David Gulpilil (Moodoo), Jason Clarke (Constable Riggs), Kenneth Branagh (Mr Neville), Deborah Mailman (Mavis)
Running time: 94 mins

BIBLIOGRAPHY

AUSTRALIA

Baxter, John (1970) *Australian Cinema*. Sydney: Pacific Books.

_____ (1986) *Filmstruck: Australia at the Movies*. Sydney: ABC.

Beilby, Peter and Ross Lansell (1983) *Australian Motion Picture Yearbook 1983*. Melbourne: Four Seasons, in association with Cinema Papers.

Berryman, Ken (ed.) (1995) *Screening the Past: Aspects of Early Australian Film*. Canberra: National Film and Sound Archive.

Bertrand, Ina (1989) *Cinema in Australia: A Documentary History*. Sydney: University of New South Wales Press.

Bertrand, Ina and Diana Collins (1981) *Government and Film in Australia*. Sydney: Currency Press.

Blonski, Annette, Barbara Creed and Freda Freiberg (eds) (1987) *Don't Shoot Darling: Women's Independent Filmmaking in Australia*. Melbourne: Greenhouse.

Caputo, Raffaele and Geoff Burton (eds) (1999) *Second Take: Australian Filmmakers Talk*. Sydney: Allen and Unwin.

Carlsson, Susanne (1989) *Charles and Elsa Chauvel, Movie Pioneers*. Brisbane: University of Queensland Press.

Chauvel, Elsa (1973) *My Life with Charles Chauvel*. Sydney: Shakespeare Head Publications.

Clark, Alan (1994) *Making Priscilla*. Melbourne: Penguin.

Coleman, Peter (1993) *Bruce Beresford: Instincts of the Heart*. Sydney: Angus and Robertson.

Collins, Diane (1987) *Hollywood Down Under – Australians at the Movies: 1886 to the Present Day*. North Ryde, Sydney: Angus and Robertson.

Collins, Felicity and Therese Davis (2004) *Australian Cinema after Mabo*. Melbourne: Cambridge University Press.

Cunningham, Stuart (1991) *Featuring Australia: The Cinema of Charles Chauvel*. Sydney: Allen and Unwin.

Dawson, Jonathan and Bruce Molloy (1990) *Queensland Images in Film and Television*. Brisbane: University of Queensland Press.

Dermody, Susan and Elizabeth Jacka (1987) *The Screening of Australia, vol 1: Anatomy of a Film Industry*. Sydney: Currency Press.

_____ (1988) *The Screening of Australia, vol 2: Anatomy of a National Cinema*. Sydney: Currency Press.

_____ (eds) (1988) *The Imaginary Industry: Australian Film in the late '80s*. Sydney: AFTRS Publications.

French, Lisa (ed.) *Womenvision: Women and the Moving Image in Australia*. Melbourne: Damned Publishing.

Hall, Ken G. (1980) *Australian Film: The Inside Story*. Sydney: Summit Books.

Hall, Sandra (1985) *Critical Business: The New Australian Cinema in Review*. Adelaide: Rigby.

Halliwell, William (1985) *The Filmgoer's Guide to Australian Films*. North Ryde, Sydney: Angus and Robertson.

Herd, Nick (1983) *Independent Filmmaking in Australia, 1960–1980*. Sydney: Australian Film and Television School.

Hinde, John (2001) *Other People's Pictures*. Sydney: ABC.

Hodsdon, Barrett (2001) *Straight Roads and Crooked Lines: The Quest for Film Culture in Australia from the 1960s*. Perth: Bernt Porridge Group.

Jennings, Karen (1993) *Sites of Difference: Cinematic Representations of Aboriginality and Gender*. Melbourne: Australian Film Institute.

Langton, Marcia (1993) *'Well, I heard it on the radio and I saw it on the television...' An Essay for the Australian Film Commission on the politics and aesthetics of filmmaking by and about Aboriginal people and things*. Sydney: Australian Film Commission.

Lansell, Ross and Peter Beilby (eds) (1982) *The Documentary Film in Australia*. Melbourne: Cinema Papers.

Lewis, Glen (1987) *Australian Movies and the American Dream*. New York: Praeger.

Lovell, Patricia (1995) *No Picnic: An Autobiography*. Sydney: Pan Macmillan.

McFarlane, Brian (1987) *Australian Cinema 1970–1985*. Richmond, Melbourne: William Heinemann Australia.

McFarlane, Brian and Geoff Mayer (1991) *New Australian Cinema: Sources and Parallels in American and British Film*.

Melbourne: Cambridge University Press.

McFarlane, Brian, Geoff Mayer and Ina Bertrand (eds) (1999) *The Oxford Companion to Australian Film*. Melbourne: Oxford University Press.

Mathews, Sue (1984) *35mm Dreams: Conversations with Five Directors about the Australian Film Revival*. Sydney: Penguin.

Molloy, Bruce (1990) *Before the Interval: Australian Mythology and Feature Films, 1930–1960*. Brisbane: University of Queensland Press.

Moran, Albert (1991) *Projecting Australia: Government Film Since 1945*. Sydney: Currency Press.

Moran, Albert and Tom O'Regan (eds) (1985) *An Australian Film Reader*. Sydney: Currency Press.

_____ (eds) (1989) *The Australian Screen*. Sydney: Penguin.

Mudie, Peter (1997) *Ubu Films: Sydney Underground Films, 1965–1970*. Sydney: University of New South Wales Press.

Murray, Scott (ed.) (1980) *The New Australian Cinema*. Melbourne: Nelson/Cinema Papers.

_____ (1988) *Back of Beyond: Discovering Australian Film and Television*. Sydney: Australian Film Commission.

_____ (ed.) (1994) *Australian Cinema*. Sydney: Allen and Unwin.

_____ (ed.) (1995) *Australian Film, 1978–1994*. Melbourne: Oxford University Press.

O'Regan, Tom (1996) *Australian National Cinema*. London: Routledge.

Pike, Andrew and Ross Cooper (1998) *Australian Film, 1900–1977*. Melbourne: Oxford University Press.

Rattigan, Neil (1991) *Images of Australia: 100 Films of the New Australian Cinema*. Dallas: Southern Methodist University Press.

Rayner, Jonathan (2000) *Contemporary Australian Cinema: An Introduction*. Manchester: Manchester University Press.

Reade, Eric (1970) *Australian Silent Films: A Pictorial History of Silent Films from 1896 to 1929*. Melbourne: Lansdowne.

_____ (1972) *The Talkies Era: A Pictorial History of Australian Sound Film Making, 1930–1960*. Melbourne: Lansdowne.

_____ (1975) *The Australian Screen: A Pictorial History of Australian Film Making*. Melbourne: Lansdowne.

_____ (1979) *History and Heartburn: The Sage of Australian Film, 1896–1978*. Sydney: Harper and Row.

Robson, Jocelyn and Beverley Zalcock (1997) *Girl's Own Stories: Australian and New Zealand Women's Films*. Sydney: Scarlet Press.

Sabine, James (1995) *A Century of Australian Cinema*. Melbourne: Mandarin.

Shirley, Graham and Brian Adams (1983) *Australian Cinema: The First Eighty Years*. Sydney: Currency Press.

Stratton, David (1980) *The Last New Wave: The Australian Film Revival*. Sydney: Angus and Robertson.

_____ (1990) *The Avocado Plantation: Boom and Bust in the Australian Film Industry*. Sydney: Pan Macmillan.

Tapp, Peter (ed.) (1995) *Australian Feature Films*. Melbourne: Informit, Royal Melbourne Institute of Technology and The Australian Catalogue of New Films & Videos Ltd (CD-Rom).

Thoms, Albie (1978) *Polemics for a New Cinema: Writings to Stimulate New Approaches to Film*. Sydney: Wild and Woolley.

_____ (2000) *Surfmovies*. Sydney: Shorething Publishing.

Tulloch, John (1981) *Legends on the Screen: The Australian Cinema, 1919–1929*. Sydney: Currency.

_____ (1982) *Australian Cinema: Industry, Narrative and Meaning*. Sydney: Allen and Unwin.

Verhoeven, Deb (1999) *Twin Peeks: Australian and New Zealand Films*. Sydney: Damned Publishing.

White, David (1984) *Australian Movies to the World*. Sydney: Fontana and Cinema Papers.

Wright, Andree (1986) *Brilliant Careers: Women in Australian Cinema*. Sydney: Pan Books.

NEW ZEALAND

Barclay, Barry (1990) *Our Own Image*. Auckland: Longman Paul.

Blyth, Martin (1994) *Naming the Other: Images of the Maori in New Zealand Film and Television*. Metuchen, NJ: Scarecrow Press.

Cairns, Barbara and Helen Martin (1994) *Shadows on the Wall: A Study of Seven New Zealand Feature Films*. Auckland: Longman Paul.

Churchman, Geoffrey (ed.) (1997) *Celluloid Dreams: A Century of Film in New Zealand*. Wellington: IPL Books.

Coombs, Felicity and Suzanne Gemmell (eds) (1999) *Piano Lessons: Approaches to The Piano*. Sydney: John Libbey.

Dennis, Jonathan and Jan Bieringa (eds) (1996) *Film in Aotearoa New Zealand*. Wellington: Victoria University Press.

Holmes, Cecil (1986) *One Man's Way*. Melbourne: Penguin.

Horrocks, Roger (1985) *New Zealand Film Makers at the Auckland City Art Gallery, 1984–1985*. Auckland: The Gallery.

_____ (2001) *Len Lye: A Biography*. Auckland: Auckland University Press.

Horrocks, Roger and Philip Tremewan (1989) *On Film II*. Auckland: Heinemann.

Lennox, Bill (1985) *Film and Fiction: Studies of New Zealand Fiction and Film Adaptations*. Auckland: Longman Paul.

Margolis, Harriet (ed.) (2000) *Jane Campion's The Piano*. Cambridge: Cambridge University Press.

Martin, Helen and Sam Edwards (eds) (1997) *New Zealand Film, 1912–1996*. Auckland: Oxford University Press.

O'Shea, John (1997) *Documentary and National Identity*. Auckland: Centre for Film, Television and Media Studies, University of Auckland.

Price, Simon (1996) *New Zealand's First Talkies: Early Filmmaking in Otago and Southland, 1896–1939*. Dunedin: Otago Heritage Books.

Rayner, Jonathan (1999) *Cinema Journeys of the Man Alone: The New Zealand and American Films of Geoff Murphy*. Nottingham: Nottingham Trent University.

_____ (2000) 'Paradise and Pandemonium: The Landscapes of Vincent Ward', in Ian Conrich and David Woods (eds) *New Zealand – A Pastoral Paradise?* Nottingham: Kakapo Books, 39–51.

Reid, Nicholas (1986) *A Decade of New Zealand Film: From Sleeping Dogs to Came A Hot Friday*. Dunedin: John McIndoe.

Robson, Jocelyn and Beverley Zalcock (1997) *Girl's Own Stories: Australian and New Zealand Women's Films*. Sydney: Scarlet Press.

Shepard, Deborah (2000) *Reframing Women: A History of New Zealand Film*. Auckland: HarperCollins.

Sowry, Clive (1984) *Film Making in New Zealand: A Brief Historical Survey*. Wellington: New Zealand Film Archive.

Verhoeven, Deborah (1999) *Twin Peeks: Australian and New Zealand Films*. Sydney: Damned Publishing.

Wilmington, Michael (1993) 'Firestorm and Dry Ice: The Cinema of Vincent Ward', *Film Comment*, 29, 3, 51–4.

INDEX